The inducements elsewhere must be remarkably
large to pay a man for moving.

Peter R. Knights

Yankee Destinies

The Lives of

Ordinary

Nineteenth-Century

Bostonians

The University of North Carolina Press

Chapel Hill and London

© 1991

The University of North Carolina Press

All rights reserved

Manufactured in the United States of America

The paper in this book meets the guidelines for
permanence and durability of the Committee on
Production Guidelines for Book Longevity of the
Council on Library Resources.

95 94 93 92 91 5 4 3 2 1

Library of Congress Cataloging-in-Publication
Data
Knights, Peter R.
   Yankee destinies: the lives of ordinary
nineteenth-century Bostonians / by Peter R.
Knights.
      p.   cm.
   Includes bibliographical references (p.   )
and index.
   ISBN 0-8078-1969-7 (cloth : alk. paper)
   1. Boston (Mass.)—Biography.   2. Boston
(Mass.)—Social life and customs.   I. Title.
F73.25.K55   1991
974.4′00992—dc20
   [B]   90-23936
                       CIP
Frontispiece: from H. L. Reade,
Money and How to Make It (Norwich, Conn.:
Reade Publishing Company, 1872).

TO MY MOTHER,

who deserves to have

more books dedicated to her,

and to my severest critics

—the 2,808

Contents

Tables

Maps

Acknowledgments

For many years I have wondered which group was the larger: the 2,808 subjects of this study or the multitude lending greatly appreciated help to its author. As it turned out, the latter group was smaller, but just barely. By far the largest number of people I should thank replied kindly to a letter from a stranger and supplied a datum that vanished into the computer's maw. These helpful individuals were so numerous that I hope a heartfelt thank you will suffice for all.

No social-historical research project lasting a sixth of a century can survive long without funding, and I have been very fortunate in receiving it, beginning with a Research Grant from the National Foundation for the Humanities that released me for research during the 1972–73 academic year. For that year the Social Science Research Council also tendered me a Faculty Research Grant, which I had to decline, but I remain grateful for its vote of confidence in my project.

Beginning in 1971–72, and again in 1972–73, 1973–74, 1980–81, and 1985–86, York University provided Minor Research Grants to purchase supplies and materials. York awarded me a Faculty of Arts Fellowship for 1980–81, which released me from two-thirds of my teaching and permitted extensive searching of census microfilms.

For the summer of 1975, the Earhart Foundation of Ann Arbor, Michigan, granted funds to buy census microfilms, which I then desperately needed.

During 1976–77, a Canada Council [Sabbatical] Leave Fellowship supplemented my sabbatical salary and allowed me a full year off for research.

Beginning with the 1980–81 academic year, I was extremely grateful to start receiving research support from the Social Sciences and Humanities Research Council of Canada, which then awarded me a Small Research Grant, following it in 1981–83 with a Released Time Fellowship and Major Research Grant. This provided two-thirds time off in one year and full time in the other and gave major impetus toward ending this project, which I was beginning to think could never be completed without substantial released time. Then in 1983–84, the council continued its aid with a sabbatical Leave Fellowship. Last, the council awarded me a Released Time Stipend for the 1987–88 year, again providing full release from teaching duties, permitting me to begin writing and to finish most of the manuscript of this book. To all these agencies and organizations, I can but express the hope that they will find the results worthy of their investment in the research. Their generous support of the research underlying this book should not, of course, be taken to indicate that they are responsible for its findings.

Colleagues, especially those at York University, have been supportive in offering suggestions and constructive criticism, even though I suspect some of them were bored to distraction by this research, or at least by hearing me talk about it. Among the members of the United States field in York's Departments of History, participants in our informal research seminar read several chapters in manuscript and helped me translate my prose into English: Robert D. Cuff, Marc M. Egnal, Joseph A. Ernst, Yves Frenette, Gerald A. Ginsburg (especially helpful on methodology), and Edward Hagerman. They caught quite a few, mostly minor, errors, but I am confident that I still slipped some others past them. Gabriel Kolko gave ongoing advice on applying for research support. History (Arts) Department chairs were also cooperative, both in arranging leave time and in encouraging me to finish this research. Richard C. Hoffmann, Susan E. Houston, Paul E.

Lovejoy, and Paul D. Stevens held that position at various times, ably seconded by Russell E. Chace, who also gave useful advice on personal computing. Thank you, one and all.

York University is fortunate in having at its Office of Research Administration wonderful people who know where to apply for research funds. They also commiserate with the unsuccessful and assist the successful in dealing with granting agencies. My gratitude goes to Noli Swatman, executive officer, and Carol Irving.

Within the academic community I was fortunate to induce several colleagues to read chapters in homeopathic doses. Kathleen N. Conzen and Michael P. Conzen, David P. Davenport, Edward J. Davies II, Jo Ann Parkerson and Donald H. Parkerson, Leo F. Schnore, and Margaret Walsh all were kind enough to look at and comment on a chapter or two. Richard A. Schwarzlose stole time from his monumental *The Nation's Newsbrokers* to read several chapters and to show me that his copy-editing students get full value for their dollar. Another longtime friend, Donald L. Shaw, also looked at two chapters. A former collaborator, Richard S. Alcorn, commented trenchantly upon my material as well. All of these people labored mightily to save this manuscript from a variety of deficiencies. Although he was spared the ordeal of reading chapters, over the years Professor Everett S. Lee has encouraged me to press on with this research. His conviction that "all that work" was indeed worthwhile was a mighty sustainer. Professors J. Morgan Kousser and Sam Bass Warner, Jr., read the manuscript for the University of North Carolina Press, and I am indebted to them for their patient criticism.

Special thanks are due to Professor David P. Davenport, who drew the maps for this book. How he had the patience and steady hand to place hundreds of tiny dots so accurately I shall never understand. His reaction when I told him that I had sent him incorrect lists of locations of out-migrants as of 1870 and 1880 ("Well, back to the drawing board") was in the best traditions of geography. Trudie Calvert, who copy-edited the manuscript, recalled to me several basic grammatical rules, cut hundreds of commas, saved me from a flock of inconsistencies in the footnotes, and will doubtless improve this sentence, too.

Without libraries this project could never have gotten off the ground. At the Inter-Library Loans office in York University's Scott Library, Mary Hudecki, the late Gary D. MacDonald, and John O. Carter patiently sent off to the Center for Research Libraries in Chicago scores of requests for census microfilms, answered querulous telephone calls asking why those microfilms had not arrived instantly, and generally restrained themselves gracefully from committing mayhem on this faculty member. They will be glad to learn that most of their problems are over—for a while. To the Center for Research Libraries my thanks as well for sending out so many reels over the years.

Another library that vitally sustained this project for many years was that of the New England Historic Genealogical Society (NEHGS), Boston, directed during most of the period by Ralph D. Crandall. The research of many genealogists who have "joined the majority" was also often helpful beyond measure, and there was the ideal place to consult it. Particularly helpful at the NEHGS were David C. Dearborn, Fellow, American Society of Genealogists (FASG), who introduced me to dozens of valuable sources and answered many inquiries by mail; Jerome E. Anderson; and Gary Boyd Roberts, the only person I have ever met who can recite genealogies of well-known people, so complete is his knowledge of their pedigrees. George F. Sanborn, Jr., allowed me to borrow, gradually, the society's microfilm run of the *Boston Evening Transcript*, 1830–75. At the society I met Robert C. Anderson, FASG, who has taken time from his research into early migration to New England to read some of my chapters on later migration within it. Roger D. Joslyn, FASG, kindly checked on some deaths that occurred in New York State, as well as on some vital events in Charlestown, Massachusetts, that will be included in the second volume of its *Vital Records*, which he is compiling.

Virginia S. Doane, Librarian Emerita of the Brooks Free Library, Harwich, Massachusetts, has contributed considerably to this study over the last decade or so, ranging from the occasional provision of interlibrary loans through making available facilities for copying microfilms (particularly of the *Boston Evening Transcript*) and books. The library's collection of the Massachusetts *Vital Records* series was also of material assistance. Jean Stone was also helpful; my thanks to both.

From time to time I have turned to the Massachusetts State Library for help in obtaining copies of nineteenth-century state publications; it never failed. State Librarian Gaspar Caso and his staff help preserve Massachusetts's working memory.

For many years the Boston Athenæum Library has sent me a reader's ticket, allowing access to its collections; especially useful was the typescript index to death notices in the *Boston Evening Transcript*, 1830–74, compiled by Mrs. Jacob Wirth, and kept in the fourth-floor vault. (This index amply deserves publication, or at least reproduction and limited distribution.) My thanks to Rodney D. Armstrong for that largess.

Vital statistics data were the sine qua non of this study, and I was glad to complete most of my work with the Massachusetts records before microfilms of them replaced the actual volumes. Although this effort is to be applauded as preserving the original records, working with the microfilms, particularly those for the post-1895 era at the Massachusetts Department of Health, now accessible to researchers only twelve and a half hours a week, drastically slows the pace of research. Fortunately, the NEHGS has the pre-1896 vital records on microfilm, and it is open more than thirty-five hours a week. At the then Massachusetts Division of Vital Statistics, successive registrars (the late Edward C. Kloza, Herbert Risser, and the present registrar, Elaine Trudeau) kindly permitted me reasonable access to the original records. Among individuals at the Massachusetts Division of Vital Records and Statistics of the Department of Health (150 Tremont Street, Boston), Harold Leonard, Kevin B. Roche, and John W. Dolan (since retired) deserve singling out for their helpfulness. At the Massachusetts State Archives at Columbia Point, Herb Van Dam cheerfully answered many inquiries by mail and in person. The Massachusetts records were the principal base of this study, and all these people contributed importantly to easing the way.

The records at the Boston City Archives are accessible only four hours a day on Tuesdays and Thursdays, but for some aspects of this study, such as checking on marriage intentions, obtaining nearly complete lists of all children born to specific parents and learning where sample members (who died in Boston) were interred before about 1890 (state records begin showing this datum about then), they were essential. Shay Allen was in charge of the office until budgetary cutbacks forced the city to ask the NEHGS to provide volunteers to take over. Virginia Hartshorn did so and has since replied to a multitude of rather unusual questions; mere words of appreciation to both ladies will have to suffice.

During my few quick visits to the Waltham, Massachusetts, Federal Archives and Records Center, the staff and director James W. Owens were always helpful. Most of my searching in the 1900 Soundex index microfilms occurred there.

Some of the men in the study died in other jurisdictions, and I wish to express my gratitude to those officials in vital statistics offices outside Massachusetts who bore the brunt of my requests for information and who sometimes authorized "look till you find that record" searches: Merton S. Honeyman, Connecticut Department of Health Services; Michael Fish, Cook County (Illinois) Bureau of Vital Statistics; Marian B. Perkins, Maine Department of Human Services; Charles E. Sirc, New Hampshire Bureau of Vital Records and Health Statistics; Donald L. Lipira, New Jersey Department of Health; and Lera O'Hara, Rhode Island Division of Vital Statistics. Hundreds of town, city, county, and probate court clerks from Maine to California also replied to individual inquiries, often adding useful suggestions as to where to look next for information if they could not provide it. These kind people effectively demolished the myth that government agencies are staffed by unfriendly grouches; their constituents are fortunate.

Boston's oldest cemeteries, despite their need to attend to current affairs, were tremendously helpful in tracing their nineteenth-century clients. Duncan C. Munro, superintendent of Mount Auburn Cemetery, Cambridge, who had allowed me access to the cemetery's interment index for the research underlying *The Plain People of Boston*, did so again for this study, and the late Axel H. Pamp, and Wilfred C. Ells, successive superintendents of Woodlawn Cemetery, Everett, loaned me a few of its nineteenth-century suburban directories, some for as long as twelve years, which sets new standards for "extended loans"; in addition, Mr. Ells arranged for lists of "missing" sample members to be looked up in the cemetery's interment index. At Forest Hills Cemetery, Hazel T. Marshall, treasurer, checked two long and several short lists of sample members' names for possible clients of her cemetery. Al Morelli of Mount Hope Cemetery allowed me to spend several hours checking missing sample members' names in its interment index. All four cemeteries, together with many others in eastern Massachusetts, responded to occasional letters of inquiry and last-minute telephone calls for "just another name." Thank you all.

Many clerks and officials at the probate courts of Suffolk, Middlesex, Norfolk, Plymouth, and Barnstable counties in Massachusetts also took a few moments to explain how a filing system worked, or where "Vault B" was, earning my gratitude. As well, clerks or registrars of probate in many other states provided pieces of the puzzle.

Among colleagues who responded to inquiries for specific pieces of information, I should single out for thanks Alan A. Brookes, of Guelph, Ontario, who was then researching his dissertation in Boston and who took time out to check an occasional vital statistics record; Professor Carl V. Harris, University of California, Santa Barbara, who found the death record of a "long-distance" out-migrating sample member; Professor Theodore Hershberg, University of Pennsylvania, whose Philadelphia Social History Project was able to round up all my out-migrants to that city; and Professor John Modell, Carnegie-Mellon University, who checked on some Minneapolis death records.

Individual genealogists pursuing researches into their local or family backgrounds, true to tradition, were without exception willing to help set a historian straight, even though they may have wondered at his studying people he was not related to. (The NAME in the list that follows is that of the family on which the genealogist provided information.) Thanks are due to Jerome E. ANDERSON, NEHGS, Boston; Mrs. C. D. Logan, Denison, Texas (ATWOOD); Mrs. Bernice B. Smith, Norridgewock, Maine (BLAISDELL); Mrs. Jane BLINN, Sun City, Arizona; Mrs. Jane F. Fiske, Boxford, Massachusetts (COOK); Alicia C. Williams, C. G. S., Hingham, Massachusetts (CRANE); Harold E. CURTIS, Madison, New Jersey, and Wells, Maine; Mrs. Harold G. Bruce, Arlington, Massachusetts (FERNALD); Mrs. Barbara L. Gill, Sandwich, Massachusetts (FISH); John A. GAGE, Toledo, Ohio; Robert C. Anderson, FASG, Salt Lake City (GAY); Gregory H. Laing, Haverhill, Massachusetts (KIMBALL); John W. McCRILLIS, Newport, New Hampshire; Denis S. MORSE, Willowdale, Ontario; Donald F. PRINCE, Framingham, Massachu-

setts; Thomas PRINCE Riley, Brunswick, Maine; Betty J. Meloy, Lew-
iston, Idaho (PUTNAM); Royal D. SIBLEY, Pawtucket, Rhode Island;
James S. SIBLEY, Midlothian, Texas; and Herbert E. Adams, Dedham, Massachusetts (TUFTS). Many other genealogists kindly answered specific questions, but these went far beyond mere helpfulness.

During the last year or so, when I was finishing the manuscript,
Lauren V. Zeilig, M.D., of Toronto, and William A. Rhodes, D.O., of
Brewster, Massachusetts, engaged in helping me keep body and soul
together, took time to discuss and clarify points concerning medical
nosology; I appreciated their aid (first and otherwise) and interest in
this part of the research.

Four long-suffering individuals have acted as my research assistants. Over a decade ago, Charles M. Flickinger toiled a summer at
the Massachusetts Division of Vital Statistics "killing off" and "marrying off" sample members. Van J. Newell at York University spent a
year assigning ZIP codes to over 10,000 geographical locations associated with the sample members and likely remains Canada's leading
expert on the ZIP code. Beth Phillips and Nola Freeman, then of Salt
Lake City, checked for deaths of sample members' wives, using the
microfilms of the Massachusetts vital records available at the Utah
Genealogical Society (which is open over 100 hours a week). I hope
you are as happy with the results of your labors as I am grateful for
your aid.

For several summers Joseph M. and Marcia C. Glynn permitted me
to stay overnight once a week at their Newton, Massachusetts, home
so as to be able to put in two consecutive days at the Division of Vital
Statistics without having to return to Cape Cod. Not only did this save
wear and tear on me, but it also saved me money (which was then in
short supply) and time. Their hospitality remains a pleasant memory.

Finally, a few—all too few—words of appreciation to my mother
and stepfather, who have doubtless regarded this project with a certain bemused tolerance all these years. My mother has allowed me to
use her home on Cape Cod as a base of operations from which to
venture to Boston during summers and, during leave or sabbatical
years, at other seasons. She has put up with the disorder attending
the research and writing of a historical work involving the collection

and digestion of millions of pieces of information, each of which probably tracked some dirt into the house. My stepfather has abandoned hope that the Boston Red Sox will ever again win a league pennant, but he usually finds time to listen to most of their games and to discuss them with me. For forbearing and supporting, my love and thanks.

Harwich Port, 1 September 1989

Yankee Destinies

Introduction

This inquiry afforded a striking illustration of the fact that many men, whose life careers were highly useful, who held positions of trust and influence, and as to whose history and characteristics there might well be a more widespread interest than that of their personal circle of friends, were themselves careless of posthumous fame, and have left insufficient memorials; while their descendants are too much absorbed in the affairs of the moment to assist in recalling the things of the past which would increase the importance and add to the instructiveness of these histories. So when some of these histories appear brief,—limited possibly by the facts that this or that man lived, was of us, was "successful," and passed on,—the reader will kindly note that it is not for want of effort to obtain them that we fail to present more extended details. For like reasons there may be errors as well as omissions.

—Albion Bicknell, in Massachusetts Charitable Mechanic Association, Annals, *1892*

If it be objected that too large a portion of the representatives are New England men, we reply, it is the fault of facts, which like the laws of the Medes and Persians, are unalterable: for, in the cities of Philadelphia and New York, as well

> *as in Boston and Providence, men of New England origin*
> *are first in Manufactures, first in Commerce, and first in the*
> *appreciation of means to make money or wisely expend it.*
> —*Edwin T. Freedley,* United States Mercantile
>   Guide, *1856*

This book is about ordinary people who resided for most of their lives in Boston, Massachusetts, during a large part of the nineteenth century. It is the second and concluding report on research that began in the fall of 1965, the first part of which appeared as *The Plain People of Boston, 1830–1860: A Study in City Growth* (New York: Oxford University Press, 1971).

The Plain People of Boston treated the lives of 1,540 men and women, heads of household, chosen randomly, 385 each, from Boston's population censuses of 1830, 1840, 1850, and 1860, and traced backward to their origins (if they were native-born) or to their arrival in Boston (if they were foreign-born). As well, I tried, with partial success, to learn what became of them in later life; again, the native-born could be traced much more easily than the foreign-born, primarily because so many of the foreign-born in that study were Irish, whose names lacked uniqueness and who thus could not be discriminated from their fellow countrymen with the same name.

The considerable labor involved in tracing the 1,540 people in the first study led me to two conclusions: first, longitudinal studies of individuals in nineteenth-century U.S. society were probably the only way that historians were ever going to learn what ordinary people's whole lives were like then. Cross-sectional studies (which are valuable as "snapshots" of populations at various times) do not follow their subjects who left the community, and since mobility was ubiquitous in nineteenth-century U.S. society, most of the people in cross-sectional studies disappear from view. Second, I concluded that a study of the lifetimes of ordinary people would have to be selective about its subjects. Desirable as it might seem to try to examine the lifetimes of a cross section of some population, the difficulties attending the tracing of people with common names would guarantee that success rates emanating from this tracing would be so low among some ethnic groups that any conclusions about members of those groups would be worthless. In surveying the field of social history, I decided that it was highly unlikely that any of my colleagues in it would carry out such a study any time soon and that the chances of someone's undertaking such a task as a dissertation topic were lower yet because of the considerable time required to complete the research. Another very important factor entering into this calculation was that I possessed a certain aptitude for and skill in doing this research and had invested several years in becoming familiar with the sources and techniques connected with it. Summing up these considerations, I determined to do a second study, centered once again on Boston, that would focus more narrowly upon that portion of its mid-nineteenth-century population most easily traced but would attempt to follow its members through their whole lives. The subjects of inquiry would be the white native-born male heads of household, with both parents native-born, known familiarly as "Yankees." These men, until the great influx of Irish immigrants in the late 1840s, were the typical everyday people of Boston—and, for that matter, of the rest of New England. Although their influence diminished, at first only politically, their social, economic, and cultural power was to endure longer, in some cases to the present.

Although deciding whom to study and how to do it probably did not require more than fifteen seconds, its consequences have required more than fifteen years to work out. At least one part of it has proved true: no one has produced a study examining the whole lives of any large group of representatively chosen ordinary nineteenth-century people. There has even been a decline in the cross-sectional studies of communities. I hope that the appearance of this book will inspire others to raise high the banner of community studies once again and to move forward against our ignorance about ordinary people of the past; certainly the task will become easier with advances in computers and data processing.

The basic inquiry animating this study has been simple. If you were able to talk for an hour or two with someone from the nineteenth century—not someone famous, but an ordinary person—what would you want to know? Suppose this individual said, "I'll tell you anything you want to know that you could find out by yourself, but nothing more," wouldn't you still say, "Something is better than nothing," and enjoy a fascinating conversation?

Social historians who want to know about the lives of ordinary people in the nineteenth century find that these people will indeed "talk" to them but will disclose only what those historians can find out. No miracles aid these historians; no ethereal voices answer their penetrating questions. Instead, the replies emerge from the detailed consultation and analysis of primary sources such as birth records, marriage records, death records, population censuses, newspapers, and credit reports and of secondary sources such as family histories and— all too seldom—autobiographies, biographies, or short life sketches of the people being studied.

Several major trends marked the progress of the United States during the nineteenth century, prominent among them urbanization and industrialization. This book deals with urbanization at its most basic— the movement of people to a city, what they did there, and what some of them went on to do elsewhere. It focuses on two groups of men who resided in Boston, Massachusetts, in 1860 or 1870. Because these men were to be sought in all the various sources listed above, they had to *be* traceable.[1] They also had to have moved from the countryside to the city. To satisfy these conditions, I required that the men be native-born, with both parents native-born, and that they be white. That the study concentrates on men, rather than on, say, equal numbers of men and women, to compare their experiences, results from my having decided to exclude women because of the difficulties in tracing them. The recent rash of finding aids, especially indexes to the 1850 and 1860 population censuses, together with indexes to the 1870 census (which seem inevitable), should make studies of samples of women ever more practicable.

The sample members were selected from the manuscript population censuses of Boston for 1860 and 1870. In 1972, when I began drawing the samples for this study, only four such censuses (1850–80) which contained name-by-name listings were readily available to researchers, so by starting in the middle I could search backward *and* forward. Later the 1900 and 1910 censuses were opened for research (1890's was accidentally burned in 1921), but only 27.1 percent of my subjects survived to the time of the 1900 census so it proved of limited usefulness (its index also omits many of those survivors). From the 1860 manuscript population census of Boston, Dorchester, and Roxbury, I selected every tenth head of household who satisfied my criteria, and from the 1870 census of Boston (which had annexed Roxbury in 1867 and Dorchester in 1869) I drew every eleventh eligible household head. Eventually (after checking on the men and their parents and replacing those who proved to have a foreign-born parent) the samples contained 1,405 and 1,403 men, respectively. Some 2,165 of the men turned out to be the in-migrants who were to feature in this study, while the remaining 643 were natives of Boston, Dorchester, or Roxbury. (Only four overlapped from the samples drawn for *The Plain People of Boston*.)

After selecting the men, I investigated them, trying to learn where they were born, when and where they married, when the in-migrants among them came to Boston, how they made a living, when (or if) they became parents, what befell them in Boston, how well they did financially, how long they stayed in Boston, when they left (most stayed), whither the out-migrants among them went from Boston, and when, where, and how the men died.[2] These inquiries, of course, address only the outwardness of the men's lives. Others, such as, What did the men think? What did they believe? Whom did they associate with? touch the inwardness of their existence. Ordinary people do not usually record these concerns except in letters and diaries; so few of these survive from the nineteenth century, and then primarily from atypical individuals, that one is hard put to infer from them much about ordinary people's attitudes.[3]

All too often since the autumn of 1972, I have imagined an assembly of the 1,400 or so men of either sample. In this fantasy, I hired a large hall in Boston, then placed notices (of course in the *Transcript* and the *Advertiser* but also in the *Atlas* and even in the *Herald*) admonishing the men, on pain of being omitted from the study, strictly to attend. The dates were set: 1 June 1860 and 1 June 1870; even a few days' delay would have seen some of the men carried off by death.

At these imaginary meetings the men looked different from modern men. A present-day observer would probably notice first the griminess of most of them, then their aroma. Both resulted from the infrequent "washing up" typical of the nineteenth century and visible in so many photographs of its people.[4] Amid the crowd, the observer would notice the slimness of most of the men: "At the Mechanics' Fair, in Boston [in the summer of 1860], 10,000 adult people were weighed on Howe's standard scales—and the average weight of the women was 116 lbs. 9 oz., and of the men 146 lbs. 13 oz."[5] Many of the sample members wore beards; I have several photographs of the more prosperous, and only one or two appear clean-shaven.

Of course, the really interesting part of my daydream would have been the extended interviews to be arranged with the men, with their wives, their children, and their co-workers, trying to elicit a sense of their everyday existence. Usually the men were just lining up at tables where my corps of assistants waited to sign them up for the interviews when I woke up, or the traffic light turned green, or a colleague recalled me to the reality of a department meeting.

Here are my best efforts to answer some of the questions I (and, I hope, you) would have asked in those interviews, as well as some the men themselves would not have been able to answer. To do so I have turned to and exploited the records made about the men by members of the new bureaucracy: census enumerators, city directory canvassers, tax assessors, sometimes even newspaper reporters—all people I suspect my sample members avoided or were glad to see gone. This may explain why some of them do not appear in some censuses, were omitted from the city directory, failed to be assessed, or did not get their names in the newspaper.

Studying the lives of 2,808 men makes one yearn for the comparative ease and simplicity of more nearly finite tasks, since additional labor always produces information on someone; the intervals between input and output merely become longer. Eventually, the researcher must decide that the research has ended. Analysis, contemplation, and writing must begin. This decision becomes easier when one's colleagues ask, "Have you started writing?" and when funding agencies indicate that the bucks stop here. All of these having occurred, I invite you to step back with me to the nineteenth century—another world, vanished, but not (let us hope) completely irretrievable.

To provide some idea of what may be recovered about the lives of ordinary people, here are three brief biographies, arranged in ascending length. Asterisks (*) indicate that the man was selected in one of the two population samples drawn for the study.

Anson Hardy – The Bare Minimum

In 1860 *Anson Hardy resided at 231 Shawmut Avenue in Boston's South End. He was born 27 April 1824 in Chatham, Massachusetts. Presumably by the time he moved to Boston in the late 1840s he had already traveled to Liverpool, England, because the notice of his marriage to Fanny Howe of Boston in 1848 describes him as "of Liverpool, England." Anson, Jr., was born in Boston in August 1849, and sometime during the next ten months or so the Hardys were off to Liverpool, where Francis A. was born in January 1851. By early 1855 they were back; Anson was an agent for the "Cutting Machine Mfg. Co.," and they boarded in Dorchester, where Helen was born in May 1855. Three more children appeared from 1856 to 1866, making six in all. In 1860, Hardy called himself a "merchant" and said he had $3,000 in personal property. He sold safes in partnership with Milton B. Bigelow. By 1870 he was once more an agent, for the "Tremont Safe & Machine Co." He claimed neither real nor personal estate but was assessed for $1,000 in personal property. In early 1872 he moved to suburban Newton, where he died of "general periostitis" in 1876, aged 52.[6]

Warren Lincoln – A Few More Details, Courtesy of a Family History

*Warren Lincoln did well in Boston. He was born in Hingham, Massachusetts, in 1801, and, his family's chronicler continues, finished his education at an early age and, having served an apprenticeship at the gilding and framing business with Kidder & Carter of Charlestown, Mass., set up in that business for himself, on Washington street, Boston, near Dock square. His work was of such superior quality that he greatly prospered. . . . He was of slender frame and nervous temperament. . . . He bore a spotless reputation throughout his business career. Both he and his wife were members and conscientious supporters of the Unitarian church.[7]

Lincoln joined the Massachusetts Charitable Mechanic Association in 1833, and his obituary in its *Annals* noted, "He was a man of marked social characteristics, very gentlemanly in his deportment and bearing."[8] Although the Lincolns had a son and five daughters, at his death in 1885 only four daughters survived him; his son perished in the Civil War, one daughter died at the age of 4, another at 31. His four married daughters produced only six grandchildren, of whom four died before the age of three. One granddaughter lived to be 42 but did not marry. His only grandson married but does not appear to have had children. By about 1920 his posterity was no more.[9] Financially, Warren Lincoln did well: in 1830, he was assessed for $400 in personal estate. In 1839 he moved to Salem Street, in Boston's North End, where he was to reside until 1871, long after all but a few other native-born residents had left that area. His 1840 tax assessment, $5,000 real and $5,000 personal estate, reflected considerable progress. By 1850 it had risen to $5,300 real, $15,000 personal. Just before the start of the war, his 1860 assessment had dropped back to $6,300 real but only $8,000 personal. Still, these amounts placed him in the top third of the city's taxpayers after about 1840. In the 1870 census he claimed $6,000 real and $15,000 personal estate, suggesting a recovery from 1860.[10]

*Ephraim H. Hall – Preserved by the Bureaucrats

*Ephraim H. Hall was a native Bostonian, born in 1841. His father, Solomon, was a carpenter from Falmouth, Maine, born about 1793, who by 1850 headed a household composed of himself, his wife, Eliza, age 30 (likely his second wife and Ephraim's mother), sons aged 18, 15, 10, 8 (Ephraim H.), 7, and 4, and a 2-year-old daughter, as well as four other females, aged 54 (his wife's mother, three years younger than Solomon), 34, 16, and 4—a total of 13, all in rented accommodations at 19 Dover Place. Solomon Hall claimed no real or personal estate in the 1850 census, and Charles Henshaw, the 71-year-old grocer who enumerated Ward 11 in 1860, seems to have missed the Solomon Hall household, which was presumably much smaller by then. By 1861 *Ephraim H. had followed his eldest brother George L.'s choice of occupation, brassfinisher. He and his next older brother Edward G. rushed to answer the call to the colors, joining Company F of the First Regiment of the Massachusetts Volunteer Infantry in May 1861; their father died that July, but Ephraim and Edward G. stayed in the army until their three years were up in May 1864. About five or six months of that period they were separated, when Ephraim was imprisoned in Richmond, Virginia, for some months after the Battle of Chancellorsville.

After being mustered out, Ephraim worked for a couple of years as a clerk, his occupation when he, aged 24, married Mary L. Milliner, 17, in Boston in June 1866. The couple appears to have left the city; their daughter Mary E., born in 1868, was born in Massachusetts, but not in Boston, and Ellen S., who came along in 1869, was born in Scarborough, Maine. When Ephraim reappeared in Boston in 1870, he was once again a brassfinisher, but this interlude was brief: the 1873 city directory shows him as a carpenter, his father's longtime livelihood and the occupation Ephraim followed through 1883. The 1880 census shows Ephraim, his wife, Mary, and Ellen S., their 11-year-old daughter. Their other daughters, Mary E., Jennie, and Susan, born in the 1870s, fell victim to scarlet fever. Late in the 1870s Ephraim and Mary abandoned the familiar stamping grounds of the Hall family in the South End–Washington Village neighborhood for the

open spaces of Jamaica Plain, West Roxbury, where there was probably more work for carpenters without extensive experience.

In about September 1883, as Ephraim admitted in 1915, "I left
Mary A Hall in 82 I think she was a Dope [addict?] and [she] went
off nights and stayed all night. She got a Divorce in 87 I did not
Protest."[11] Ephraim went west, first to Miles City, Montana, then to
Idaho for two years, settling in Omaha, Nebraska, in 1887. His first
wife filed for a divorce in June 1888, and Ephraim sent a telegram
from Omaha in June 1889, "Will not contest." As her grounds for
divorce Mrs. Hall alleged adultery by Ephraim. No final decree was
issued. Meanwhile, Ephraim had married Julia E. Kinneer in Omaha
in October 1887 so he would have had weak grounds for "protest-
ing." He lived in Omaha until 1905 (marrying a third wife, Winnie
Jane Shellhart, in October 1903), then moved to Benson, Nebraska,
where he resided in 1907. That year he "took up a claim" in Boyd,
Wyoming, and apparently remained nearby until his death in November 1918.[12]

The lives of this trio—*Anson Hardy, *Warren Lincoln, and
*Ephraim H. Hall—though differing markedly in character from
each other nevertheless present certain features common to many of
the lives of the native-born men who resided in Boston in the mid-
nineteenth century. About three-quarters of the native-born men of
native-born parentage in Boston had moved in from elsewhere, as
had Lincoln and Hardy. About 7 percent of the men served in the
Civil War, as Hall did. About a sixth of the men were rather successful, like Lincoln, another sixth, like Hardy, had limited success, and
more than half, like Hall, never paid a property assessment tax.
About a third of the men, like Hall, practiced a "skilled" occupation;
about a quarter of them, like Lincoln, were "major" proprietors, managers, and officials, and like Hardy, about a seventh of them filled
"clerical and sales" positions. Ultimately, like Lincoln, about 61 percent of the men died in Boston, like Hardy another 7 percent died in
the nearby suburbs, and like Hall, a small fraction, say 11 percent,
died at considerable distances (about 18 percent died within the state
but beyond the suburbs).

Their stories also reflect, roughly, the quantities of information
about individual "ordinary" people that can be grubbed from the

nineteenth century's legacy. *Anson Hardy was mentioned briefly in the genealogies both of the Hardy family and of the Howes, his wife's family, but that information consisted of bare pedigrees sufficient to trace his relationship to other family members. He was enumerated in the federal censuses of 1860 and 1870, was missed in 1850 because he was in England, and died before the 1880 census. He was probably assessed in Boston by 1860 and definitely in 1870. He appears not to have been mentioned in the *Boston Evening Transcript*, except perhaps in the "marriages and deaths" column, between 1830 and 1870. Accordingly, information on him is sparse, and his biography is necessarily brief.

With *Warren Lincoln we are on firmer ground. He occupies about a page in a family history which attempts to give more information about its subjects than is usual for such histories, including physical appearance, character, and religious preference. As a member of the Massachusetts Charitable Mechanic Association, Lincoln received two inches of tribute in its *Annals*. As a well-to-do Bostonian from the late 1830s to 1885, he was assured of the annual ministrations of the city assessors. His biography can be even longer and more detailed than Hardy's.

Since *Ephraim H. Hall served in the Civil War and later received a federal pension, a file on him in Washington permits fairly extensive reconstruction of his peregrinations. It does not, interestingly enough, indicate how he earned his daily bread at any time in his career except that, at his enlistment, he was a brassfinisher. We have advanced even farther as to specificity, however, than with *Warren Lincoln: *Ephraim H. Hall, on enlisting, stood five feet six and a half inches tall, whereas Lincoln was "slender" and Hardy of unknown stature.

Ideally there would be a full-dress biography for every sample member, but this was so only for *Thomas Bailey Aldrich, *Dr. James Ayer, *Dr. Henry I. Bowditch, *Rev. Sylvanus Cobb, *Horatio Hollis Hunnewell, *Dr. Edward Jarvis, *Dr. Dio Lewis, *Frederic Walker Lincoln (a memorial volume), and *Reverend Baron Stow, or about 0.2 percent of the 2,808 sample members (see the Bibliography for appropriate citations). Everyone else fell short, to a greater or lesser— usually a vanishing—degree.

When historians encounter this dearth of information on ordinary nineteenth-century lives, they may choose from two strategies: ignore the situation because it has gone away, or seek safety in numbers. This study chose the latter. Since it is highly unlikely that any single piece of information, apart from an individual's name, will be learned for all the people in a study of this kind, one must locate as much information as possible on its subjects so that its sheer mass will crush most obstacles. The story may then, one hopes, be reconstructed. Let us turn to it.

Origins

"Why, what did he go to Boston for?"

"Well, that's a pretty question! That's the only place to go to! Why, if a man wants anything he allus goes to Boston. Everything goes there, just as natural as if that city was the moon, and everything else was water, and had to go, like the tides. Don't you know all the railroads go to Boston? and sailors say—you ask Tommy Tafts—if you start anywhere clear down in Floridy and keep up along the coast, you will fetch up in Boston."

—Henry Ward Beecher, Norwood, *1868*

Another class of the sons of our farmers are not contented to gain their living by the sweat of their brow, but they must act (or rather ape*) the* gentleman*—crowd our cities as clerks in stores, or in other occupations, which they consider more* genteel, *more* respectable *than farming. They look upon farming as degrading, instead of being, as the beloved Washington designated it, "the most healthful, the most useful, and the most noble employment of man." This ought not so to be.*

—S. C. Charles, in New England Farmer *24 (2 July 1845): 4*

Seven brothers lately met at concord, N.H., whose united ages are 453 years. Not one of them remembers ever seeing the seven all together.

*—*Scientific American *1 (11 September 1845): 3/3*

Nineteenth-century observers spoke of cities' "magnetic attraction," which drew multitudes from the hinterlands. A closer look, however, shows that many aspects of this cityward movement were, and remain, unknown. Reality was, as usual, rather more complex and less straightforward than myth. Clergymen who inveighed against evil Boston's corrupting rural youth did not know that about half of the men moving to Boston from its environs were already "family men," hence presumably less susceptible to the Sirens' call of debauchery.[1] But that is getting ahead of our story.

During about the first three-quarters of the nineteenth century, Boston drew its migrants (all references to "migrants" are to native-born unless otherwise specified) from an area extending from the coast of Maine across New Hampshire and Vermont, then contracting to the south to include Massachusetts east of the Connecticut River, a sliver of northern Rhode Island, and the peninsula of Cape Cod (see Map 1.1). The city's attraction seems to have been augmented by ease of travel and reduced by the competing attraction of other urban areas. Few Massachusetts men came to Boston from west of the Connecticut River, for New York City dominated that area.[2] Of the 2,808 men in this study, Massachusetts provided about 40 percent of the 2,165 who were in-migrants to Boston (there were 643 Boston natives), followed by Maine (about 25 percent) and New Hampshire (about 22 percent). Allow Vermont a mere 7 percent and but 6 percent remains for "others." These proportions held, with minor variations, at least from the 1820s through the Civil War.

Changing Sources of Migrants

Early in the century, before the development of New England's extensive railroad network, migrants to Boston tended to hail from areas from which the journey to the city was easier: the coastline and along well-traveled interior routes (rivers and, later, turnpikes and canals). With the spread of rails throughout New England after the mid-1840s, more men from the interior towns began to arrive, changing the mix of skills they brought to the labor market away from maritime

MAP 1.1
Birthplaces of All In-Migrant Sample Members

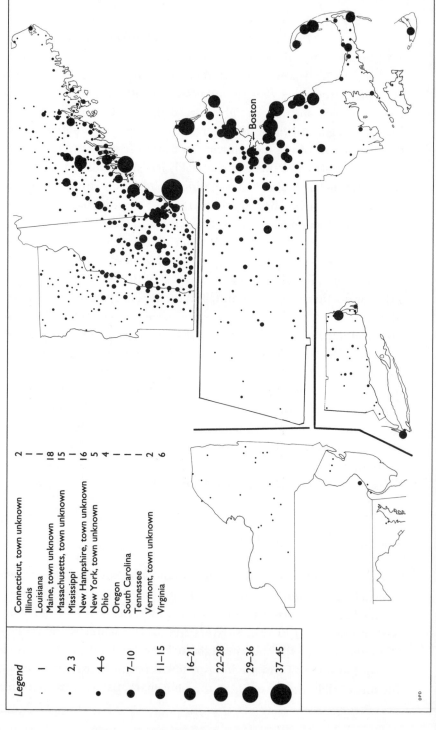

Legend

·	Connecticut, town unknown	2
	Illinois	1
	Louisiana	
·	Maine, town unknown	18
2, 3	Massachusetts, town unknown	15
	Mississippi	
·	New Hampshire, town unknown	16
4–6	New York, town unknown	5
	Ohio	4
●	Oregon	1
7–10	South Carolina	
	Tennessee	1
●	Vermont, town unknown	2
11–15	Virginia	6

16–21

22–28

29–36

37–45

Boston

DPD

and toward agricultural. Of course, after about the 1830s they could not farm in Boston so they had to take on new occupations there.

The spatial distributions of these earlier and recent in-migrants, separated into those who entered Boston before 1841 and those who arrived after 1845, are presented in Maps 1.2 and 1.3. Before 1841 New England's railroads were concentrated near Boston and presumably transported few in-migrants from distant places, whereas after 1845 the system began penetrating to all parts of the region. Comparing the maps one may note the striking opening up of interior regions as sources of migrants.

Most of the men who moved to Boston came from communities within 100 miles of the Hub: about a third moved less than 50 miles from their birthplaces to Boston, another third between 50 and 115 miles, and the remaining third over 115 miles. Since New York City was 240 miles distant, this suggests the relatively compact area from which most in-migrants came. As one might anticipate (see Table 1.1), those who moved the longest distances to Boston were probably the least well off and thus were destined not to do as well as those who had some family nearby (fuller details on the concept of "assessment wealth group" appear in the next chapter).

The maps of sample members' birthplaces, separated by sample (Maps 1.4 and 1.5), can only suggest what statistical inquiry reveals: the group of native-born men residing in Boston as of 1870 had come from a larger number of different communities than had their predecessors of 1860, and these communities tended to be farther away; the average distance to Boston from in-migrants' birthplaces rose from 97 to 104 miles during the Civil War decade. The increase, though small, was statistically significant. (Although married sample members tended consistently to come from slightly farther away from Boston than did the bachelors, this difference was not statistically significant.)

Most migrants to Boston came from small towns; apart from the few major cities in the region, small towns were the norm.[3] These men came from farms, even though their fathers might not have called themselves farmers, because farms constituted the settlement pattern in those towns. Almost every rural family grew something, kept some animals, resided by itself in a structure separate from the residences

MAP 1.2
Birthplaces of In-Migrants to Boston before 1841

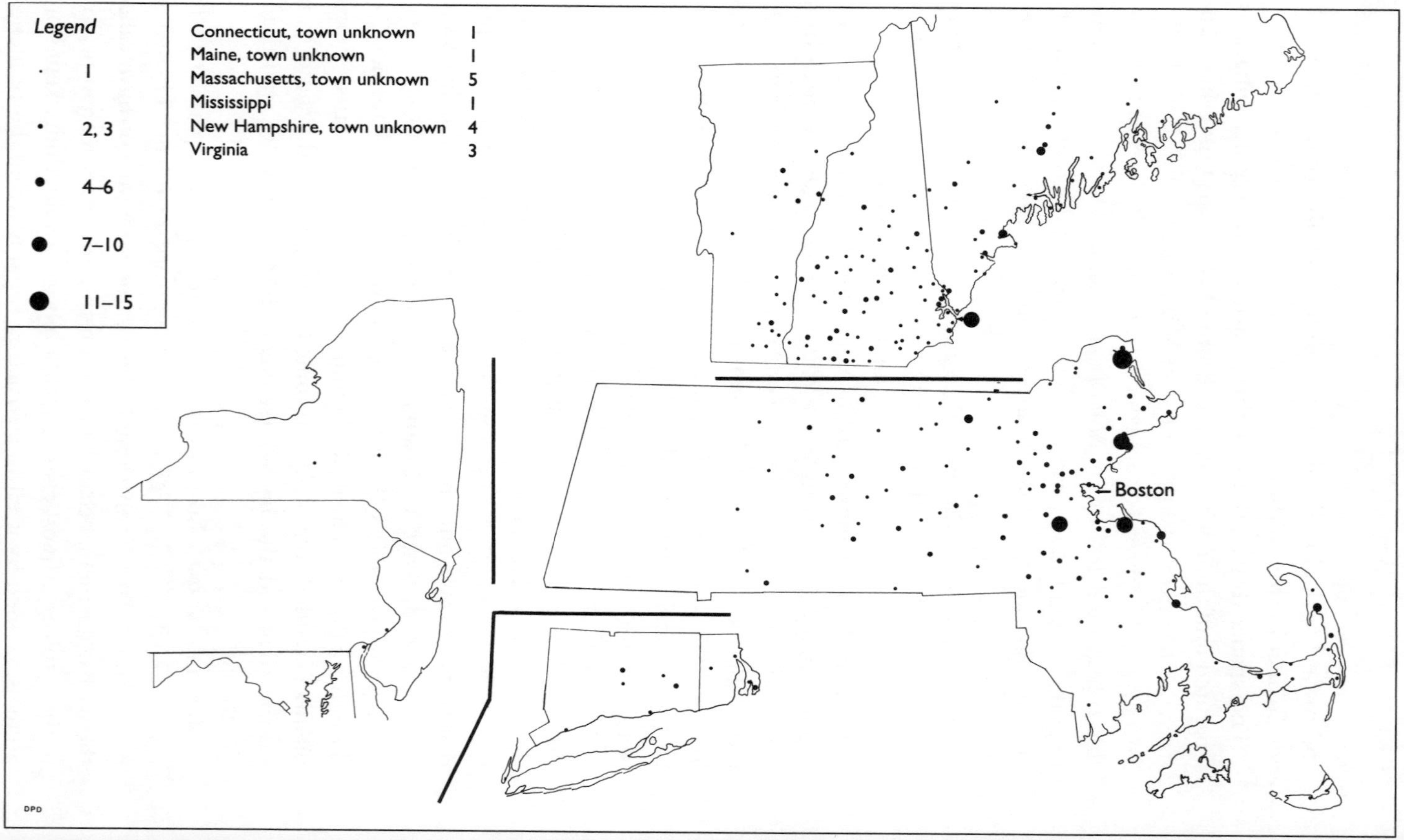

Legend

Connecticut, town unknown	1
Maine, town unknown	1
Massachusetts, town unknown	5
Mississippi	1
New Hampshire, town unknown	4
Virginia	3

·	1
•	2, 3
●	4–6
●	7–10
●	11–15

Boston

DPD

MAP 1.3
Birthplaces of In-Migrants to Boston after 1845

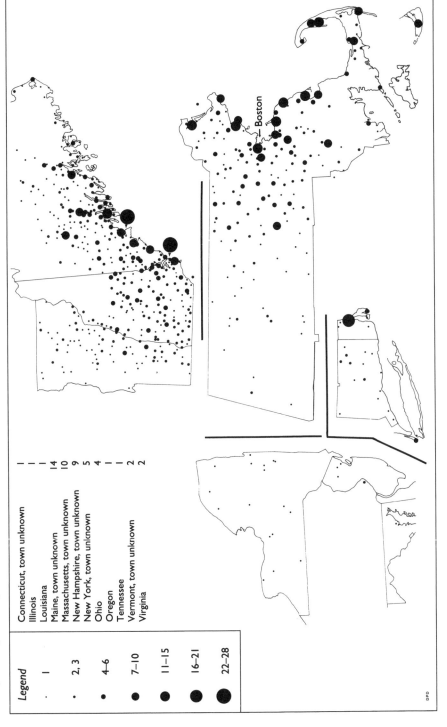

Legend

Connecticut, town unknown	1
Illinois	1
Louisiana	14
Maine, town unknown	10
Massachusetts, town unknown	9
New Hampshire, town unknown	5
New York, town unknown	4
Ohio	1
Oregon	2
Tennessee	2
Vermont, town unknown	
Virginia	

Legend	
·	1
.	2, 3
●	4–6
●	7–10
●	11–15
●	16–21
●	22–28

Boston

DPD

Table 1.1

Assessment Wealth Group Compared with Distance Traveled to Boston,
Both Samples Combined

Assessment	Distance traveled to Boston from birthplace (miles)			
wealth group	< 50	50–115	> 115	Totals
3 (highest third of positive assessments)	128	105	65	298
2 (middle third of positive assessments)	107	119	110	336
1 (lowest third of positive assessments)	111	121	102	334
0 (not assessed)	375	378	444	1,197
Totals	721	723	721	2,165

Source: All tables in this chapter are based on sample data. Chi-square significance
> 0.0001. Regression equations relating assessed wealth to distance from birthplace
to Boston were not statistically significant.

of other households (in nineteenth-century census listings of New
England's towns, the virtual one-to-one correspondence of houses
and households is notable).[4] The migrants, then, typically grew up in
towns of less than a thousand population; the families in such towns
were dispersed over the countryside in farms which, by 1850, averaged about 125 acres each and of which, again on average, about a
third was cultivated, with the rest in pasture and woodlots.[5]

In Maine, New Hampshire, and Vermont, the 1850 census enumerated just over half the adult males as farmers. In Massachusetts, Connecticut, and Rhode Island, where the trend toward urbanization was
much more pronounced, only about a third were farmers.[6] Among
the men in the study, the proportion of migrants coming from outside
Massachusetts whose fathers were described as farmers was 49 per-

MAP 1.4
Birthplaces of In-Migrants to Boston, 1860 Sample Members

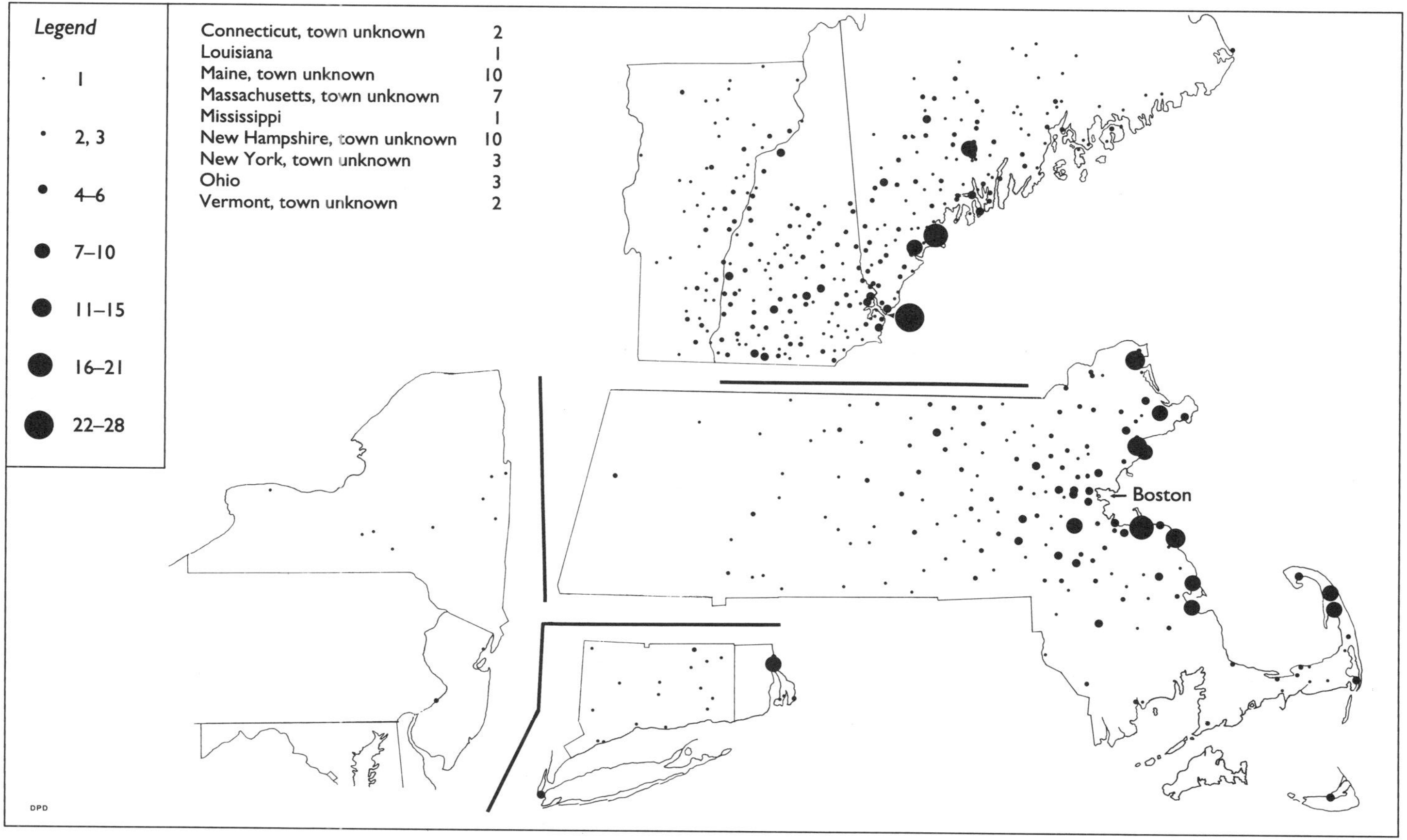

Boston

Legend

Connecticut, town unknown	2
Louisiana	1
Maine, town unknown	10
Massachusetts, town unknown	7
Mississippi	1
New Hampshire, town unknown	10
New York, town unknown	3
Ohio	3
Vermont, town unknown	2

.	1
•	2, 3
●	4–6
●	7–10
●	11–15
●	16–21
●	22–28

DPD

MAP 1.5
Birthplaces of In-Migrants to Boston, 1870 Sample Members

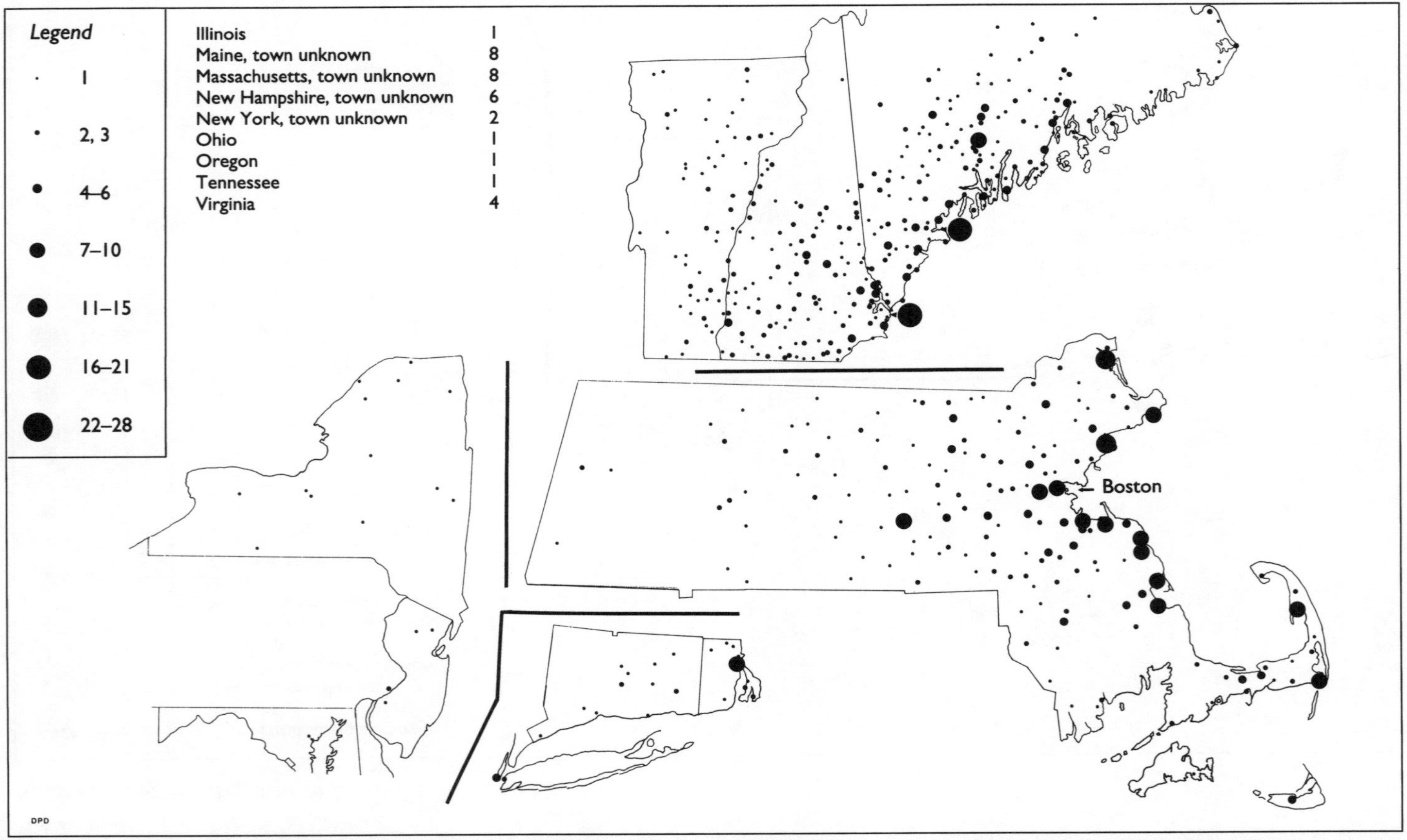

Legend

.	1
•	2, 3
⬤	4–6
⬤	7–10
⬤	11–15
⬤	16–21
⬤	22–28

Illinois	1
Maine, town unknown	8
Massachusetts, town unknown	8
New Hampshire, town unknown	6
New York, town unknown	2
Ohio	1
Oregon	—
Tennessee	—
Virginia	4

Boston

DPO

cent; for those from within Massachusetts the fraction fell to 26 percent. Neither value departs markedly from the census norm so it appears that migrants' fathers were farmers to about the extent usual around 1850 in New England.

Fortunately for historians, Lee Soltow has chosen three rather large nationwide samples of free adult males in the U.S. population as of 1850 (size 10,393), 1860 (size 13,696), and 1870 (size 9,823). He did this by obtaining National Archives population census microfilms, inserting them in a microfilm reader, and turning the crank handle a predetermined number of times until an eligible male's entry appeared (hence his designation of "spin samples").[7] In 1850, according to Soltow, the nationwide average value of real estate owned by native-born farmers was about $1,400.[8] He does not break down the 1850 wealth figures for native-born farmers by age, but if the trend is similar to that he reports for 1860, the average value of real estate owned by native-born farmers aged over 40 in 1850 would have been about $2,250.[9] These figures permit rough comparisons concerning the prosperity of the families from which the migrants came. As is usual in census-based studies, there is considerable attrition: by 1850, at least 631 of the 2,165 migrants' fathers were already dead, leaving only 1,534 who might have reported wealth in the census. Of them, 406 reported zero wealth to the enumerators, leaving 1,128 who might have possessed wealth; of them, 717 reported some wealth; the other 411 fathers could not be located in the census (likely because some of them were dead). The oldest third of these 717 fathers, aged 62 and over as of 1850, averaged about $3,600 in real estate, while the middle third, aged 51 to 61, averaged $3,100. The youngest third, aged 50 and under, averaged $2,750. Some 77 percent of native-born farmers nationwide who were aged 40 and over reported *some* wealth to the census enumerators,[10] as compared with 717 of the 1,129 sample members' fathers (64 percent). Adding in the 406 fathers who reported no wealth yields an overall average wealth for the sample members' fathers of just about $2,000. Taking into account the slightly lower than average wealth reported and the markedly lower than average proportion of fathers who reported any real wealth at all, it would appear that the migrants left from homes somewhat less well off than the average.

Leaving Home

A "typical" migrant to Boston was born in a town of under a thousand population, spent the first 18 years or so of his life in or near that town, and was then ready to strike out on his own.[11] This was not a sudden change in status for him because from about age 15 he was likely to have been working "out" for other farmers, usually within a few miles of home, or to have been learning a trade. David W. Galenson's examination of the biographies of almost 300 "New England manufacturers" memorialized by one J. D. Van Slyck in 1879 suggests that the mean age of leaving home for the 233 men for whom that datum was provided was 18; more than 80 percent of them had left by age 21. Interestingly, about 52 percent of their fathers had some connection with agriculture, as against 49 percent of the men in this study. Galenson suspects that his manufacturers may have departed a bit earlier than was usual for those who would go into nonmanufacturing pursuits. He also found that having a father who was a farmer tended to delay a son's departure.[12] The data in this study were more precise but do not speak directly to the same question because a sample member's age at departure from home was almost never recoverable from the nineteenth-century sources. As Table 1.2 shows, however, one may place an upper limit on the age at departure from home for those sample members who arrived in Boston unmarried by examining their ages at arrival in the city. This distribution would indicate that about half of the single in-migrants to Boston arrived during their early twenties, but since the principal source for determining their arrival in the city was the city directory, which tended not to list men under age 21, it is likely that quite a few of them arrived a year or two before that, in their late teens. Assuming that they had moved directly to Boston with no stops along the way, this accords well with Galenson's finding of a large clustering of departures from home around age 18.

One may obtain some blurred glimpses of the in-migrants "on the road," so to speak, since several of them appear twice in the manuscript population census of 1850 or 1860, once with their families "at home," again with a farm family a few miles away, listed as "laborer." *Aaron B. Hayden was enumerated 29 August 1850, aged 19, with

Table 1.2

Age Cohorts at Arrival in Boston of Unmarried In-Migrants, by Sample

Age cohort	1860 sample	1870 sample	Totals
0–10	18	28	46
11–20	78	85	163
21–25	255	219	474
26–30	130	95	225
31–35	32	30	62
36–40	6	8	14
41–50	4	4	8
51–60	1	0	1
Totals	524	469	993

Source: Sample data. Chi-square test for differences between the two samples was not significant.

his family in East Livermore, Maine, and also that day as a "farmer" in nearby Jay.[13] (He became a tailor and married Mary H. Orne of Lebanon, Vermont, in Boston in 1853; see Appendix C.) His apparent duality of residence could reflect that work for payment was going on or perhaps it indicates "labor exchange," a method by which farmers traded work at slack times of the year in return for aid at their busy times. The result was the same: the temporary removal of the migrant from his home family. Most of the workers so listed were in their late teens. It would seem reasonable that parents would be more prepared to allow a son to go off to Boston after he had spent a few months or even several years working "out" for nearby farmers, or after he had learned a trade, than if he had always worked "in" for the family. Consider the case of Asa G. Sheldon, who well remembered that "On April 14th, 1797, being still in my ninth year, Mr. Daniel Parker came to my father's house to get a boy to live with him. Mother said he might take his choice, Samuel or Asa. 'I will take Asa,' he said, 'because he is the youngest.'" Asa spent almost the next seven years residing with and working for the Parkers.[14] Legally, of course, all sons remained subject to their parents until they reached 21, the then age of majority, but it seems to have been usual to "give sons their time," thus allowing them to work for themselves, sometime between the ages of 15 and 18, depending on family situation. Among the men in this study, fathers who were farmers kept their sons home, on average, a year longer than did fathers who followed other occupations.[15]

About one-third of the migrants were the eldest son of their family, somewhat more than one would anticipate if birth order played no role in the decision to leave home (Galenson's manufacturers showed a proportion of 46 percent eldest sons for the 102 men for whom that information was available[16]). Historians still do not know a great deal about inheritance patterns in rural nineteenth-century New England, but there are strong indications that, if there were more than one son in a family, the eldest son did not usually inherit the family farm.[17] The average farmholding of about 125 acres did not permit a farm's subdivision into self-sustaining smaller units; 125 acres was about as small as a one-family farm could get and still support that family.[18] As a former resident of New Hampshire explained, "A farmer-proprietor, having from one hundred to three hundred acres of land, 'suitably divided into arable, pasturage, and woodland,' might have half a dozen sons and as many daughters. Such a farm does not divide to advantage. One son, not always the eldest, takes the homestead, assuming the support of his parents in their old age, and any unmarried aunts or sisters; the rest go out to make their way in the world."[19] Since rural men usually married in their mid-to-late twenties, by the time the eldest son reached age 18 or so, his father was probably in his late forties and hence not yet likely to turn over operation of the farm to the next generation.

The Sons' Dilemma

Surprisingly, one finds few discussions of farm succession in nineteenth-century sources. Likely the practice was so typical and the solution so obvious that it was commonplace.[20] It does seem plausible that, from early on, eldest sons knew that their chances of taking over someday as proprietor of the family farm were low. They had several options. They could decide to stay in farming and hope eventually to own a farm nearby, but for many this seems to have been impossible. Once gained, rural real estate tended to be retained: in four small New England towns analyzed in connection with this study (Eastham, Massachusetts; Greenwood, Maine; Rumney, New Hampshire; and West Fairlee, Vermont), the decadal persistence rates[21] during 1850–80 for farmers owning their farms were above 60 percent (i.e., at least 60 out of every 100 farmers who headed households and who were present in, say, 1850 were still there in 1860, at least 60 out of every 100 present in 1860 remained there in 1870, and so on). In a town of 30 square miles composed entirely of 125-acre holdings, there would be about 180 farms, so in a decade about 72 of them (or 40 percent) might become available (assuming 60 percent persistence), but of these the great majority would be inherited by other family members. So perhaps only two or three farms per year might enter the real estate market in any given town. Lee Soltow has estimated, as we have seen, that the average farmer over age 40 was worth only $3,000 as of 1850; if that sum equaled the cost of acquiring a farm, eldest sons desiring to purchase their own farms could not have looked to their parents for meaningful financial aid. They would have been trying to amass, even as down payments on their own farms, amounts representing a considerable fraction of their fathers' wealth.[22]

To raise money for their own farms sons could work "out" for other farmers at a dollar or so a day for years and hope to save enough to buy their own farms, they could perhaps go off to work in a mill or factory and also save, they could set up locally in a newly learned trade, or they could go west in search of cheap land. Or they could give up entirely the idea of farming and move to the city.[23] By the 1830s and 1840s, as employment opportunities beckoned in New England's mills and factories and on the new railroads, more and more young men seem to have decided that farming, at least in New England, was not for them. That they made this decision reluctantly is shown by their lifelong nostalgia for the family farm and by the efforts of the successful among them to reproduce in the suburbs the amenities of rural living without the attendant hard work.[24]

By the mid-1840s another factor had obtruded itself: the astound-

ing influx of Irish immigrants into New England. The federal population census of 1850 tabulated nativities of the population only at the
state level, but even then, only five years after the start of the Irish
mass emigration, Maine showed 2.4 percent of her population as having been born in Ireland, New Hampshire 9.8 percent, Vermont 4.9
percent, Massachusetts 11.7 percent, Rhode Island 10.8 percent, and
Connecticut 7.2 percent.[25] The Massachusetts state census of 1855 is
the only New England state census of the 1850s to have gathered
town-level data on nativity. By 1855, 16.0 percent of the Bay State's
population had been born in Ireland; if we count, as did those who
took the Boston city census of 1855, the children of foreigners as foreigners, the state figure would reach about 22 percent, or between
one-quarter and one-fifth. More important, by 1855 the foreign-born
were literally everywhere in Massachusetts; although they were concentrated in the cities, even Bristol County, the gateway to Cape Cod,
showed 18.0 percent foreign-born. Only the distant western and the
maritime counties had less than 10 percent foreign-born.[26]

The advent of these masses (most of the immigrants were adults
ready to enter the labor force) seems to have resulted in a lowering of
agricultural wage rates and to have increased for native-born sons of
farm families the attractions of factory work or of moving to the city.[27]
Although specific wage data are lacking, there was no shortage of
complaints about the newcomers. As early as 1847, the *Boston Evening
Transcript* quoted approvingly the "Native American State Committee" of Massachusetts's plaint that "a foreigner can live in Massachusetts for one third of what it costs a native citizen. . . . By such men
the native laborer is completely forced out of employment. He is un-
derbid in his wages at every step. The price of labor is reduced to a
scale, at which no man can live, but in the most abject relation to the
rest of the community, a mere fixture upon the soil."[28] At least some
of the pressures acting on Boston's in-migrants, then, were so-called
push factors.

From their parents, who could not usually send them into the great
world with much cash, the migrants received the experience, often
painful, of continued grinding physical labor associated with farm
life. Most family farms were too small for any labor-saving devices,
such as were then being adopted in the Midwest,[29] to be profitable,

even if they could have been afforded. Work was performed by muscle power—human or animal. It is noteworthy that the reported value (in current dollars) of farm implements, as a proportion of the value of farms, actually *declined* between 1850 and 1860 in New Hampshire, Vermont, and Connecticut. It rose only 0.7 percent in Maine, 3.1 percent in Rhode Island, and 7.5 percent in Massachusetts, suggesting an extremely slow (or even retrograde) mechanization of antebellum New England farming.[30] Almost every farm migrant's autobiography dwells on the hard work, the long hours, and the exhaustion involved in family farming; some gave these as reasons for their moving to the city.[31] More important, though, were the skills learned by the sons because they would base their careers in Boston on those skills.

The Importance of Skills

In discussing the acquisition of skills, it is important to distinguish those sons whose fathers were farmers from those whose fathers were not. Farmers taught their sons relevant agricultural skills, including crop management, manuring, animal husbandry, minor carpentry, teaming, implement maintenance and repair, and harvesting techniques. As a Bostonian, identified only as "L.," put it, "Farmers' sons are *born and brought up* in an agricultural school; and hence, if they intend to become farmers, they are as well prepared for it as a medical student is prepared to practise medicine, after passing through a course of study, and receiving his diploma."[32] But only a few of these skills, no matter how hard won, were directly transferable to the urban environment: teaming, animal husbandry, and simple carpentry. Farmers' sons who moved to Boston tended overwhelmingly to pursue occupations involving those skills, especially teaming and animal management, which translated in Boston into jobs as teamsters or stablers. Unfortunately for them, in the city such occupations did not lead to any considerable wealth, as will be shown in Chapter 3.

The sons of nonfarmers tended, in three-quarters of the cases, not to follow their fathers' occupations but still to acquire a nonfarming skill, which they took with them to Boston.[33] Here is yet another puzzle of nineteenth-century rural life. Why would a rural father pos-

sessing a nonagricultural skill not pass on its rudiments to his eldest
sons, knowing that someday they would have to make their way in the
world? How did the sons obtain their skills if their fathers did not take
advantage of their unpaid labor as a household income supplement?
Likely the sons were bound out (formally or informally) as apprentices to local craftsmen; this would have reduced household expenses
while ensuring their training and the loosening of home ties. The
brief obituaries of members of the Massachusetts Charitable Mechanic Association (of which more in Chapter 3) suggest that they
learned skills different from their fathers'. Perhaps fathers reasoned
that their sons would pick up, merely by being around, the rudiments
of the fathers' skills and that explicit training in another skill gave
the sons second strings for their bows.[34] Much more research is required in this obscure area: finding father-son pairs will be time-
consuming.[35]

Out-migration of the rising generation depleted the already sparse
"service sector" of the rural economy. In the four small towns mentioned earlier (Eastham, Massachusetts; Greenwood, Maine; Rumney,
New Hampshire; and West Fairlee, Vermont), there was a consistent
decline during 1850–80 in the size of the nonfarming sector of the
local occupational distribution. Blacksmiths, masons, and millers
tended to move to larger or more central locations. Occupationally,
most of New England's smallest towns seem to have become more
homogeneous during the nineteenth century, as farming or other
more specialized agricultural activities (dairying, truck gardening,
sheep raising) spread.[36]

Getting a Job in Boston

Sons of nonfarmers who moved to Boston did not have to worry
about fitting into the occupational hierarchy; they entered, usually as
skilled workers, into an economy eager for skilled workers. Between
1830 and 1870 the city's population rose from at least 60,000 to at
least 250,000, a net gain of about 200,000 in forty years, or about
5,000 per year or 13 every day.[37] The total number of dwelling houses
rose from 6,141, containing an average of 9.99 people each, in 1830,

to 22,542, sheltering an average of 9.02 each, in 1870 (in that part of 1870 Boston contained in the 1830 boundaries). Thus within the older core of Boston an average of one and one-eighth new houses was added to the city's stock *every day* for forty years—besides repairs, modifications, and replacement of that stock.[38] Add to that the food to feed these thousands of newcomers, garments to clothe them, wood to fuel their cooking fires, coal to heat their homes, and water for their kitchens, the streets and omnibuses or horsecars for their travel, the police and fire departments to protect them, railroads and ships to supply their wants and export their products, and banks, insurance companies, physicians, attorneys, clergymen, and government officials to care for them, mulct them, and bury them, and this will include almost all of the areas of the local economy dominated and administered by native-born men, three-quarters of whom had come to Boston from its hinterland.

Boston's "Magnetic Attraction"

Almost all migrants to Boston possessed some common characteristics: they were literate, having endured perhaps six years of sporadic attendance in local common schools; they were Protestant, of a patchwork of denominations;[39] and probably they already knew, or knew someone who knew, a Boston resident. The processes by which migrants moved to nineteenth-century Boston (or any other U.S. city, for that matter) remain obscure. Common sense suggests that migrants tend to prefer destinations about which they have *some* information over those about which they have little or none. How might they have obtained such information, or, in other words, how did Boston exert its magnetic attraction in the countryside?

Boston's newspapers circulated widely in New England; every little country weekly carried "exchange" items clipped from them, together with price and market information.[40] In addition, from early on the city was linked to the countryside by an extensive system of express wagons and stagecoaches connecting it to the farthest corners of Maine, New Hampshire, Vermont, and western Massachusetts (hence its nickname, the Hub).[41] Several migrants' autobiographies tell of their traveling to Boston on the local "express wagon," which carried to the city goods for sale and brought back newspapers, hardware, and "notions." The extension of the railroads throughout the region in the 1850s reinforced these patterns of communication and Boston's regional dominance.[42]

Boston also acted as a market for farm goods over a surprising distance. It was long supposed that the transportation of farm goods in the early nineteenth century over distances of, say, more than twenty miles was uneconomic, but recent research has revealed more or less regular visits to the city by enterprising farmers as far away as Worcester County and even Vermont.[43] In the winter it was much easier to travel (by sleigh) than it was by wagon at warmer (and muddier) times of the year. A few migrants' autobiographies or life sketches note that they hitched a ride to Boston with an obliging neighbor farmer needing help with a load going to the city. Once the railroads were completed, convenience of travel was multiplied, and migrants and their families could even return to the countryside for visits, just as their rural relations could visit them,[44] or perhaps send along a child to stay and attend the city's schools.[45] Later it will be useful to distinguish between the young single men, who seem to have moved directly from their hometowns to Boston without intermediate stops, and the married migrants, who sometimes did not.

Friends in the City

It seems likely that almost all migrants to Boston knew someone, or knew someone who knew someone, in Boston before they arrived. The retrospective tracing of residents of the four small country towns mentioned earlier revealed that, as of 1860, each town contained at least one household head who had resided in Boston in 1850, and these were towns whose populations ranged from 779 to 1,103 in 1860. There seems to have been extensive communication between Boston and the multitude of communities in its migrationshed.[46] This is suggested by the 1860 census of Ward 1 in Boston, the North End, where most of the city's "immigrant reception area" boardinghouses, for foreign- as well as native-born migrants, were clustered. Fortunately, the ward's census enumerator, William B. Tarlton (a native of Portsmouth, New Hampshire), noted the community of birth for almost all native-born and many foreign-born residents of the ward.[47]

Tarlton's returns show that boardinghouses were overwhelmingly ethnically specialized and that mixing of foreigners and native-born in the same house was rare (except, of course, for the presence of Irish servants in native-born households). This will not surprise anyone familiar with a census return of a mid-nineteenth-century city, but, more important, Tarlton's careful lists of the birthplaces of the boardinghouses' native-born denizens demonstrate areal specialization of boardinghouses, usually clustering around the birthplace of the proprietor. One can easily imagine that the parents of a son intending to move to Boston who had no friends or relatives there would inquire for the name of a reliable former resident, or friend of a resident, to whom they could entrust their son for the beginning of his stay in Boston. All the better if that proprietor came from their town or a few miles away. Certainly the lists of birthplaces of the native-born boarders in those houses show areal concentrations from small regions often far from Boston.[48] Given the networks of family and friends, it is likely that these boardinghouses accommodated a small minority of Boston's in-migrants.

Moving in with Co-workers

Those migrants who initially stayed in boardinghouses do not seem to have remained in them very long; expense alone would have dictated a brief sojourn.[49] Also, most jobs for skilled workers were not within easy walking distance of the North End. Analysis of where the migrants resided just before their marriages suggests that they soon shifted to boarding with the families of co-workers, which often explains the presence in the census of several unrelated individuals within a household who followed the same occupation as the head of household. When his children were young, taking in as boarders some of the household head's co-workers may have provided a useful supplement to his income; as his children got older, he may have reduced the number of boarders, perhaps because the children were

starting to contribute to the family's income. When the ties to co-
workers were reinforced (e.g., the boarder was a relative of the household head or his wife or came from the same town), the likelihood of
the boarder's marrying into the household increased. Boarders not
from the same geographical area as the household head or not following the same occupation were apparently less likely to marry into the
household. The migrants usually boarded somewhere until they married and set up their own households; even after marriage, some continued to board or to rent a house, apparently not from choice but
from economic necessity.[50]

Concentrations of Skills Lead to Geographical Concentration

Because these migrants came from areas where particular skills, usually agricultural or maritime, predominated, their occupations in Boston were largely predetermined. But in midcentury Boston almost no
occupations were evenly dispersed throughout the city; to the con-
trary, many productive[51] occupations tended to be concentrated. An
excellent example is shipbuilding, which was almost entirely centered
in East Boston. Few in this industry were landlubbers: the birthplaces
of most lay along the coast from Maine to Cape Cod. The conse-
quence of this concentration in East Boston was an ingathering of
men from only a few places (because only men from those places
could have learned shipbuilding) in a restricted area, East Boston. To
glance through that neighborhood's census returns is to become
aware of the great numbers of men from coastal Maine, New Hampshire (almost exclusively Portsmouth), and coastal Massachusetts who
resided there. But when one consults as well the lists compiled in 1859
of the city's residents who were natives of New Hampshire or Maine[52]
and matches their towns of birth to the listings in the census returns,
one sees that entire streets in East Boston were the domains of particular towns or groups of towns in Maine or New Hampshire (and
presumably Massachusetts also). Early occupational training in a specialization confined to a few small geographical areas of New England
had led to a reconcentration within Boston of men from those areas.
The friendships, kinship networks, and communications patterns

within East Boston (or the city's other similar neighborhoods) cannot be recaptured, but the high proportions of endogamous marriages within East Boston provide partial confirmation of their intensity and extent.

Native-born migrants to Boston in the period roughly from 1820 to 1870 came overwhelmingly from Massachusetts, Maine, New Hampshire, and Vermont, in that order, with a scattering from other states. They came from households apparently typical as to wealth and father's occupation, spending their late teen years working "out" for neighbors or learning a skill and gradually loosening home ties. They do not seem to have learned these skills from their fathers if the fathers were not farmers, which suggests that many may have worked locally for men with those skills or have been bound out as apprentices. When they left home, the single men in their late teens to early twenties usually moved directly to Boston without spending time at intermediate locations, whereas those already married (who by then were in their mid-thirties) had made one or two intermediate stops.

In Boston, the bachelors resided at first in boardinghouses, soon moving to board with families, usually of their co-workers. The married couples were more likely to set up independent households when they arrived; they were older and usually had already maintained their own households for at least ten years. The migrants' skills tended to redistribute them spatially in the city so that men with similar or identical skills often resided near each other. Those who applied their non-agricultural skills did better than those who used agriculture-based skills. Men who arrived unmarried in Boston and wed well there compiled the greatest gains, suggesting the desirability of a close look both at the married migrants and at the meaning of marriage in nineteenth-century Boston.

Marriage and Children

A MAN'S WEALTH *depends more on his wife than [on] his income. Some women will cause their husbands to become rich on five hundred a year; others can scarcely keep out of jail on five thousand. Saving has made more fortunes than getting one. If married men are poor, in nine cases out of ten, it is their wives' fault.*

–Boston Evening Transcript, *13 May 1853, 4/1*

DEATH THROUGH IGNORANCE. *The [Boston] Commonwealth states that in Roxbury, yesterday, an Irishwoman named Toomey, having heard that a quantity of tobacco steeped in milk would operate as an excellent* vermifuge *for children, procured the wicked dose and administered it to her own child, only a year old, causing its death in less than an hour and a half.*

–Boston Evening Transcript, *8 July 1851, 2/3*

A MOTHER'S LOVE. *We learn from the [Boston] Journal that Mrs. *Daniel Warren of 528 Commercial street, on Tuesday afternoon missed her little son [Charles M.], eighteen months old, and found him at the eaves of the roof, sitting in the gutter with his feet hanging over the outer edge. The little fellow was screaming with all his might, and without for a moment thinking of the danger to which she was exposed, she slipped down the roof to the eaves, and seizing her darling boy, bore him in safety to the attic, when she instantly fainted, and it was with much difficulty that she was restored to consciousness.[1]*

–Boston Evening Transcript, *12 July 1855, 1/5*

Almost any issue of almost any antebellum daily newspaper (usually they ran four pages) probably contains some reference to marriage. Editors delighted to run items such as "Choice of a Wife" or to point out in death notices that the deceased was survived by 10 children, 66 grandchildren, 160 great-grand-children, and 12 great-great-grandchildren,[2] all of whom had crowded around the deathbed to speed the parting matriarch. To judge from today's newspapers, it seems that there has been a considerable shift in society's concerns over the last century or so.

Expectations about Marriage

In the early nineteenth century people expected that every young man and woman physically capable of marrying would do so someday; in their study of northern antebellum agriculture, based on sample households drawn from the census of 1860, Jeremy Atack and Fred Bateman suggest that, as of 1860, about 69 percent of the native-born women in the Northeast were married, and this proportion would rise if it included all women who ever married.[3] Yet historians know less about how marriages occurred than they would like to.

As a corollary to universal marriage, people assumed that every marriage would produce, or attempt to produce, children. Among the sample members, a considerable countertrend seems to have begun in the antebellum era and to have extended at least to the 1870s.

Once married, a couple would live together, as they had vowed, "until death us do part." This assumption glossed over the fact, which occasionally protruded from newspaper accounts, that there were sometimes considerable stresses within marriages:

ADMITTED TO BAIL. *Ansel L. Flanders, who has been lying in jail for two or three weeks past, awaiting the convalescence of his wife, upon whom he made a murderous assault with a hatchet, was brought up for the third time in the Police Court this morning. Mrs Flanders was able to appear, though still very feeble, and he was formally admitted to bail in the sum of $1000

to appear at the next Municipal Court, but in default thereof he
was again committed.

Flanders is a mason by trade, resident at the South End,
and committed the assault through the influence of jealousy.
The appearance of both husband and wife, as they confronted
each other, was that of respectability, and the case altogether is
but another illustration of the evil power of the "green-eyed
monster."[4]

Separation and even desertion by husbands was much more frequent
among the couples in this study than was divorce. Divorce was expensive and time-consuming because it involved a hearing before a
county supreme judicial court.[5] Desertion or separation achieved
many of the desired results at no cost. (The title *widow* appended to
women's names in nineteenth-century city directories was sometimes
a polite fiction for deserted wife.) But among the couples in the study,
divorce, desertion, and separation affected less than 5 percent of the
marriages; in over 95 percent of the cases, death *did* them part.

One would like to know how young men and women met—
seemingly a more mysterious process in the city than in the countryside.[6] It would be desirable to know more about the economic circumstances of marriage: did grooms anticipate that marrying a particular
bride would give them a financial boost, or was that a minor or negligible consideration?

Ideally we would like to peep into our couples' bedrooms to learn
the most intimate details of their wedded lives, but the dearth of public information on these questions is notorious. Possibly some letters
and diaries may illuminate this obscurity. The public records permit
conjecture about some aspects of marital behavior (or its lack) because
of the appearance (or nonappearance) of children. These records
give indications about premarital sex, the spacing of children, their
quantity, and their parents' presumed practice of birth control. One
may surmise from this evidence that couples adopted various strategies concerning the timing and production of children, because patterns in their appearance (and in the cessation of their appearance)
emerge from the analysis of the sample members' 2,775 first marriages (492 of them married twice, 62 three times, 6 four times, and

1 entered into a fifth marriage [*Brown P. Stowell married first at the age of 22; each of his first four wives died within four years of marrying him, and he died while fighting a fire, aged 43, after less than five years of a fifth marriage. He also found time to serve twice in the Civil War, for 90 days and two years, spending a year and a half in a Confederate prison in Galveston, Texas.]).[7]

The Timing of Marriage

The record[s] of the City Registrar in Providence [Rhode Island], show that Thursday is the best marrying day in that city. Singular to state, it is ten per cent. better on that day than [on] the other days of the week.
—Portsmouth *(N.H.)* Morning Chronicle, *1 December 1860, 2/2*

As was mentioned in Chapter 1, not quite half of the migrants among the 1860 sample members were already married when they arrived in Boston; the corresponding proportion for the 1870 group was just over half. Table 2.1 compares those who were already married when they arrived in Boston with migrants who were single at their arrival and suggests that (as one might anticipate) moving to Boston was associated with a delay in marriage. The average ages at marriage of 583 male natives of Boston, 26.3, and of 573 of their brides (about three-fifths of whom were in-migrants), 22.8, agree with the pattern among the total in-migrant group. These figures suggest that Boston natives were marrying, on average, about a year or so earlier than their country cousins and that those men who came to Boston single usually were able to find a bride with only slightly more difficulty than were the city's male natives.

The sample members who arrived already married tended to be appreciably older than the single arrivals; the age distributions of those men already married when they arrived appear in Table 2.2. (Soon we shall see that there were interesting differences between the prosperity of the two groups as well.)

Men who married after their arrival in Boston tended to select as brides women who were younger, as measured by the difference in ages between the spouses, than had the men who were already mar-

Table 2.1

Average Age at First Marriage for In-Migrants and Their Brides

	Arrived single		Arrived married		Totals	
		Average		Average		Average
	N	age	N	age	N	age
In-migrants	987	27.3	784	24.3	1,771	26.3
Their brides	973[a]	23.4	754[b]	22.3	1,727	22.9

[a]About three-quarters of these brides were also in-migrants.
[b]About nine-tenths of these brides were also in-migrants.

The average age differences between both in-migrants arriving married and in-migrants arriving single and between their brides arriving married and brides acquired in Boston are significant at the 0.0001 level. Unless otherwise stated, all tables in this chapter are based on sample data.

Table 2.2

Age Cohorts at Arrival in Boston of Married In-Migrants, by Sample

Age cohort	1860 sample	1870 sample	Totals
17–20	0	3[a]	3
21–25	42	68	110
26–30	133	126	259
31–35	89	125	214
36–40	88	81	169
41–50	91	98	189
51–60	39	44	83
61–70	4	9	13
71–80	1	1	2
Totals	487	555	1,042

Chi-square test for differences between the two samples was not significant. Compare Table 1.2.
[a]The ages at arrival of these three married men were 17, 18, and 20.

ried when they got to the city (see Table 2.3). The trend toward an increasing age differential between spouses, with the average age of the grooms rising faster than that of their brides, was of long standing, as Table 2.4 shows. The statistics do not bear out the theory that the men who arrived unmarried selected brides who were appreciably their juniors so as to be able to sire larger families. Those who were bachelors on arrival fathered families slightly smaller than did those men who arrived already married (3.16 as against 3.43 children for fruitful couples in first marriages). The data provide no explanation for this trend, but possibly considerable out-migration from Boston of young unmarried women forced in-migrating bachelors to select wives from the pool of remaining, slightly younger, women.

The two great in-migratory streams thus consisted of young bachelors and men who were already married upon arrival in Boston, who averaged about 36 years of age at arrival, and who had been married about 11 years. They arrived with a wife and (usually) had had all, or almost all, their children. In contrast, men who were single on arrival were aged about 22 when they came to Boston so they faced five years or so of life in boardinghouses or residing with co-workers before setting up their own households. They were most likely, as well, to complete having their children before leaving Boston. These two groups demonstrate other interesting differences.

Married In-Migrants

Migrants who were already married when they arrived in Boston tended to have wed women, also from the countryside, who had been born nearby; only about 10 percent of their brides were natives of Boston (this may have encouraged such couples' moving to Boston). By the time they arrived in Boston, these men were already established in their careers, but their financial success before arrival appears to have been mixed. Of the 1,405 men in the 1860 sample, some 216 resided outside Boston and headed their own households in 1850. Only 73 of them reported real wealth to the census enumerator, and this averaged about $2,900; eliminating the five wealthiest among

Table 2.3

Average Difference in Age between Spouses (Husband's Age–Wife's Age) in
First Marriages, by Marital Status of Husband on Arrival in Boston

| | Husband arrived | |
	Single	Married
Average difference in ages between spouses (husband–wife), in years (all couples)	3.92***	2.78***
N	1,009	974
Average difference in ages between spouses (husband–wife), in years, for couples with children	4.13***	3.00***
N	850	859
Average number of children produced in first marriage (for couples with children)	3.16*	3.43*
N	867	925
Childless couples	168	151

Asterisks will be used to indicate significance levels of differences, with one asterisk
per zero, as a mnemonic aid:
*Single/married difference is significant at the 0.01 level.
***Single/married difference is significant at the 0.0001 level.

them, who reported $10,000 and over, yields a more realistic figure
of $1,620. The men were then in their early thirties; Lee Soltow's
figures from the 1850 census show an average wealthholding nationwide for men aged 30 to 39 to have been $835, somewhat less than
the average for our group, $980, which includes the 143 men report-
ing zero wealth. But Soltow also indicates that in 1850 about 50 percent of all native-born males aged 30 to 39 owned some real estate,
though the rate among the 1860 sample group was only 34 percent.[8]
    The situation looked better for the 1,403 sample members from
1870, for 150 of them resided outside Boston as of 1860, and 121

Table 2.4

Average Differences in Ages of Spouses (Husband–Wife), among Sample Members, by Decade of Marriage, 1797–1879

Decade of first marriage	Average difference in ages of spouses (husband–wife), years	N
1790–1799	3	1
1800–1809	4.04	10
1810–1819	3.32	40
1820–1829	2.85	202
1830–1839	2.96	390
1840–1849	3.30	655
1850–1859	3.54	796
1860–1869	3.76	374
1870–1879	3.62	25
Totals	3.36	2,493

No consecutive interdecadal differences between averages were significant at below the 0.05 level.

reported some real or personal wealth, averaging $4,100 or so; dropping four wealthy souls who reported over $30,000 in wealth lowers that average to a more realistic $2,500. Soltow's countrywide average for all native-born men aged 30 to 39 in 1860 was $2,444, and the proportion of them who possessed wealth remained at 50 percent.[9] Among those who had moved to Boston between 1860 and 1870, as of 1860 the corresponding proportion was 121/150, or 81 percent. In current dollar terms, then, the typical married migrant of the 1870 group was considerably more prosperous than his predecessor ten years before had been, perhaps even as prosperous as the typical native-born male of his age, and he was much more likely to have reported owning some real or personal wealth. But this wealth did not necessarily confer any special advantage on its possessors, for married migrants in both samples numbered disproportionately in the city's poorer tax-assessment wealth groups. The best predictor of how well a migrant to Boston would do financially was the nativity of his wife. Probably without their knowing it, migrants' choice of a wife helped shape their later success—or lack thereof.

Selecting a Wife

In antebellum Boston whom one married (or had already married) was related to one's economic success, at least as measured by the city's tax assessors. If we divide wealthholders into three roughly equal groups, based on their tax assessments in the year they were sampled, and divert the nonassessed into a fourth group, then examine their marriage patterns in Table 2.5, this observation becomes more specific. There was a slight but definite trend toward delayed marriage among men of the higher wealth groups, but not among their wives. The average age of the men at the time of these assessments was 41, which gave them more than a decade to accumulate wealth after their marriages. Nativity and wealth accumulation were related. One would anticipate finding native Bostonians disproportionately among the richest because wealth accumulation takes time, and the longer one's family has resided in a place, the more opportunities one's forebears have had to "get in on the ground floor" of accumulation, especially in real estate, which accounted for the bulk of Boston's wealth.[10] But there was always an inflow of ambitious men from the countryside who made their mark and their fortunes. The origins of their brides were certainly connected with their success, especially for the most successful of them, as one may see from Table 2.6.

These results suggest that the optimal marital behavior for an ambitious young man was to move to Boston at about age 22, work hard for about five years, making as many local contacts as possible, and marry a local woman. This strategy could not have guaranteed success, but it certainly would have helped. Why could such differences

Table 2.5
Average Age at First Marriage, by Assessment Group, Both Samples

Assessment group	Groom's average age	N	Bride's average age	N
Richest third	***27.3	387	23.1	376
Middle third	*26.6	389	**23.5	378
Poorest third	26.4*	343	23.0	340
Not assessed	*,***25.8*	1,238	**22.6	1,209

*Difference is significant at the 0.01 level (i.e., among grooms, middle third and not assessed, poorest third and not assessed).
**Difference is significant at the 0.001 level (i.e., among brides, middle third and not assessed).
***Difference is significant at the 0.0001 level (i.e., among grooms, richest third and not assessed).

Because of the higher mortality rates for women in the early years of marriage, it is more difficult to learn their age at marriage; thus the N's for them are smaller than for the men.

Table 2.6
Birthplace of In-Migrant's Wife, Compared with His Assessment Group, for Men Who Arrived in Boston Unmarried

Assessment group	Wife born in Boston		Wife also in-migrant		Totals
	N	%	N	%	
Richest third	55	35.0	102	65.0	157
Middle third	38	24.4	118	75.6	156
Poorest third	52	33.1	105	66.9	157
Not assessed	122	25.4	358	74.6	480
Totals	267	28.1	683	72.9	950

Percentages sum horizontally (chi-square significance > 0.037).

in wealth status have been associated with one's wife's birthplace? For some possible answers let us glance at the nature of business in ante-bellum Boston.

Business Organization in Antebellum Boston

Almost every business enterprise in antebellum Boston was con-ducted in the name of one or more individuals, as the city directories show. Very few businesses, except for banks and insurance compa-nies, sheltered behind the anonymity of a corporate name.[11] The style of most firms was "A, B, & Co.," or "A, B, C, & Co."; the city directory revealed who the "& Co." were. In the case of large commission mer-chant firms, as many as six or seven principal partners might be listed, but most firms consisted of only two or three individuals and were partnerships, usually entered into for a set period (often five years). The city's newspapers ran many notices of partnerships established and dissolved, especially around 1 January and 1 July. Most firms did not command substantial resources, and turnover among them was high; over the years most sample members who had partners had a series of them.[12] Since many partnerships were small operations, they probably relied heavily on word-of-mouth advertising or recommen-dations from friends or relatives. Self-employed sample members with limited resources would have been especially dependent on in-formal networks. It seems reasonable that a Boston-born wife would know more local people and be related to more others than would be a wife from outside the city; too, if she disposed of any capital re-sources, they were most likely local. These may seem slim advantages, but some combination of them may help explain the slightly greater success of in-migrants with Boston-born wives.

Death Did Them Part: The Length of Marriages

The average Yankee couple residing in antebellum Boston could look forward (had they but known) to almost 34 years together. Table 2.7 indicates that more husbands than wives died first.[13] For about the

Table 2.7

Average Duration of First Marriage, by Cause of End of Marriage

Cause of marriage's end	Average duration of marriage (years)	N	Average number of children (for couples with children)	N
Husband died first	38.6	1,184	3.49	1,208
Wife died first	29.0	907	3.32	890
Wife died first, but date is unknown	[26.1]ᵃ		(for all couples) 1.82	246

ᵃEstimated using the regression equation: years married = 2.75 times (number of children from first marriage) + 21.

first 26 years of a first marriage, the wife was the more likely to die, probably because of the dangers associated with childbirth; after about 26 years, the husband was more likely to die first. An average family's three children would be born over a period beginning about a year and a half after marriage and lasting about eight and one-half years (as explained below) so that by the tenth year of marriage child-bearing would be completed. If the mother of our average family died first, the youngest child would have been about 15, the oldest 23 or 24. If the father died first, the eldest child would have been about 37, the youngest around 29; in such cases the "nest" would have been empty for several years. Entirely apart from practical considerations of survival (as described by Ruth S. Cowan[14]), the presence of young children obliged their widowered father to remarry (half of the widowers from a first marriage remarried within two years)[15] or to make long-term paid domestic arrangements. In a few cases, the widower married a younger sister of his late wife, converting an aunt into a stepmother; this seems to have become less common with time.

Table 2.8

Average Duration of First Marriages and Reason for Their End,
for Marriages Begun in Three Different Time Periods

Period during which first marriage began	N	Average duration (years)	N	Husband died first	Wife died first
Before 1843	722	37.8***	940	439[a]	501[a]
1843–1853	664	***33.7***	873	459[a]	414[a]
After 1853	727	***31.2	844	491[a]	353[a]
Totals	2,113	34.2	2,657	1,389	1,268

*** Differences significant at the 0.0001 level.
[a] Chi-square significance > 0.001.

The trend, as Table 2.8 indicates, was toward marriages of shorter duration. The trend also was for more marriages to be terminated by the death of the husband, since for the three periods analyzed, the average age at death for husbands who married in those periods declined from 74.0 (N = 944) through 69.0 (N = 879) to 66.1 (N = 865) (differences significant at the 0.0001 level). Clearly some factors were operating to reduce the life expectancy, over time, of the sample members. As well, they were having fewer children.

Children: A Vanishing Breed?

YOUNG AND OLD MOTHERS. —*In the Portland [Maine] Advertiser is an item stating that while the census-taker was collecting his statistics in Searsmont [Maine], he found a very young woman, only thirteen years old, who was the mother of a child of ten months.*

On the other extreme, the Cincinnati [Ohio] Express mentions that a lady of that city, Mrs. Alice W., . . . is over 57 years of age, having been born in April, 1803. . . . About a week ago, Mrs. W. gave birth to a pair of boy-twins.

—Portsmouth *(N.H.) Morning Chronicle, 30 August 1860, 2/1*

The principal reason for marriage, according to some nineteenth-century writers, was to perpetuate the race.[16] Boston's migrants and natives at midcentury probably would have agreed—up to a point, for in some ways Boston does not seem to have been a hospitable environment for children.[17] High rates of infant mortality in American cities of the nineteenth century have long been remarked on,[18] but there are other, more subtle indications of what was occurring. Rates of childlessness among the city's couples who married after arriving there (16.3 percent) were higher than for in-migrating couples who had married elsewhere (14.0 percent), and, as one would expect, completed families were smaller. Nevertheless, the 2,775 first marriages of sample members produced at least 7,687 children (424 first marriages were childless), and all marriages of the sample members accounted for at least 8,653 children (only 326 marriages were childless, i.e., 98 sample members who had no children in a first marriage later fathered at least one). The children of first marriages made up 88.8 percent of all the children.

Smaller families were a long-term trend among the samples' couples, among whom at least three reasons for smaller family size may be discerned: delayed marriage for men; lengthening of intervals between children, starting with the first; and an ever-earlier end to childbearing by wives.

It proved possible to determine the interval in days between the date of marriage and the date of birth of a couple's first child in 1,232 of the 2,351 first marriages of sample members who had children. The intervals ranged from −40 days (the couple married 40 days after birth of their first child), through 0 days (a tie), to 5,357 days, which is just over 14.5 years. There were some extremely interesting differences among the sample members, as Table 2.9 suggests. This agrees with Atack and Bateman's finding that in the Northeast levels of fertility were lower in the countryside than in the cities.[19] Over time there was a distinct prolongation of the interval to the first birth (see Table 2.10). Most of the increase in the interval to the birth of the first child would appear to have occurred early in the century. Looked at by marriage cohorts, as shown in Table 2.11, the first-birth interval seems to have been lengthening at least since the 1820s.

In midcentury Boston, strong relationships are evident between the

Table 2.9

Average Interval from First Marriage to First Birth, by Nativity of Father

Fathers were	Average birth interval (days)	N
Natives of Boston	583**	327
In-migrants	718**	905
Single on arrival	735	529
Married on arrival	693	376

**Difference significant at the 0.001 level.

Table 2.10

*Average Interval from Marriage to First Birth, by Period of Marriage,
for First Marriages*

	Married before 1843	Married 1843–1853	Married after 1853
Average interval to first birth (days)	**549***	**705	734***
Number of cases	276	432	524

**Difference is significant at the 0.001 level (i.e., between Married before 1843 and Married 1843–1853).
***Difference is significant at the 0.0001 level (i.e., between Married before 1843 and Married after 1853).
Difference between Married 1843–1853 and Married after 1853 was not statistically significant.

variables describing the beginning and ending of child "production" and the extent of that production; for example, among couples who produced children in their first marriage, for each year younger at which the wife had her first child, the couple would average 0.106 additional children; the average age at having the first child for these wives was 24.6. The corresponding figures for the fathers were 0.073 and 28.1, so obviously the wife's age was the more important factor in

Table 2.11

Average Number of Children in First Marriage (for Couples with Children) and Average Interval to Birth of First Child, by Decade of Marriage

Decade of first marriage	Average number of children (for couples with children)	N	Average interval to birth of first child (days)	N
1797–1806	5.5	2	420	2
1807–1816	4.31	26	346	15
1817–1826	4.50	125	476	64
1827–1836	***4.16	287	493	100
1837–1846	***3.48**	454	649	180
1847–1856	3.15**,***	645	710	490
1857–1866	2.61***	352	770	290
1867–1876	2.54	97	727	89
1877–1879ᵃ	2	2	742	2
Totals	3.35	1,990	682	1,232

**Interdecadal difference significant at 0.001 level.
***Interdecadal difference significant at 0.0001 level.
No interdecadal differences among average birth intervals were statistically significant.
ᵃThe last sample member's first marriage occurred in 1879.

this consideration (both sets of relationships were significant well beyond the 0.00001 level). Carl N. Degler suggests that in the early nineteenth century women were gaining ever more control over the timing of child production, a finding these figures do not controvert.[20]

Children and Occupation

Since wealth and family size were closely related, the number of children produced by parents should have varied with the father's occu-

Table 2.12

*Average Total Number of Children Produced by Couples Who Had Children
in Their First Marriage, by Major Occupation Group*

Major occupation group (and average age when sampled)	Average number of children (for couples with children)	Number of couples with	without children (%)	
Semiskilled & Service (42.0)	3.37	323	65	16.8
Clerical & Sales (38.3)	2.82	239	53	18.2
Skilled (42.5)	3.25	1,021	170	14.3
Proprietors, Managers, & Officials (50.6)	3.57	598	97	14.0
Professionals (47.0)	3.31	105	24	18.6
Totals	3.31	2,286	409	15.2
All couples	3.33	2,351	424	15.3

pational group (these groups will be discussed more fully in the next chapter), and they did, as one may see in Table 2.12. Lower economic standing did not prevent couples from having greater numbers of children; three of the groups poorer than those in Clerical and Sales had more children, on average, than did members of that group. Childlessness did not seem to be related to poor circumstances either, for among the second wealthiest group, Professionals, almost one marriage in five was without issue, while the wealthiest group, the Proprietors, showed the lowest rate of childlessness and the highest average number of children. Prosperity conduced only very slightly toward larger families, as may be demonstrated by a regression equation involving assessed wealth and number of children produced in the 2,351 fruitful first marriages: predicted number of children = 0.00000449 times (assessed wealth) + 3.284027. This would suggest that couples worth, say, $10,000 would produce about 3.25 children, and couples twice as well off would average only about 3.3 children. Really large differences showed up only at very high assessment levels. The youngest members of society were also the most receptive toward family limitation, a conclusion reinforced here by the strong connection between average age among occupation-group members and total number of children. The high rates of childlessness among the Clerical and Sales and Professional groups, often mentioned as those most closely associated with "modernizing" tendencies, also suggest that the decline in child production may have begun among these groups.

The Timing of Children

About one-third of the men had begun to become fathers by the age of 25.7 and two-thirds by the age of 29; the corresponding figures for their wives were 22 and 25.9. When their last child was born, the analogous figures for fathers were 32.6 and 39, for mothers 29.4 and 36. By their late thirties, then, two-thirds of Boston's native-born parents had completed their families. These ages are much lower than those found by Atack and Bateman in their study of antebellum northern agriculture centered on 1860: the average farm wife in the Northeast had her last surviving child at age 39.4 and the average nonfarm wife at 40.4.[21] Since death rates among women of childbearing age were probably higher in Boston than in rural areas, the couples may have curtailed their childbearing so as to shorten the period during which wives were at risk from such diseases as childbed fever.

There were also significant differences among the various groups in the sizes of their completed families, as Table 2.13 demonstrates. For each calendar year earlier couples married, on average they produced an additional 0.047 child, suggesting a decline in that average of about one full child in 21 years, a rapid fall for this important

Table 2.13

Average Number of Children, in First Marriage, of Couples Who Had Children in First Marriage, by Migration Status of Husband and Period of First Marriage

Husbands were	Married before 1843		Married 1843–1853		Married after 1853	
	Average number of children	N	Average number of children	N	Average number of children	N
Natives of Boston	3.93	156	3.60***	166	***2.77	173
In-migrants Single on arrival	3.88**	225	**3.21**	276	**2.67	323
Married on arrival	4.07***	302	***3.20*	233	*2.71	134
Totals	3.98***	683	***3.30***	675	***2.70	630

*Interperiod difference significant at the 0.01 level.
**Interperiod difference significant at the 0.001 level.
***Interperiod difference significant at the 0.0001 level.
Only consecutive periods were tested.

demographic measure. In a relatively short time, all major components of the native-born population of Boston curtailed the sizes of their families.

The production of children also seems to have been related to a couple's ability to afford them. Separating the sample members by assessed wealth (or its absence), and determining each group's average child production, one obtains the data in Table 2.14. The wealthy did have more children, while those less fortunate had significantly fewer. One may view this production-limitation process in action by looking at Table 2.15, which details the various average ages at which

Table 2.14

Average Number of Children, in First Marriage, of Couples Who Had Children, and Number and Percent of Childless Couples, by Assessment Group

Assessment group	Couples with children		Number of childless couples	% of total assessment group
	Average no.	N		
Richest third	3.90***	362	49	11.9
Middle third	3.29	356	52	12.7
Poorest third	3.21	386	75	16.3
Not assessed	3.21	1,247	248	16.6

***Intergroup difference significant at the 0.0001 level for richest third as against any other group.

parents had their first and last children. For the entire group, the average beginning and ending ages were 28.1 and 36.1 for men and 24.6 and 32.6 for women; thus the average couple produced its children in about eight years. To learn how it did this, we may examine the characteristics associated with the size of completed families (there were too few cases of six or more children to give good results). To have two children took about 4.9 years, to have three required approximately 8.4 years, to have four demanded about 10.7 years, and five necessitated about 12.8 years. The ages at which fathers and mothers began their families varied little after the total of two children was reached; having a large family involved keeping on, not starting very early. In other words, though one might anticipate that especially philo-progenitive parents would wed early and beget often, to take advantage of the wife's greater childbearing capacity in her early twenties, this was not usually so (except for births resulting from premarital intercourse, as explained below). Couples appear to have continued to produce children, though at lengthening intervals after the second, and then they stopped. Given the parlous state of techni-

Table 2.15

Average Ages at Which Parents Had Their First and Last Children,
by Number of Children, up to Five, in Their First Marriage

	Total number of children									
	One		Two		Three		Four		Five	
Average age of father at birth of		N		N		N		N		N
first child			28.4	506	28.0	463	27.7	313	27.4	226
	30.0	452								
last child			33.3	514	36.4	468	38.4	324	40.1	229
Average age of mother at birth of										
first child			24.7	492	24.4	460	24.3	309	23.6	222
	26.9	431								
last child			29.7	500	32.8	462	35.0	320	36.4	225

cally based contraception in the mid-nineteenth century, it seems likeliest that ending of child production was achieved by cessation of relations or by withdrawal. There were few instances of rather long intervals between a penultimate and an ultimate child; these usually indicate a failure of contraception. Whichever techniques these couples used, they were highly effective.

Evidence from Birth Intervals

One may analyze further the couples' early sexual behavior by recurring to the data in Table 2.16 on interval between first marriage and first birth. The gestation period for a child in the mid-nineteenth century had to approximate 270 days because physicians then could not save premature babies. Setting several lower bounds for that birth

Table 2.16

Numbers of First Children Born N Days after First Marriage

Number of days after first marriage	Cumulative number of children born by then	Cumulative percent of total (1,232)
300	264	21.4
270	147	11.9
260	122	9.9
250	109	8.8
240	103	8.4
230	97	7.9
200	82	6.7
150	54	4.4
100	32	2.6
50	15	1.2
30	11	0.9
Before marriage	8	0.7

Each group includes all the cases below it.

interval provides some notion of the minimum extent of premarital sexual contact among the sample members. (Naturally some couples could have had premarital sex that did not lead to a pregnancy.) Depending on where one draws the line, it would appear that at least about one-tenth of the sample couples indulged in premarital intercourse.

Considering finally (in Table 2.17) the 147 couples whose first child was born less than 270 days after their marriage, their early start seems to have accelerated their other procreative activities. The pattern of their first child's arriving some three to four years earlier than for an average couple did not persist to the end of the precocious couple's production; they stopped a year or two earlier than did the average couple. Their earlier start, in the years of easier childbearing

Table 2.17

Characteristics of 147 Couples Whose First Child Was Born Less Than 270 Days after Their First Marriage

		N
Average number of children	3.78	147
Average age of father at		
birth of first child	26.1	147
birth of last child	34.8	146
Average age of mother at		
birth of first child	22.1	147
birth of last child	30.9	146

for the wife, also meant that their average total of children was about 0.5 more than the 3.30 mark attained by the 2,204 presumably less forward couples.

People of the mid-nineteenth century anticipated that virtually everyone capable of marrying would do so, and they expected these marriages to be terminated by the death of a spouse. Less than 5 percent of the sample members' marriages ended in divorce, desertion, or separation. The average sample member's marriage lasted about 34 years—more if the husband died first, less in the wife's case. Nativity of one's bride appears to have been associated with achieving financial success in antebellum Boston, with advantage going to men who arrived in the city single and married local women. Over time successive marriage cohorts of the couples in the study markedly curtailed the number of children issuing from their marriages: men married slightly older as time went by; the couples lengthened the intervals to their first child and between their subsequent children; and the couples applied, at comparatively early ages, as compared with other areas in the United States, an almost completely effective contraceptive method to terminate child production while both parents were still in their thirties. At least one couple in ten seems to have produced a "premature" first child and as well to have had slightly more children because of this comparatively early start. Marriage and children were, of course, intimately connected with making one's living, as we shall see.

Making
a Living

Whatever of worldly prosperity may have fallen to his lot is but the natural result, under Providence, of patient, persevering industry, guided by an ordinary sense of prudence and common sense. No golden prospect of acquiring sudden wealth by speculation was ever able to tempt him from the "even tenor of his way," [he] deeming a slow but less uncertain prospect of gain more conducive to rational and permanent happiness. [The above biographical sketch of Solomon Piper has been inserted at the particular request of friends.]

—*Solomon Piper*, Genealogy of the Family of
  Solomon Piper, 1849[1]

John Springer joined our association, as a carpenter, in 1838. Not being able to obtain any particulars of his life, none can be given.

—*Albion Bicknell, in Massachusetts Charitable Mechanic*
  Association, Annals, *1892*

*Solomon Piper was among the top dozen or so wealthiest of the 2,808 men in this study. In 1860, he was the 140th most heavily assessed taxpayer in Boston, the 76th most heavily assessed individual (most of the difference of 64 positions was accounted for by corporations). It is an interesting, perhaps inexplicable, paradox of life in mid-nineteenth-century Boston that, despite all the advantages the Yankee portion of society enjoyed, some 1,516 of the study's 2,808 sample members, or about 54 percent, possessed so little personal property (let alone real property) that the city's assessors charged them only for a poll tax; in fact, only 10,727 of the city's total of 34,449 polls (31.1 percent) were taxed for more than a poll tax in 1860.[2] Why should so few men have been assessed for real or personal property? The assessors may have been incompetent or excessively lenient, neglecting to assess some of these men for relatively trifling amounts, reasoning that any attempt to collect even a few dollars in taxes from this poorly off group would have been more trouble than it was worth. Evidence to resolve this question is conflicting: the lowest amount of property for which sampled individuals were ordinarily assessed in 1860 and 1870 was $200, although in 1860 one sample member was doomed for only $100, and in 1870 one was assessed for $60 and another for $100. The tax rates in 1860 and 1870 were $9.30 and $15.30 per $1,000, respectively, so someone assessed for $200 would have owed $1.86 in 1860 or $3.06 in 1870. Because of the expense of making up and sending out bills for such small amounts, the assessors may have agreed that $200 was a practical minimum and neglected to value people's holdings below that amount. The ledger volumes compiled to keep track of whether people paid their assessments and poll taxes in 1860 and 1870, however, contain many notations of "g.c.f." among the names of those assessed for only the $1.50 poll tax. This notation was an abbreviation for "gone, can't find," indicating that City Hall must have been trying to collect those bills for $1.50. As is evident from Table 3.1, those who paid only the $1.50 poll tax were small potatoes. By far the greatest portion of Boston's assessments was accounted for by its wealthiest taxpaying entities. Until and including 1865, the assessors prepared annually and the city published a report listing all those individuals and groups assessed above some certain value, together with the amounts of their real and personal assessments and the tax due on those amounts. For the year 1860, the minimum total assessed amount required for inclusion in the report was $10,000. The report for 1860 contains the names of 4,719 taxpaying entities. Slightly more than half of these, 2,569, were individual men; the next largest group, 1,024, was partnerships, and some 394 payers were designated as "heirs." Another 313 taxpayers were characterized as administrators, trustees, guardians, agents, executors, or attorneys, and 293 more were individual women (their total assessment amounted to 4.8 percent of the city total). The smallest groups were 120 corporations, 5 assignees (presumably of bankruptcies), and 1 noted as "in possession." In all, these 4,719 prosperous taxpaying groups accounted for $237,138,000, or 85.6 percent, of Boston's total assessed valuation of $276,861,000 in 1860.[3] This left only some $39,723,000 in assessed wealth to be spread among the remaining taxpaying groups, of whom there were at least 8,158 individuals, together with an unknown number of partnerships, heirs, administrators, women, corporations, and assignees. The conclusion is inescapable: wealth in pre–Civil War Boston was very unequally distributed, even among those of the favored Yankee group.

To appreciate some of the differences in Bostonians' individual economic achievements, let us examine the work careers of four men, one from each wealth group used in this study. Wealth group 0, the largest, took in the slight majority of sample members who, according to the Boston or Dorchester assessors, possessed no wealth.[4] Groups 1, 2, and 3 were defined to contain, respectively, the bottom, middle, and top thirds of those sample members whose wealth was rated above zero by the assessors (see Table 3.2).

The Rise of *Silas B. Jaquith (Wealth Group 0)

Born in Gardiner, Maine, in 1825, to John and Elizabeth Jaquith, Silas began his career as a millman (probably in a planing mill). About 1848 he married Cevilla M. (family name unknown), who was about 15, a native of Castile, New York. Between 1849 and 1867 they became the

Table 3.1

Poll Tax Receipts as a Proportion of Boston's Tax Revenues, 1860 and 1870

Year	Number of polls	Maximum possible[a] poll tax receipts at $1.50 per poll	Total taxes	Poll tax as % of total taxes
1860	34,449	$51,673.50	$2,479,519.34	2.08
1870	56,926	85,389.00	9,106,481.77	0.94

Source: Charles P. Huse, *The Financial History of Boston from May 1, 1822, to January 31, 1909* (Cambridge, Mass.: Harvard University Press, 1916), 370, 376, 377.
[a]Assuming everyone paid his tax.

Table 3.2

Assessment Wealth Group, by Sample

Wealth group	1860 sample N	1870 sample N	Totals
3 (highest assessed)	215	210	425
2	239	219	458
1 (lowest assessed)	206	203	409
0 (not assessed)	745	771	1,516
Totals	1,405	1,403	2,808

parents of four sons and five daughters. No son survived past the age of five, but all the daughters married.

In 1860, the Jaquiths still resided in Gardiner. That year's census shows Silas as a laborer; his 27-year-old wife, a year-old son (who would die in 1864), and two daughters, 11 and 6, rounded out his household. He claimed neither real nor personal estate, even though he was then 34. By early in 1861 the Jaquiths had removed to Boston, where Silas found work as a carpenter—the most popular occupation among native-born Bostonians.

Silas changed from carpentry to teaming in 1868; the 1870 census lists him, his wife, and three of their daughters (aged 16, 6, and 3). Silas still claimed no real or personal wealth, and the Boston assessors doomed him for a poll tax only. Considerable changes occurred in Silas's life in the late 1870s. His marriage ended. Perhaps his wife died (though there is no record of her having done so in Massachusetts), or the couple may have divorced or separated. In late 1878 or early 1879 he removed to Alameda, near San Francisco, California, and resumed carpentry. This western interlude was brief, for he returned to Boston and married Anastacia Walsh about 1885 (again, there is no Massachusetts record of this event). They produced a son in 1886 and a daughter in 1894. Silas kept on as a carpenter until his death in Boston from pneumonia, aged 63, in 1898. He does not seem ever to have owned any real estate in Boston.[5]

Several of Silas's characteristics worked against him. His parents had removed from Maine before 1850 (perhaps to Wisconsin, where his father is said to have died in 1898—aged 104). Any economic support they might have offered would have been at best remote. Second, he married a woman whose family origins also lay at some distance. Her tender age at marriage suggests that her family's household had broken up recently, or that she and Silas were compelled, by an impending birth, to wed (or both). Soon their children began appearing, about every other year, permanently removing Cevilla from the paid labor force. Most of Boston's more successful men married about four years older than had Silas and delayed having their first child almost another two years. This gave them an advantage of at least five—perhaps six—years during which their economic burden was minimal and allowed them to build up a stake, possibly enhanced toward the end of that period by a wife's labor contribution. This delay was important, as is evident from Table 3.3.

Silas Jaquith seems never to have gone into business for himself, even as a teamster; to do so would not have required more than a few hundred dollars in capital. Likely this lack blocked his ascent to higher wealth groups, for only clerks in mercantile houses normally achieved, say, wealth group 1 membership while yet remaining em-

Table 3.3

Average Age of Sample Member at His First Marriage, at Birth of His First Child,[a] and Average Number of Children in His First Marriage,[a] by Wealth Group

	Wealth group				
	None	Poorest		Richest	
	0	1	2	3	Totals
Sample member's average age at his first marriage	25.8	26.4	26.6	27.3	26.3
(N)	1,236	343	389	385	2,353
Sample member's average age at birth of his first child[a]	27.7	28.2	28.8	29.0	28.2
(N)	1,220	335	385	353	2,293
Average number of children born in sample member's first marriage[a]	3.22	3.25	3.27	3.87	3.33
(N)	1,250	340	397	364	2,351

[a]Only for those marriages that produced children.

ployees. All in all, one must conclude that the deck was stacked against Silas B. Jaquith. His economic experience was the norm for some 1,197 of the 2,165 in-migrants (55.3 percent).

The Rise of *Silas Foss (Wealth Group 1)

Silas Foss's career can be sketched rapidly. He was born in 1832 in Dover, New Hampshire, to Clark and Mehitable Foss. There is no sign of them in the 1850 census of New Hampshire, which lists him as aged 15, a farmer residing in a Dover household. Perhaps they were already dead. About 1859, Silas Foss arrived in Boston, accompanied by his recent bride, the former Margaret M. Kierstead, a native of Maine. The 1860 census shows the newlyweds as East Boston residents, listing him as age 27, a mason with $100 in personal estate, and her as 20. The city records list no births for the Fosses between 1849 and 1869, and no children appear in any census so, like about one-sixth of the couples in the study, they were probably childless.

The 1870 census found Silas and Margaret still residing in East Boston; Margaret's mother, Abigail, had joined them. Silas reported that he was worth $3,000 in real and $600 in personal estate, but the Boston assessors rated him for $2,200 in real estate. Late that year, or early in 1871, the Fosses moved to nearby Everett, where Silas continued as a brick mason until his early death in 1883 from dropsy at the age of 50.[6]

Silas Foss typifies a fairly large number of skilled workers who were able, after considerable effort, to amass a respectable but not surprising amount of wealth: 334 of the 2,165 in-migrants reached this wealth group (15.4 percent), most of them not surpassing a valuation of $10,000. Although Silas Foss married a nonlocal woman, and thus presumably would have been disadvantaged thereby, the couple's lack of children may have permitted economies that helped them amass above-average wealth. There are no indications that Foss built on his own account or became a building contractor, as did the most successful master masons.

The Rise and Disappearance of *Silas D. Bryant (Wealth Group 2)

One of the more mysterious members of this study was *Silas D. Bryant, born about 1820 in Rochester, New Hampshire; his parents' names are unknown. During the 1840s he married Mary J. Pinkham, a fellow native of Rochester about three years his elder. In all they appear to have had two sons and a daughter in the period 1844–54. He practiced the trade of harnessmaker, at least from his first appearance in Boston in 1843, when he was about 23, until he vanished into the historical mists in 1881.

Bryant seems to have done well at his trade. The 1850 census, which found the family in South Boston, noted that Albert was aged six and Mary E., six months; Silas claimed no real estate. Ten years later, however, he reported $10,000 in real and $3,000 in personal estate—evidence of solid prosperity, even if the assessors credited him with but $4,000 in real and $2,000 in personal estate. This still sufficed to place him in the middle third of Boston's assessed citizens. Of the 2,165 in-migrants, only 336 (15.5 percent) reached this level.

In 1865 the Bryants moved to a recently purchased home on Clarence Place in Dorchester; Silas continued commuting to work on Federal Street in Boston. In 1873, however, he may have suffered reverses in that year's panic: his city directory listing became merely "house Clarence Place." On 2 January 1879, Mrs. Bryant died at their home, aged 60, and the 1880 Boston city directory does not list him. The last trace of his existence is in the 1881 city directory of Des Moines, Iowa: "harnessmaker W. B. Mitchell & Co., boards 533 6th." He is not listed in the 1882 directory, nor was he found in the 1880 census, of Des Moines. Wherever he died, his body was not returned to Boston's Cedar Grove Cemetery to lie beside Mary J., so that which God had joined together, man had put asunder.[7]

In an age when horses were the principal motive power on farms and for transportation in cities, the harnessmaker, like the blacksmith, was indispensable. Yet blacksmiths were much more common. In 1855, Boston contained 4,800 horses and 877 blacksmiths but only 222 harnessmakers.[8] Silas D. Bryant's choice of vocation was intelligent: the possibilities of adding value by manufacture were probably greater for harnessmakers than they were for blacksmiths, assuming that blacksmiths dealt principally in services (horseshoeing and metal repairs). Although harnessmakers doubtless also did repairs, harness likely cost much more than did horseshoes. The 1855 Massachusetts census of manufactures found 39 "Saddle, Harness and Trunk Manufactories" in Boston; the value of their product amounted to $757,200, their capital invested came to $169,100, and their employees numbered 378, suggesting an average product per employee of over $2,000. Blacksmiths' products were not separately enumerated.[9]

The Rise of *Silas P. Meriam (Wealth Group 3)

Those who bought and sold in quantity predominated among Boston's richest men; prominent in this group were the wholesale grocers, of whom *Silas P. Meriam serves as a good representative.[10] He was a "Harvard man," having been born in that Worcester County town on the last day of 1801, and come to Boston in 1825. He married Harriet B. Sullivan in Boston in 1828; she died childless in 1834, and in 1836 he married Susan M. Briggs; they had three daughters between 1837 and 1844. The youngest, Frances H., married an attorney, *William W. Burrage. Mrs. Meriam was a sister of *Edward T. Briggs, and Silas's cousin, *William Meriam, was also sampled. Theirs was a well-represented family.

The 1850 census snapshot of the Meriam household on Bowdoin Street, just off Beacon Hill, reveals Silas as head of an otherwise all-female contingent: his wife (aged 40), three daughters (19, 13, 9), and two Irish domestics. He claimed no real wealth. By 1860 the Meriams had relocated up the hill to Temple Street. The eldest daughter had married, leaving two, aged 21 and 20. One Irish domestic had been replaced by a 12-year-old American girl. Silas claimed $15,000 in real and $30,000 in personal estate. The assessors estimated his real wealth at $13,000 and rated his grocery firm at $18,000 in personal estate. He thus ranked in the top third of Boston's assessed; only 298 of the 2,165 in-migrants (13.8 percent) reached this summit.[11]

The 1870 census found the Meriams still in Temple Street; only their middle daughter, Susan M., remained with them. Their two domestics came from Ireland and Canada. Silas did not indicate any wealth, though it probably had not decreased during the 1860s.[12] By 1880, two years after Susan's marriage, Mr. and Mrs. Meriam had moved to a residential apartment house, the Commonwealth Hotel, on Washington Street, Meriam & Meriam & Co. had been dissolved, Silas alone retaining the firm's old stall in the South Market—and he had made his will. (The Meriams were not located in the 1880 census.) Silas died of paralysis at the Hotel Pelham in 1885, aged 83.[13]

Silas Meriam's success was aided by his younger brother William and their partner, Thomas M. Vinson, Jr.; this association lasted some thirty years (1848–77). In an era when partnerships were dissolved

and reformed almost with the regularity of square dancing, such sta-
bility was remarkable. Of course, another factor in Silas's favor was
the continuing demand for his stock in trade, food.

Unequal Achievement

Although the native-born men who moved to Boston from the countryside throughout the nineteenth century obtained the choicest positions in the city's labor force, as we have just seen they did not benefit
equally from their labors. Some jobs were much more remunerative
than others; fortunately, these connections are revealed by an examination of Boston's job structure in general, compared with the distribution of positions among members of the two study samples. Once
these differences are clear, the complex web of associations among
jobs, wealth, persistence, and even family formation may be examined.

Skills in Particular versus Skills in General

Compared with the general run of Boston's male household heads as
of 1860 shown in Table 3.4, the men in the study samples were not at
all typical. The biggest discrepancies between the general run of
household heads and the native-born household heads as of 1860 lay
in the Unskilled and Menial Labor group and in the higher reaches
of the occupational ladder: native-born men were underrepresented
in the lowest-ranked jobs and overrepresented in the higher. Ten
years later, as Table 3.5 reveals, the situation had not changed very
much. The principal shifts in Boston's distribution of occupational
groups during the Civil War decade, using the *Plain People of Boston*
classification scheme, occurred in the Semiskilled and Service and the
Skilled groups, which gained relative to the other groups, and in
Clerical and Sales and Major Proprietors, Managers, and Officials,
which declined relatively. Given the native-born domination of the
latter two groups and the continuing decline of the native-born contingent in Boston's population during the 1860s, this is to be expected.
Among the members of the study samples, however, the fluctuations

Table 3.4

Socioeconomic Status Groups of Boston's Male Heads of Household in 1860 Compared with Those in the 1860 Study Sample

Socioeconomic status group	Boston's male household heads, 1860 (sample)		Native-born household heads, 1860 (sample)	
	N	%	N	%
Unskilled & Menial	85	24.9	6	0.4
Semiskilled & Service	37	10.9	196	14.0
Petty Proprietors, Managers, & Officials	33	9.8	199	14.2
Skilled	78	22.9	436	31.0
Clerical & Sales	30	8.8	109	7.8
Semiprofessional	2	0.6	8	0.6
Proprietors, Managers, & Officials	62	18.2	360	25.6
Professionals	8	2.3	80	5.7
Retired, farmers	6	1.8	11	0.8
Totals	341	100.2	1,405	100.1

Sources: Smaller sample from Peter R. Knights, *The Plain People of Boston, 1830–1860: A Study in City Growth* (New York: Oxford University Press, 1971), 87, with lists of occupations in each group at 149–56. Larger sample: sample data. Forty-four single or widowed women were removed from the smaller sample because there are no women in the larger sample. For purposes of comparison, the classification of the 1860 study sample has been conformed to that of the *Plain People* sample.

Table 3.5

*Socioeconomic Status Groups of Boston's Male Heads of Household in 1870
Compared with Those in the 1870 Study Sample*

Socioeconomic status group	Boston's male household heads, 1870 (sample)		Native-born household heads, 1870 (sample)	
	N	%	N	%
Unskilled & Menial	71	22.5	6	0.4
Semiskilled & Service	43	13.7	205	14.6
Petty Proprietors, Managers, & Officials	28	8.9	221	15.8
Skilled	104	33.0	433	30.9
Clerical & Sales	18	5.7	128	9.1
Semiprofessional	1	0.3	10	0.7
Proprietors, Managers, & Officials	39	12.4	337	24.0
Professionals	7	2.2	52	3.7
Retired, farmers	4	1.3	11	0.8
Totals	315	100.0	1,403	100.0

Sources: Smaller sample drawn for, but not used in, Peter R. Knights, *The Plain People of Boston, 1830–1860: A Study in City Growth* (New York: Oxford University Press, 1971). Larger sample: sample data. Seventy-one single or widowed women were removed from the smaller sample because there are no women in the larger sample. For purposes of comparison, the classification of the 1870 study sample has been conformed to that of the *Plain People* sample.

were much less substantial: a slight gain among Clerical and Sales, a
slight loss among Professionals. When we remember that considerable numbers of Yankees who moved out of Boston continued to commute to the city, we realize that the change in the city's work force was
probably negligible over the 1860s.

Classified Information

Unfortunately, the socioeconomic status classification used for occupations in *The Plain People of Boston* (and in a few other urban studies)
did not wear well in the various analyses of the sample data. The
earlier scheme proved deficient in that it divided the membership of
the various groups primarily according to their wealth so that, say,
a well-to-do master brick mason could rise from the Skilled group
to the Major Proprietors group by attaining an assessment of over
$1,000. The present study, however, emphasized individuals' lifetime
achievements: it turned out that an open-ended classification system,
preserving as much of the old definitions as possible, gave far better
results. The main differences between the old and new classifications
are that the old group 3, Petty Proprietors, has been eliminated and
that some sample members have been reassigned to classifications reflecting, as best as can be determined, their original or earliest occupations. For example, under this arrangement, the wealthy master
brick mason just mentioned would be shifted from group 7, Major
Proprietors, to group 4, Skilled, regardless of his large assessment.
The reclassification produced especially striking results in the areas
of comparative child production and wealth accumulation, as will appear. (To avoid confusion, the *Plain People of Boston* classification will
be referred to as the "socioeconomic status" classification, while that
used in the present study will be called "occupational groups.")

The native-born contingent of the work force obviously enjoyed a
much more stable structure than did the work force in general. Unfortunately for most of the men in the study, even this favorable distribution of jobs, especially as compared with the immigrants at the
bottom of the occupational scale, did not guarantee them a good living. A look at wealth distribution will confirm this finding.

Wealth and Occupational Group

The wealth of sample members, as estimated by the city assessors, varied according to the men's occupational group with (as one would anticipate) those occupations involving advanced education or the management of large sums of money coming out on top. If we look at the five largest occupational groups, shown in Table 3.6, these disparities become evident. These men were, typically, about halfway through their careers in Boston. The wealth disparities among them are starkly evident. Some, who remained in Boston well into their sixties, were able to accumulate, relatively early, more than fourteen times as much wealth as were others. The surprise is that men who were not doing so well nevertheless remained in Boston almost as long as did those at the top of the economic scale. Table 3.7 indicates that there were some changes during the 1860s. The main differences appearing in the Civil War decade were that all five large occupational groups improved their average assessments (in current dollars) considerably; the advance in the price of groceries from 1860 to 1872, according to the Massachusetts Bureau of Statistics of Labor, was 32 percent, of provisions, just over 50 percent, and of fuel, about 55 percent.[14] This compares with gains of 247 percent, 61 percent, 54 percent, 28 percent, and 26 percent, respectively, for the five major occupational groups in the order listed above. The gain for all assessed sample members was just 26 percent, for all sample members only 20 percent. Thus it appears that during the war decade the major economic gainers in Boston were the members of the Semiskilled, the Clerical and Sales, and the Skilled occupational groups, in about that order. Members of the Professional and Proprietors groups, as well as assessed men and the general citizenry, fell behind (the proportion of holdings owned by non-Yankees was minuscule then so this was true for all practical purposes). Again, any adverse economic effects may have been minimized in that men who moved to the suburbs but who continued to operate businesses in the city would still have been taxed for those businesses by the city, even though their names disappeared from the census and electoral rolls.

Even though members of the Semiskilled, Clerical and Sales, and Skilled occupational groups appear to have done well collectively dur-

Table 3.6

Average Assessed Wealth of Sample Members, by Major Occupation Group,
1860

Major occupation group (average no. of years spent in Boston after age 21)	Average assessment for those assessed for more than poll tax only	N	Not assessed N	% of total	Total	Avg. age
Semiskilled & Service (34.9)	$ 2,313	45	135	75.0	180	38.6
Clerical & Sales (38.4)	5,771	48	87	64.4	135	39.8
Skilled (41.5)	8,070	224	375	62.6	599	43.2
Proprietors, Managers, & Officials (41.5)	30,578	273	93[a]	25.4	366	45.9
Professionals (45.3)	21,081	61	20[a]	25.0	82	46.4
Totals (41.4)	$18,236	651	710	52.2	1,361	42.9

[a]Members of the Proprietors, Managers, and Officials and of the Professionals
groups who resided in Roxbury in 1860 were evaluated on the basis of their census
listings because the 1860 assessment records for Roxbury cannot readily be located.

ing the 1860s, this did not create large differentials in their rates of
persistence, which ranged between 55 percent and 63 percent for all
of the major groups. In-city death rates among the major occupation
groups, as Tables 3.8 and 3.9 suggest, ranged between 9.3 percent
and 18.5 percent.

Table 3.7
Average Assessed Wealth of Sample Members, by Major Occupation Group,
1870

Major occupation group (average no. of years spent in Boston after age 21)	Average assessment for those assessed for more than poll tax only		Not assessed			
		N	N	% of total	Total	Avg. age
Semiskilled & Service (39.5)	$ 8,017	65	146	69.2	211	44.5
Clerical & Sales (38.2)	9,282	62	104	62.7	166	40.1
Skilled (41.3)	12,489	203	393	65.9	596	46.0
Proprietors, Managers, & Officials (45.7)	38,996	239	95	28.4	334	48.2
Professionals (47.9)	26,121	48	9	15.8	57	48.1
Totals (41.9)	$23,024	617	747	54.8	1,364	45.7

Taking these results together, one may speculate that, in those groups that "aged" at less than the average rate of 2.8 years for the decade of the 1860s (45.7 in 1870, less 42.9 in 1860), turnover among the membership—new recruits, as it were—was more rapid, and among groups with the highest age differences, turnover was slower. This explanation is plausible in that two of the three groups that made the greatest economic advances during the 1860s also had the slowest turnover, reflecting the superior opportunities that opened up to men well positioned as of 1860 such as *Silas S. Putnam.

Table 3.8

Persistence and Deaths in Boston, 1860–1870, of Members of the 1860
Sample, by Major Occupation Group

Major occupation group	N in 1860	Persisting in Boston, 1870	%	Died in Boston, 1860–1870	%
Semiskilled & Service	180	105	58.3	21	11.7
Clerical & Sales	135	83	61.5	19	14.1
Skilled	599	365	60.9	92	15.4
Proprietors, Managers, & Officials	366	232	63.4	62	16.9
Professionals	81	54	66.7	15	18.5
All sample members	1,405	858	61.1	217	15.4

*Intelligent Positioning: The Rise of *Silas S. Putnam*

Silas S. Putnam was born in 1822 in Hartford, New York, to Israel and Charlotte Putnam, natives respectively of Danvers, Massachusetts, and Fairhaven, Vermont. By 1848 Israel was dead, and Silas resided with his mother and a widowed sister at 20 Kneeland Street, Boston. The 1850 census shows him as a manufacturer of curtain fixtures, with no real estate indicated for his family. Just before Christmas 1850 he married Anna Maria Whitmarsh, 18, a native of Abington, Massachusetts. They took up residence in Roxbury with Silas's mother and his sister.

Apparently the curtain fixtures business prospered. Silas and Ann's first child was not born until August 1853, when Silas was about 31

Table 3.9

Persistence and Deaths in Boston, 1870–1880, of Members of the 1870
Sample, by Major Occupation Group

Major occupation group	N in 1870	Persisting in Boston, 1880	%	Died in Boston, 1870–1880	%
Semiskilled & Service	211	130	61.6	37	17.5
Clerical & Sales	166	94	56.6	15	9.3
Skilled	596	349	58.6	99	16.6
Proprietors, Managers, & Officials	334	202	60.5	50	15.0
Professionals	57	37	64.9	7	12.3
All sample members	1,403	832	59.3	214	15.3

and Ann 21. Seven others followed until 1872, a total of three boys and five girls. (All seem to have reached majority.)

The 1860 census enumerator found the Putnams fairly well off in Roxbury: Silas admitted to $1,600 in real and $500 in personal estate. The scant evidence available on Roxbury's assessments for that year does not indicate that he was assessed for more than poll tax only.

But Silas Putnam went on to greater triumphs: in the 1860s he added to his output horseshoe nails and clothes hooks, small items with high value added by manufacture. The 1870 census suggests that he had arrived: he was listed as having $50,000 of real estate, $60,000 of personal estate, three servants, and a governess for his seven resident children. Ten years later his household contained a manservant, a woman servant, and a seamstress (with two daughters, aged 19 and 18, to help in the house, presumably the Putnams required fewer maids). Silas had left manufacturing to become general manager of the New Era Coffee Company. By 1891, he had pretty much retired. He died from Bright's disease in Roxbury in 1895, a few days past his seventy-third birthday.[15]

Silas S. Putnam obviously had a few more advantages than did, say, *Silas Jaquith. Putnam enjoyed some local familial support from his mother and sister until at least 1860, some ten years after his marriage. His wife came from Abington, only 17 miles from Boston, and her father, as of 1850, was a "manufacturer" of shoes, with $5,000 in real estate. The Putnams' first child was born some three years into their marriage, which postponed some expenses. Even before his marriage, Putnam was engaged in manufacturing, if only in a small way. He selected a product in which to specialize—curtain fixtures—which was in growing demand but was not made by a crowd of competitors. (Today economists call this a "niche" product.) He diversified into closely related product lines (horseshoe nails, clothes hooks) that used similar manufacturing techniques, and he did extremely well during the Civil War decade. He sold out in his fifties and assumed a (presumably) less arduous position as a manager. Atypically, he was apparently able to retire from business in the late 1880s, having earned a "competence."

The Persistence of Persistence

Most community studies have demonstrated that persistence, or the tendency to remain in a community, is closely associated with wealth, usually the ownership of real property. When one looks within the group that owned the vast majority of that real property—the native-born of native-born parentage—one sees that gross inequalities existed even among these supposedly favored people. True, persistence in Boston was high among all native-born men (about 60 percent for household heads 1860–70 and 1870–80), and it was quite uniform across all major occupational groups. This might suggest widespread real property ownership among the men. But the truth was otherwise.

Combining the assessment data with census data, as is done in Tables 3.10 and 3.11, allows one to estimate the annual rate at which sample members' assessed wealth grew. These figures suggest that, for about a quarter or a fifth of the Semiskilled and Service group members, a healthy rate of accumulation was possible. Prominent among that group were stable proprietors and policemen, who occasionally showed rapid jumps in their claimed wealth from one census to the next. The number of policemen who eventually owned their own homes was especially noteworthy, given the apparent irregularity of their employment. (Policemen were prone to oscillate in and out of that occupation.) [16]

Using the information on average assessments and the average rate at which men in the major occupation groups accumulated assessed wealth, one may calculate the number of years required for an average sample member in an occupation group to reach his assessment. Since his average age is also known, by subtraction one may estimate the average ages at which these men began to accumulate assessed wealth. These figures, which appear in Tables 3.12 and 3.13, are *very* approximate and are used for illustration only. With the exception of the Professionals group in the 1860 sample, these results suggest that most sample members began to accumulate meaningful wealth in their early thirties, while they were still fathering children (average age at birth of first child for 2,293 fathers was 28.1 years). In his study of wealth in the United States, based on samples from the manuscript census returns of 1850–70, Lee Soltow found that "wealth accumulation begins at age 18 and is *directly proportional to adult age*." [17] Their shift to an urban residence obviously delayed the start of this process for the sample members, but their faster rates of accumulation allowed them eventually to surpass the national averages for wealth-holding.

Since about three-quarters of the men in the study consistently claimed only one occupation throughout their lives, a closer look at the connections between occupation and persistence is in order.

Persistence among the Largest Occupational Groups

Of all the sample members, about three-sevenths (1,194) practiced an occupation involving the acquisition over several years of skills usually

Table 3.10

Estimated Annual Increments of Wealth for Assessed and for All Sample
Members, by Major Occupation Group, 1860

| Major occupation group (and average assessment) | Estimated annual wealth increments ($) | | | |
| | Assessed sample members only | | All sample members | |
	$	N	$	N
Semiskilled & Service ($2,313)	52^n	45	42 ($578)	180
Clerical & Sales ($5,771)	240^n	48	116^n ($2,052)	135
Skilled ($8,069)	253	224	183 ($3,018)	599
Proprietors, Managers, & Officials ($30,578)	1,845	273	1,542 ($22,808)	366
Professionals ($21,081)	880	61	590 ($15,876)	81

Source: Sample, assessment, and census data. Average assessment in 1860 for all
assessed sample members was $18,367, and for all sample members, $8,680.

All regression estimates except those marked "^{n}" are significant at least at the 0.01
level; most are significant at the 0.001 level.

identified with particular products. Just under one-fourth of the men
(700) was classified as Proprietors, Managers, and Officials. The third-
largest component (391) consisted of so-called Semiskilled workers,
most of whom ranked in the bottom third of the city's assessed citizens or were not assessed. Not quite so large was the Clerical and Sales
group, which accounted for 301, or about one-ninth. The 139 mem-

Table 3.11

Estimated Annual Increments of Wealth for Assessed and for All Sample Members, by Major Occupation Group, 1870

| Major occupation group (and average assessment) | Estimated annual wealth increments ($) | | | |
| | Assessed sample members only | | All sample members | |
	$	N	$	N
Semiskilled & Service ($8,017)	221^n	65	143^n ($2,470)	211
Clerical & Sales ($9,282)	442	62	342 ($3,467)	166
Skilled ($12,489)	696	223	332 ($4,254)	596
Proprietors, Managers, & Officials ($38,996)	2,692	239	2,046 ($27,904)	334
Professionals ($26,120)	1,338	48	1,324 ($21,996)	57

Source: Sample, assessment, and census data. Average assessment in 1870 for all assessed sample members was $23,135, and for all sample members, $10,421. All regression estimates except those marked "^{n}" are significant at least at the 0.01 level; most are significant at the 0.001 level.

bers of the Professionals group composed the fifth-largest major occupational contingent (about 5 percent).

Among these major groups, lifetime persistence (residence in Boston until death) varied considerably, as Table 3.14 suggests. Regardless of birthplace, men in the Clerical and Sales group were the most likely to leave the city, those among the Proprietors the least. Even

Table 3.12

Estimated Age at Which Wealth Accumulation Began, by Major Occupation Group, 1860

Major occupation group (and average assessment)	Estimated annual wealth increments $	Years to accumulate assessment (=assessment/ annual rate)	Average age of men in occupation group	Estimated age at start of wealth accumulation
Semiskilled & Service ($578)	42	13.8	38.5	24.7
Clerical & Sales ($2,052)	115	17.9	39.8	21.9
Skilled ($3,018)	183	16.5	43.2	26.7
Proprietors, Managers, & Officials ($22,808)	1,527	14.9	45.9	31.0
Professionals ($15,699)	554	28.3	46.4	18.1
All sample members ($8,680)	665	13.1	43.2	30.1

All regression estimates are significant at the 0.05 level—most at the 0.001 level.

members of the Semiskilled group, who were usually the youngest among the lifetime out-migrants, averaged about 50 years of age when they departed the city. Those older than about 55 could not look forward to much of a career elsewhere unless (like *Silas S. Putnam) they had amassed a "competence" sufficient to see them

Table 3.13

Estimated Age at Which Wealth Accumulation Began, by Major Occupation Group, 1870

Major occupation group (and average assessment)	Estimated annual wealth increments $	Years to accumulate assessment (=assessment/ annual rate)	Average age of men in occupation group	Estimated age at start of wealth accumulation
Semiskilled & Service ($2,470)	143	17.3	44.4	27.1
Clerical & Sales ($3,467)	341	10.2	40.1	29.9
Skilled ($4,254)	331	12.8	46.0	33.2
Proprietors, Managers, & Officials ($27,904)	2,052	13.6	48.3	34.7
Professionals ($21,996)	1,330	16.5	48.1	31.6
All sample members ($10,421)	873	11.9	45.7	33.8

All regression estimates are significant at the 0.02 level—most at the 0.001 level.

through their declining years or had relatives on whom they could depend. Most of the men in the Proprietors group who removed from Boston shifted only to the suburbs, where they could enjoy greater amenities.

Examining the average length of stay in Boston by members of the

Table 3.14
Lifetime Persistence in Boston, by Major Occupation Group

Major occupation group (and average age at leaving Boston [out-migrants only])	In-migrants who were also lifetime				Boston natives who were also lifetime				Totals
	Persisters		Out-migrants		Persisters		Out-migrants		
	N	%	N	%	N	%	N	%	
Semiskilled & Service (50.1)	186	47.6	152	38.9	39	10.0	14	3.6	391
Clerical & Sales (53.0)	89	29.6	109	36.2	66	21.9	37	12.3	301
Skilled (54.0)	540	45.2	406	34.0	176	14.7	73	6.1	1,195
Proprietors, Managers, & Officials (58.6)	319	45.6	204	29.1	133	19.0	44	6.3	700
Professionals (59.4)	74	53.6	30	21.7	24	17.4	10	7.2	138
Totals	1,208	44.3	901	33.1	438	16.1	178	6.5	2,725

A "lifetime" persister died a resident of Boston; a "lifetime" out-migrant died a nonresident of Boston.

various major occupational groups, according to whether they were
natives or in-migrants, lifetime persisters or out-migrants, will help
sort out even more internal differences (see Table 3.15 for these figures). Even those men who moved into and later left Boston gave the
city the best part of their working lives—from the minimum average
of 23 years for Semiskilled workers up to about 44 years for Proprietors, Managers, and Officials. These men who eventually left the city
also tended to be a year or so older on arriving there than were those
in-migrants who would later die in Boston. Their sojourn in Boston
agreed fairly well with the levels of wealth achieved by the various
occupational groups—the longer the stay, the greater the wealth.
(This phenomenon will be considered in Chapter 5.)

The patterns of wealth achievement, then, appear to have been
connected with persistence, but only when the city's various population components have been separated out. If we look at the four principal population components (in-migrants and natives, out-migrants
and persisters), which are decomposed in Table 3.16, we see that
wealth was very unevenly distributed among them. During the Civil
War decade the economic gap widened between those who would persist and those who would later leave Boston, with the city's natives
notably improving their position, mostly at the expense of in-migrants
who would later leave town but also relative to native Bostonians who
would leave. There were relatively, as well as absolutely, more in-
migrants in the city's population after the war, and they were doing
less well than had in-migrants just before the war. Opportunities for
in-migrants to Boston declined over the Civil War decade; together
with the other trends—particularly that toward an increasing proportion of already married in-migrants, this suggests that the city's mag-
netism was perhaps acting more to keep established residents in the
city than to attract newcomers, as it had done for so long. This was
reflected in the rise of the average sample member's age from 43.2 in
1860 to 45.7 in 1870, a difference significant at the 0.0001 level. Ambitious young men would still move to Boston, but fewer of them
would succeed as spectacularly as had migrants in the first third or so
of the century.[18] The shift of Boston's successful men to suburban
residences was quite marked in the 1860s[19] and is emphasized (as
shown in Table 3.17) by the changes, over time, in the proportions

Table 3.15
Average Number of Years Spent in Boston by Members of Major Occupation Groups, by Migration Status

Major occupation group	In-migrants who were also lifetime				Boston natives who were also lifetime				Totals
	Persisters		Out-migrants		Persisters		Out-migrants		
	N	Years	N	Years	N	Years	N	Years	
Semiskilled & Service									
Average years spent in Boston	183	37.2	141	23.3	39	65.2	12	46.9	375
Average arrival age	183	28.3	150	28.6	39	0	14	0	386
Clerical & Sales									
Average years spent in Boston	88	40.0	106	27.0	65	66.4	37	56.1	296
Average arrival age	88	26.0	109	26.7	65	0	38	0	300
Skilled									
Average years spent in Boston	537	40.4	378	25.2	176	67.6	69	52.3	1,160
Average arrival age	537	29.0	388	30.3	176	0	73	0	1,174

Proprietors, Managers, & Officials

Average years spent in Boston	312	44.0	203	30.5	133	70.3	42	57.2	690
Average arrival age	312	27.6	204	29.4	133	0	44	0	693
Professionals									
Average years spent in Boston	72	42.5	28	26.2	24	68.0	10	62.5	134
Average arrival age	72	31.0	31	33.8	24	0	10	0	137
Totals for average years spent in Boston	1,192	40.9	856	26.4	437	68.1	170	54.6	2,655
Totals for all sample members									
Average years spent in Boston	1,216	40.9	887	26.2	457	68.0	176	54.5	2,735
Average arrival age	1,216	28.4	913	29.6	457	0	186	0	2,772

Table 3.16
Relative Share of Boston's Assessed Wealth According to Migration Status

| | In-migrants who were also lifetime | | | | Boston natives who were also lifetime | | | | |
| | Persisters | | Out-migrants | | Persisters | | Out-migrants | | Totals |
	N	Average assessment ($)	N	Average assessment ($)	N	Average assessment ($)	N	Average assessment ($)	
1860	639	$10,032	439	$5,067	239	$13,054	88	$5,017	1,405
Share of total household heads (%)		45.5		31.2		17.0		6.3	
Share of assessed wealth (%)		52.6		18.2		25.6		3.6	
1870	594	$12,408	493	$4,340	219	$21,825	97	$3,424	1,403
Share of total household heads (%)		42.3		35.1		15.6		6.9	
Share of assessed wealth (%)		50.4		14.6		32.7		2.3	

Table 3.17

Composition of Boston's Heads of Household by Nativity and Sex,
1860 and 1870

	1860		1870	
Total households 40,538		49,194		
Native-born heads	16,239		19,173	
(%)	40.1		39.0	
Male heads		14,038		15,936
(%)		86.4		83.1
Female heads		2,201		3,237
(%)		13.6		16.9
Foreign-born heads (includes native-born of foreign-born parents)	24,299		30,021	
(%)	59.9		61.0	
Male heads		20,435		[a]24,930
(%)		84.1		[a]83.0
Female heads		3,864		[a]5,091
(%)		15.9		[a]17.0

Sources: Author's counts of native-born and foreign-born household heads by sex from the 1860 manuscript population censuses of Boston, Roxbury, and Dorchester; author's count of native-born household heads by sex and total foreign-born household heads from the 1870 manuscript population census of Boston.

[a] The male/female ratio was estimated from the 1870 household-head sample drawn for *The Plain People of Boston* (N = 386).

of Boston's household heads. The trend was toward foreign-born-headed households (including as well the native-born children of foreigners) and more households headed by women. Households headed by the more successful increasingly tended to move out of Boston to such suburbs as Brookline, Cambridge, Somerville, and Malden—communities well served by the suburban commuter railroads.[20]

Occupational Nonpersistence: Some Examples

Observers of the nineteenth-century American scene often commented on the multiplicity of occupational endeavors successively undertaken by the new nation's citizens. Changing occupations was thought to be easy because few positions required licensing or were regulated. As Count Adam de Gurowski remarked, "an individual, unsuccessful in any branch or line, rises as quickly as he fell; dusts himself off, and rushes again into the same or another enterprise, without any great injury to his name or credit. An American changes place, and even occupation, pursuit, trade, running from one extreme to another, with a rapidity and ease neither thought of nor possible in crowded Europe."[21] Since about a quarter of the men in the samples listed (and likely pursued) more than one occupation during their working careers, some limited observations may be helpful.

Most of the men who listed more than one occupation were concentrated at the lower levels of the occupational ladder, as one might anticipate. Probably the most common pattern could be called "recursive," that is, the temporary deviation from one's usual line of work, followed by a return to it (as in the case of *Silas B. Jaquith). *Asa K. George provides a good example; he was born in Plymouth, New Hampshire, in 1832, the son of William and Mary George; Plymouth's historian wrote of Asa, "With the exception of a residence of a few years in Roxbury, Mass., he lived in Plymouth . . . until about 1870, when he removed to Rumney."[22] Asa K. George, like many another young single sample member, could not be located in the 1850 census, when he was 18; he was not living with his parents in Plymouth so was probably working "out." In 1860 he appears in Roxbury, Massachusetts, with his wife, Abby A., and a year-old daughter, Anna F. (the couple's first daughter, born in Roxbury in 1857, had died in 1858). He listed himself as an expressman and claimed $300 in personal estate. The Georges had a son in the fall of 1860; their next son was born in Plymouth, New Hampshire, in 1865 and the last in Rumney in 1872. The 1870 census shows Asa farming in Plymouth, with his wife, two boys, and a girl, and $600 in real and $535 in personal estate. By 1880, in Rumney, he had become a butcher, residing with his wife, a son, and a daughter. He died in Rumney in 1901.[23] For whatever reasons, his stay in the Boston area was brief. Should he be regarded as a failure who could not stand the gaff in Boston, hence retreated to the beautiful hills of Grafton County, New Hampshire? What if his goal all along was to save up to buy a farm back home? By showing over $1,100 in estate in the 1870 census, Asa K. George certainly was more financially successful than over half of the men in his cohort who had stayed behind in Boston.

Another common pattern included men who drifted into and out of a variety of low-level jobs that demanded a modicum of intelligence but no specific skills. This fuzzy area included such jobs as porter, janitor, hostler, and laborer, all among the Unskilled and Menial group, and driver, policeman, steward, fireman, and hackman among the Semiskilled and Service classification. Men in these classifications seldom rose into the ranks of the Skilled or the Proprietors, Managers, and Officials. *Philander C. Mathews, for example, was born 30 April 1831 in Norwich, Vermont, to John and Cynthia B. Mathews, who were then about 50 and 40, respectively, so he was likely their last child. By 1850, his father, who was then 69, had turned over the family farm to Charles F., an elder son. Philander was already on his way at the age of 19, working as a farm laborer in Lyme, New Hampshire. He may have met his future wife, Matilda S., then, for she came from nearby Danbury. Philander first appeared in Boston-area records in 1857, when George H., his first child, was born in Roxbury (no Massachusetts marriage record exists for the couple). Philander then called himself a teamster. The 1860 census enumerator took him as an expressman with $800 in personal estate, but the canvasser for the 1860 Roxbury city directory recorded him as a machinist. The 1868 Boston directory lists him as proprietor of the Roxbury Express between Court Square in downtown Boston and Roxbury. Both the 1870 census and directory show him as without occupation, although the census lists $4,000 in real and $600 in personal estate. He seems to have owned his house at 38 Orchard Street, with yet another older brother, William H., a teamster, next door at number 40. In early 1877 he moved north of Boston to Everett, where the 1880 census indicated that he was a laborer who had been unemployed for six months of the last twelve. He died in Everett in 1908, aged 77, from arteriosclerosis.[24]

*Philander C. Mathews's experience of several low-level changes in occupational designation was not unusual for members of the Semi-skilled group, and his apparent acquisition of a home accords with the finding that members of this group sometimes did better than did those with specific skills. They did not forgo having children to do this, for on average they had more children than did members of the Professional and Skilled groups—almost as many as did members of the Proprietors group.

A less common but still striking pattern emerges from the lives of men who do not seem to have been able to cope with the urban environment but do not seem to have done well in the countryside either, such as *James C. Chesley. Unfortunately, there is very little information on Chesley, who does not appear to have impressed those few bureaucrats who encountered him. He probably came from Barrington, a small town near Dover, New Hampshire, and was born about 1823; his parents are unknown. He resided in Barrington in 1850, a farmer claiming $500 in real estate, according to that year's census. With him were his 24-year-old wife, Maria L., and their 2-year-old son, George W. Mr. Chesley's whereabouts in the intercensal interval are unknown. In 1860 he was the superintendent of the town poor farm in Canton, Massachusetts, a suburb then just a bit too far out from Boston for easy commutation. His wife was 35, his son George W., 14; they enjoyed the services of an 18-year-old American farm laborer and a 28-year-old Irish servant girl (probably both from among the town poor) and maintained three other men and five women in the manner to which the poor were condemned to become accustomed. Chesley claimed no real or personal estate. He vanished again from modern-day ken until 1869, when the Boston city directory listed him

as "eclectic physician, 16 Salem, house d[itt]o." In the 1870 census the
enumerator misheard this as "electric magnetic physician." By con-
ventional standards of occupational measurement, Dr. Chesley had
made giant strides in just nine years, from poor-farm supervisor to
eclectic physician, seemingly impressive upward occupational mobility. Fortunately for posterity, in 1874 someone asked the Boston
office of R. G. Dun & Co. for credit information on him and his "practice" in Chelsea. The answer was as follows: "Mar. 6. 74—'C.' claims
to be a Physician; but is an ignorant man—never studied med. & takes
up the practice without any knowledge of it—Is not known to have
any Co. or Partner;—without means—& would be sold only for
Cash—"[25] By 1880 the Chesleys had left Chelsea, to disappear once
more into the historical woodwork, except for one last item: James C.
Chesley died in Dover, New Hampshire, in 1893 and was buried in
Barrington, having come full circle.[26]

Some Evidence on Careers of Skilled Workmen: The Massachusetts Charitable Mechanic Association Obituaries

During the nineteenth century one of Boston's most prominent organizations for workingmen was the Massachusetts Charitable Mechanic Association (MCMA). It was founded in 1795 as a social and
self-assistance group by skilled workmen, masters who were interested in having a law passed the better to control their errant apprentices.[27] Out of this small beginning developed a society that survived
into the twentieth century and is vaguely remembered today for its
triennial public exhibitions of skilled crafts products. In 1892 the association published *Annals* containing brief notices of 789 of its regular members who had died between 1860 and the end of 1891. Some
46 were foreign-born; of the 743 native-born men, 494 were natives
of Massachusetts (including 176 Bostonians). New Hampshire had
supplied 98 of the deceased members, Maine 69, Vermont 16, New
York 10, Connecticut 9, Rhode Island 8, and 37 came from a scattering of other states. The geographical distribution of the native-born
Massachusetts Charitable Mechanic Association members was similar
to that of the 2,808 members in the study samples, and 62 of those

743 native-born association members were also included in the study samples.

These brief obituaries permit a modest analysis of some of the relationships among location of training or apprenticeship, occupation, and later success of the Massachusetts Charitable Mechanic Association members. Some 469 of the native-born men were active in Boston at some point in their careers. At least 102 of the men received their training or served their apprenticeships in Boston. At least 140 of them learned their skills before they came to Boston, though for 227 no training locations were given in their obituaries. Since all of the men were still alive in 1860, their listings in the 1860 population census can help test whether nonlocal or local training was associated with greater wealth.

Surprisingly, given the results from the two principal samples that show greater success for unmarried in-migrants to Boston, there do not seem to have been any large differences in the average wealth of the two Massachusetts Charitable Mechanic Association groups, those trained outside Boston and those who learned their skills after arriving there. The 107 men who had received some training before they came to Boston averaged some $28,800 in total estate, while the 74 who had not averaged about $31,800 in total estate. Since these men were, on average, about 53 years old in 1860, some eight to ten years older than members of the samples, and were prominent mechanics as well, it is no wonder that their wealthholdings greatly exceeded those of the sample members. Their annual rate of accumulation was about $724, as compared with about $253 for Skilled men of the 1860 sample, or about $696 for those in the 1870 sample. This is likely a result of the acceleration of the MCMA members' accumulation in later life, but it certainly indicates that they were a breed apart from (and above) the general run of the Skilled sample members. Many MCMA members were described as having been "masters," so the additional labor of their employees went to swell their holdings.

The obituaries of the Massachusetts Charitable Mechanic Association members contain repeated references to many of the qualities and attributes stressed in success literature of the mid-nineteenth century and echoed above by *Solomon Piper: slow, steady application;

patient accumulation; honest dealing with other businessmen. Unfortunately, just as in the example of John Springer, with which this chapter began, such personal characteristics are irrecoverable for the ordinary men of this study. Further lessons to be learned from their business careers will have to be gleaned from less evanescent sources.

Perils of Everyday Life

SNAKE IN THE STOMACH. *A correspondent of the Bunker Hill Aurora states that James Oliver of South Reading, on Friday last ejected from his stomach a live snake, one foot and four inches in length, which was probably swallowed many years ago. Mr. Oliver has been for several years subjected to fits.*

–Boston Evening Transcript, *4 August 1846, 2/4*

The *Gentlemen who left a small package at a dwelling house in this city, last evening, are informed that they have been discovered, and the writer is only withheld from publishing their names by a feeling of respect for their friends.*

–Boston Evening Transcript, *30 April 1844, 2/4*

CULPABLE CARELESSNESS. *A few evenings since, as some boys were amusing themselves by shooting cats in the rear of a house at the south end, the pistol was slightly elevated, and the ball went through a fence into a dwelling-house, and dropped on the floor immediately in front of a lady whose life would probably have been taken if the ball had not spent its force before reaching the spot. Although no damage was done in this instance, yet it is a dangerous practice to use fire-arms for any purpose in the vicinity of dwelling houses. [Journal.]*

–Boston Evening Transcript, *12 April 1854, 1/5*

FIRE. *The alarm of fire at 8 o'clock last evening was occasioned by the burning of a window curtain in a house near the Roxbury line. The whole department turned out promptly, but the curtain, nevertheless, was destroyed. It was valued at 38 cents, and was not insured. [Courier].*

–Boston Evening Transcript, *9 April 1856, 1/4*

*JOHN AVERY RATHBONE ... *born July 1, 1816; married Emily Daniels, Sept. 20, 1838; she was born ——— ——. He went west, was not heard from in over 36 years. One day to her surprise he entered her house well and in good spirits.*

–*John C. Cooley*, Rathbone Genealogy

On Saturday, 7 June 1851, a man "dressed in a green sack coat, black satin vest and striped cotton pants, and who is supposed to be Ephraim G. Daggett, of Hope, M[ain]e," appeared at the Roxbury home of Dr. and Mrs. *Ariel I. Cummings. He claimed to be without money, said he was subject to fits, and asked for food and medical advice. The Cummingses gave him dinner and supper and said that he could spend the night. Daggett asked if he might do some chore and spent half an hour splitting wood. Dr. Cummings went out on a call, and Daggett went upstairs to the family sitting room, where he joined Mrs. Cummings and her four-and-a-half-year-old daughter, Ellen.

Mrs. Cummings said that Daggett appeared wild, spoke of having fits, and so scared her that she went to the window and by gesturing summoned her next-door neighbor, Mrs. Thomas Crossley, who came over and began amusing Ellen. "But she had not been in the room but a moment when Daggett sprung upon his feet and drew out a razor from one of his pockets, saying, '*It is no use, she must go*,' and with a tiger-like fierceness he seized the little girl by the hair, and throwing her head back over his knee, severed with one blow the wind pipe and most of the great blood vessels of the neck."

Mrs. Cummings wrested Ellen back, receiving a cut across four fingers, and ran screaming from the room, Daggett in hot pursuit. Thomas Crossley, having heard her cries from next door, arrived just in time to see Daggett about to slash Mrs. Cummings again and cried "Stop!" Daggett "turned half way round, and then drawing himself up to his full height, he drew his head back, and with one blow cut his own throat from ear to ear." Recalled to his home, Dr. Cummings arrived while Daggett was still in his death throes and was "so anxious to save him, being ignorant of what had happened, that he passed *his own dead child upon the piazza*, and aided in conveying the man into the house. . . . The man died in a few minutes.

"The child was buried . . . yesterday [Sunday] afternoon. . . . So great was the anxiety to see the corpse that the Sexton was obliged to bring it out into the front part of the Church and then not a quarter part of the congregation was gratified. . . . The anxiety to see the remains of the man at the Almshouse was so great that the authorities were compelled to deposit them in a tomb, where they will remain for

the present." A few days later the *Boston Evening Transcript* informed
its readers that Daggett had suffered from epileptic fits for the past
four years but had never been violent or in confinement. His remains
were to be returned to Maine.[1]

Disaster surrounded the people of mid-nineteenth-century Boston,
or so it seemed. Several times a week they read accounts of wrecked
trains, of horrific industrial mishaps (often involving, and revolving,
workers in machinery), of epidemics supposedly caused by "miasmic
emissions," of sanguinary homicides, of ordinary people who sud-
denly dropped dead for no apparent reason, or of runaway horses
and carriages. Even the grave sometimes failed to protect, as *Seth
Hall learned when two "resurrectionists" in Rochester, Massachusetts,
a physician and a medical student, dug up his recently interred father
hoping to use the cadaver for dissection.[2] Anyone who read newspaper accounts of such untoward events must have wondered, Could
that happen to me?

In attempting to learn about the lives of everyday people of the
nineteenth century, one's natural impulse is to resort to the daily
newspapers of the time, and most people will probably recall having
been struck by reading some particularly apposite quotation culled
from a daily newspaper and presented in a work of social or urban
history. Few of these are as dramatic as the brief story of the awful
tragedy that befell the Cummingses, but the article about them pos-
sesses an advantage over any story chosen from a newspaper merely
for its dramatic or didactic impact. The Cummingses were sample
members, one among 2,808 households selected for examination in
this study. Thus they were representative and, one must assume, typical of other households of the time which were visited by violent and
bloody crime. By reversing the usual procedure—by selecting first the
people to be studied, then looking for news of them in the daily newspaper—the researcher places the results of his or her quest for news
about the masses on much firmer methodological ground. Since the
sample members represented a cross section of their ethnic group
then residing in Boston, reports concerning them must also represent
a cross section of the reports about members of that ethnic group,
and hence those reports deserve much greater credence than reports
chosen for their drama, their aptness, or even their accessibility. The

problem of which Boston newspaper to consult was simple: none could be better for this purpose than the *Boston Evening Transcript*.

In the late 1840s, the *Boston Evening Transcript* began to present reports of dire events under the standing headings "accidents" and "fires," rather than distributing them almost randomly on its first and second, or "news" pages. Other events, such as train wrecks, ship sinkings, and the like, continued to receive individualized headings. From their daily perusal of this continuing chronicle of disaster, the *Transcript's* readers may be excused for perhaps thinking that the world was a dangerous place and that their hold—anyone's hold—on life was tenuous and evanescent.

In trying to understand the kinds and frequencies of events that could befall the ordinary individual in mid-nineteenth-century Boston, it is important to keep the newspaper editor in mind. The editor must create, every day, a newspaper to which people will turn for reliable news about the surrounding world, but there is a fine line between informing and alarming. Too much emphasis on crime can have undesirable social consequences and can needlessly inflame the citizenry.[3] One may well imagine the hue and cry if Ephraim G. Daggett had fled instead of killing himself. But too little mention of crime can lull readers into a false security that may cost them dearly (what if Thomas Crossley had been less alert?). The editor well knows that only a very small proportion of the day's events is written up; from that an even tinier part can be presented in the newspaper. No editor could (or can) apply selection criteria consistently, day after day, month after month, so types of stories often came in spates for a few weeks, then vanished for months (e.g., stories about remarkable achievements of dogs; since editors at the mid-nineteenth century were much more likely to copy items from other newspapers than are today's editors, such stories spread by exchanges).

These dual considerations, the balance between informing and alarming and the ability to present only an infinitesimal portion of the day's theoretically newsworthy events, fatally flaw any effort to quantify precisely what readers got from their daily paper at the midcentury. Accordingly, these observations derive from an inspection of every issue of the *Boston Evening Transcript* available on microfilm from the paper's founding in July 1830 through the end of 1860. The *Tran-*

script appeared six days a week, or about 312 times a year, so about 9,500 issues were scrutinized. Reporting of interesting local tidbits ceased almost completely with the onset of the Civil War and does not seem to have resumed so only notices of marriages and deaths were checked daily from 1861 through the end of 1875, a further 4,680 issues.

The Newspaper

The *Boston Evening Transcript* (officially the *Boston Daily Evening Transcript*) seemed to be an ideal source from which to glean insights into the world of the samples' members. It appears to have shared much readership with the *Daily Advertiser*, a morning Whig publication that emphasized economics and politics (the *Advertiser* was probably the local newspaper most often quoted by the *Transcript*). The *Transcript* was more a general-interest paper. It was founded in July 1830 as an adjunct to their printing business by *Henry W. Dutton and James Wentworth.[4] From its beginning the *Transcript* was unusual for a metropolitan newspaper. In an era of intense political partisanship, when almost every daily paper cast its lot with a group or a party, the *Transcript* professed political independence. Unlike other dailies, it never wafted a party banner over its editorial column or ran the names of its candidates for election atop that column for weeks on end. It did support candidates (almost always Whigs) editorially, but it did so calmly and did not repeat that endorsement ad nauseam. One might best describe the paper's editorial stance as crypto-Whig until the breakup of that party left it disoriented for a while; one suspects that its proprietors would have liked to shift over into the Republican ranks but that they were at first insufficiently concerned by the slavery issue to do so. The use of federal power in 1854 to return an escaped slave, Anthony Burns, from Boston to captivity seems to have been the tipping point; warily thereafter the *Transcript* toed the antislavery waters, staying perhaps just a bit ahead of genteel Boston opinion.[5]

The world of the *Transcript* consisted of two unequal groups: "we" and "they." "We" were native-born, middle or upper class, mildly progressive concerning women's rights (between 1842 and 1847 the paper was the first metropolitan daily in the United States to be edited by a woman, Cornelia Wells Walter, who resigned to marry *William Bordman Richards[6]). Despite the rural origins of a large part of the *Transcript*'s readers, it viewed farmers ambivalently. They were almost exclusively native-born and so qualified as members of "us," but news reports about farmers in Boston usually depicted them as trusting or incautious souls gulled by urban sharpers or victimized by the city's thieves (presumably mostly "them").

"We" were willing to hear both sides of most political questions argued, but politely and without vituperation, in readers' letters. "We" were prudent, temperate, thoughtful, and (like the unfortunate Cummingses) dispensed charity to the deserving poor. "We" attended church on Sundays, read the Bible (though "we" were sometimes chary of using it as a clinching argument in nonreligious matters), and, above all, "we" were decent folk.

"They" were much more numerous, but until about the mid-1840s "they" were generally outside Boston. "They" were unpredictable, spontaneous, uncouth, usually lower class, and, increasingly, foreign—Irish in particular. "They" often refused sincerely offered genteel enlightenment and probably never heard Ralph Waldo Emerson lecture. When the Famine struck Ireland in the mid-1840s, the *Transcript* at first reported the plight of the Irish sympathetically. As it became ever more evident that the Famine-inspired migration was adverse for "us," the *Transcript* gradually became alarmed.[7] It thought the primary responsibility to relieve the problem lay with the British government; if it did not act, Ireland would lose her most enterprising and productive citizens.

As the immensity of the population movement unleashed by the Famine became clear, the *Transcript* claimed that Great Britain was dumping her unwanted people upon the United States. Their arrival was bound to upset the labor market and to bring hard times upon the native-born worker (as may have occurred; see Chapter 1). The *Transcript* never descended to the depths of the Know-Nothings's sweeping xenophobia, but it did want the federal government to assert more control over immigration. It early accepted stereotypes of Irish irresponsibility and unpredictability: "A RAILROAD OBSTRUC-TION.—The West Watch report for last night says: 'Mary Barnes was found lying directly on the [Boston &] Maine Railroad track. Fearing she might be an obstruction, or cause some damage to the locomotive, she was brought in and kept till morning.' "[8] The *Transcript* favored (without saying how this could be done) slowing the influx of Irish so as not to swamp Boston's capacity to support the newly arrived poor. It desired a waiting period to keep recent immigrants from gaining citizenship quickly and then taking control of places where they had just arrived. What could "we" do? "We" believed in majority rule, but what would happen when that majority had nothing in common with "us"? The dilemma of democracy versus demography was never re-solved satisfactorily in the *Transcript*'s columns; meanwhile, the pa-per's readers voted with their feet: Boston's population became less and less "we" after 1850, and many of "our" household heads contin-ued to work in Boston while commuting from the suburbs. In 1885–88 Boston got its first Irish-born mayor.

After about 1850 the paper's concerns with vague external threats revealed themselves in more and more reports about "local matters." Previously, most local matters had consisted of short items of political or religious interest, interspersed with stories on fires and accidents. By about 1850, however, there appeared a subtle change in emphasis: some of those events that sent a frisson of horror down readers' spines were not the result of blind chance, Atropos cutting the thread of life. They were the result of deliberate acts of men. At first, the *Transcript* wished to dismiss some of these reports as based on insane or aberrant behavior, not crediting that such "fiends in human form" could exist. But it became apparent that "incendiaries" were deliber-ately igniting hayricks and burning barns, while depraved others were disabling machinery or malevolently opening railroad switches that should have been closed. How could such actions be reconciled with the *Transcript*'s worldview? It had little room for irrationality; insanity such as Ephraim G. Daggett's was acceptable—and the *Transcript* was much in advance of most of its contemporaries[9] in viewing insanity as a disease perhaps curable—but deliberate evil was not. Usually the *Transcript*'s editors resisted the temptation, indulged in by its contem-poraries, to identify evildoers with "them." There is a glimmer of sus-picion that somehow all this was bound up with "progress" and that some modern Luddites, unbalanced by civilization's onrush, could not cope with it, hence struck out blindly at it, trying to retard it wherever and however they could. The *Transcript's* mildly Whiggish soul was revolted by such behavior.

There were definite connections between some events and the march of progress, however; many accidents were obviously the result of human, not Divine, intervention, and the *Transcript's* comments on railroad calamities soon changed from entreating a calm acceptance of God's wishing to call His children home, to asking what could be learned from particular accidents to avoid similar recurrences. "Although ship mishaps were considered normal," says the historian of the Boston & Albany Railroad, "no tradition prepared people for spectacular land wrecks." [10]

In this context appeared thousands of reports about thousands of incidents over the 30-year period examined. In looking through the *Transcript*, I strove to note every mention of any of the 2,808 sample members in a news item, excluding advertisements and reports of political meetings (a very few men usually appeared in these repeatedly). Even though the sample members represented about 10 percent of the native-born male household heads of native-born parentage who resided in Boston between about 1855 and about 1875, the vast majority of sample members was, apparently, never mentioned in news items during the entire period surveyed. The events concerning individuals that were reported in the *Transcript* over the 30 years may be divided conveniently into accidental and deliberate. The former were much the more numerous.

Accidents

Accidents, at least as the *Transcript* reported them, were gender-oriented, presumably reflecting the proper spheres of society. Accidents in the workplace involved men; accidents in the home involved women almost exclusively (occasionally a man was injured at home attempting to extinguish a woman's burning clothing). [11] Women could be injured out-of-doors, usually in traffic; sometimes they fell on icy sidewalks in the winter. Gradually accidents also took on some ethnic coloration: certain kinds involved primarily Irish victims, oth-

ers almost exclusively native-born. These reinforced ethnic stereotypes. Irish dockworkers, presumably because of a little too much of
"the creature," fell into the holds of ships they were unloading. Reports of laborers injured in a collapsing excavation were sure either
to give Irish names or to note the victims' nationality.

In contrast, native-born workers more often fell from high places,
from scaffolding especially, than did foreigners. For one sample
member, this had fatal consequences:

> FATAL RESULT.—Mr. *Thomas Palmer, a well-known and skil-
> ful master mason and builder, died on Wednesday, at his resi-
> dence, 4 Staniford place, from the effects of an accident which
> occurred some weeks since. He was in the 63d year of his age.[12]

As would be expected, nonfatal falls were much more usual than fatal
ones:

> GENERAL.—... Yesterday morning as *Abner Libby was at
> work putting up an iron awning frame on Hanover street, the
> iron work gave way, causing him to fall to the pavement, breaking
> one of his wrists and one of his ankles. The First Police conveyed
> him to his residence, 72 Brighton street.[13]

> ACCIDENTS .... William Deering, four years old, son of Mr.
> *Dexter Deering, fell from a platform attached to Simmons's car-
> penter's shop, at the foot of Lime street, into the Charles river,
> yesterday noon, and after sinking twice, was fortunately rescued
> by two boys named Parker and Gulon.[14]

A frequent kind of fall involved an inattentive man's stepping into
a building's "scuttle" and being precipitated to the basement. In buildings where workers hoisted goods between floors for storage, the
scuttle, a series of openings in each floor combining to create a shaft
from basement to top floor, was employed. Although scuttles were
equipped with trapdoors on each floor to close them off, these seem
often to have been left open for convenience in shifting goods, for
ventilation, and for communication from one floor to another. (Scuttles left open in locked stores were blamed several times for the rapid
spread of flames within those buildings; the Great Fire of 1872 was

supposed thus to have gotten its rapid start.[15]) Of course, employers warned their men to be cautious around scuttles, but every few weeks, especially in the summer, another "scuttle fall" story would appear. Most of the victims tended to be younger employees relegated to a building's upper floors. The *Transcript* never suggested that scuttle accidents could be avoided by installing safety rails or by requiring that trapdoors be kept shut except when goods were being hoisted. Its editors may have felt that the law of gravity was beyond legislation.

Another feature of the 1850s was an increase in reports of people's encounters with machinery, especially rotating parts thereof:

> NARROW ESCAPE.—Mr. Charles W. Emery, machinist, at the corner of Hawkins and Ivers streets, was caught and carried round a shaft several times, there being just room for his body to pass under the ceiling without being crushed. His clothes were torn off, and he was somewhat bruised, but no bones were broken. His escape from imminent death was but a hair's breadth.[16]

Sometimes it was not even necessary to become entangled with the machine:

> NARROW ESCAPE IN ROXBURY. At *Ebenezer Ryerson & Son's manufactory of leather-splitting and planing-machine knives, on Kemble street, yesterday afternoon, Mr. Ryerson had just stepped away from a large grindstone some eight feet in diameter, where he had been at work, when it burst in halves, one piece going out through the side of the building—which is of brick—and the other directly opposite. The stone was revolving at great speed, and Mr. Ryerson's escape seems most providential.[17]

Occasionally the victim was not so lucky:

> ACCIDENT IN CHARLESTOWN. Yesterday afternoon, as ex-Alderman *Salma E. Gould, of East Boston, was engaged in driving piles in Charlestown, his right hand was crushed and mangled in a shocking manner by the large iron weight of a pile driving machine. At the time of the accident he was adjusting the pile, when the weight fell. It was found necessary to amputate a portion of the hand.[18]

In reporting such machinery accidents, the *Transcript* never suggested that they could be avoided by installing guards, relocating belting, or arranging for emergency shut-off switches.

Fires

Boston's fires had no lack of combustible materials. Scholars have truly called the early nineteenth century the Wooden Age: wood was cheap and easily worked so it furnished the material for most structures, it was the raw material of most of the furnishings within those structures, and until coal supplanted it in the 1860s it was Boston's principal heating and cooking fuel. Clothing was made of natural fibers, and because of people's less frequently washing it (and themselves), and less often changing it (since people had few changes of clothing), clothing tended to become greasy with time and thus even more of a fire hazard. (Other materials, such as fashionable crinoline, would seem to have been invented to help incinerate their wearers.) In the days before domestic electricity, illumination was by fire, candle, or lamp; fires threw off sparks, candles burned down or fell over, and lamps, particularly those employing volatile camphene, or "burning fluid," tipped over or even exploded. With the combination of flammable clothing and precarious or open flames in most homes, it is a wonder that more people did not become human torches:

EXPLOSION OF CHEMICAL FLUID.—About 10½ o'clock on Saturday night, a glass lamp, containing a small quantity of Porter's Chemical Burning Fluid, exploded in the house of Col Abram Moore, Province House Court, badly burning his son, a young man about 19 years of age. There were two tubes to the lamp, one of which was not prepared with a wick, as it should have been, and Mr Moore being ready to retire to bed, got up and took the lamp, giving it a swinging toss upwards in order to make it burn more freshly. . . . A sudden and loud explosion was produced. . . . The burning fluid fastened on the vest, a double breasted one, of the young man, burnt the front away, burnt his arms, hands and thighs, so that the skin came off in peels, and also consumed a portion of his hair and burned one of his temples. The application of water had no effect in extinguishing the burning clothes . . . and he was not relieved until they were cut off, when every remedy was administered by Dr. O. W. Holmes . . . and we are happy to learn this morning that he [Moore] is doing very well.[19]

Structure fires, not necessarily involving loss of life, were frequent in midcentury Boston; they were probably so common that many were never reported in the newspapers.[20] They usually started from a spark or coal in a fire that presumably had been extinguished for the night but was biding its time to consume its surroundings. After the introduction of piped water in the mid-1840s, Boston was better off than most other large cities because its firemen had access to a system of hydrants. Unfortunately, a combination of unusual conditions still could, and did, cause widespread havoc, as during the Great Fire of 1872.[21] House fires were almost uniformly blamed on sparks escaping from heating fires supposedly banked or extinguished for the night. Daytime home conflagrations were apparently less frequent because someone was watching the cooking fire or stove; they usually started from cooking, rather than heating, fires.[22]

Workplace fires were especially prone to begin near machinery because of the heat generated and the customary presence of combustible materials:

DESTRUCTIVE FIRES.—Yesterday afternoon, at half past two o'clock the carpenter's shop of Mr George Nowell, at the foot of South Cedar street took fire, and the wind being fresh from the southwest it speedily communicated to the adjoining buildings in that street and the foot of Piedmont street, and was not arrested until upwards of twenty-five dwelling houses, chiefly of wood, were destroyed. Some of the furniture of the occupants was removed several times, and some burnt in its last place of deposit. . . .

The following are some of the names of the sufferers.

On South Cedar street . . . Mr. *Elisha Atwood, fish dealer, dwelling. . . .

Mr *Seth Hall, sexton of the Methodist Church, who resided under the Church, had his furniture badly injured by hasty removal. . . .

The alarm a little before 7 o'clock this morning, came from the Looking Glass Manufactory of Mr *Samuel Curtis, 47 Washington street. Little or no damage. . . . From 2 o'clock yesterday the department has been constantly on the run or hard at work, many of the members are completely exhausted from over exertion. A relay of men will have to be put on, if the fires and alarms are continued.[23]

Accidents Involving Transportation

Until the advent of the horsecar, most traffic accidents involved horses and horse-drawn vehicles: carriages, wagons, buggies, and the like. They were straightforward. A horse or horses became alarmed and rushed wildly through the streets:

RUNAWAY HORSES ON WASHINGTON STREET.—Three horses, one attached to a baker's wagon, belonging to *J. A. Brigham, another to a buggy belonging to O. H. P. Burnham, and the third to a wagon, became frightened on School street, near the *Parker House, yesterday forenoon at about half-past ten o'clock, and ran toward Washington street. While running, the foremost horse was seized and stopped by a young man. This action blockaded the street in such a manner as to prevent the other teams from passing, and a possible catastrophe was averted. The buggy was badly broken.[24]

Pedestrians were also fair game:

ACCIDENT.—As Mr. *Alvah Skinner, of the firm of Skinner & Sweet, jewellers, 49 Hanover street, was passing through Congress street, yesterday, he was knocked down by a hack, very hastily and carelessly driven. His head was somewhat bruised, and one of his fingers dislocated. He had several hundred dollars, in bills,

in his hands at the time, which were freely and abruptly circulated. The money was nearly all gathered up subsequently.[25]

Drivers also had their problems:

NARROW ESCAPE. On Tuesday afternoon, *John Souther, Esq.,
proprietor of the Globe [Locomotive] Works, South Boston, was
considerably injured by jumping from his wagon, his horse having become unmanageable, near the Worcester [Railroad] depot.
His hand was badly torn, his right leg bruised, and his whole
frame jarred and seriously injured.[26]

Ironically, as a leading manufacturer of locomotives, *John Souther
helped the transportation system of the United States through some
rapid changes between about 1850 and 1870.[27]

It is difficult to know whether, around the midcentury, steamboats
or railroads killed more people,[28] but a steamboat accident had to
be truly spectacular to receive extended treatment in the *Transcript*.
Railroad accidents were reported in stages. First came a telegraphic
dispatch of a "disaster" involving several deaths. Within a day or
so appeared more detail, including victims' names (interest grew if
Boston-area residents were involved). A "round-up" item a few days
later would arrange all available information into a coherent narrative
and attempt to ascribe causation. Perhaps some weeks or months later
still, if an inquest or a government investigation inquired into the disaster, a report of those proceedings would appear.

Almost from the beginning of such reports, the *Transcript*'s editors'
implicit position was that, though God permitted such accidents to
occur, they were not to be regarded in the same light as deaths from
most other accidents or from disease: He was not working through
the railroads to call His children back to Him. People could escape
death in rail accidents "by Providence," but the accidents themselves
were not providential. Most often, people were responsible for
them.[29] The railroad also could provide (I believe) a clever means of
suicide:

DEATH OF *NOAH STURTEVANT.—*Noah Sturtevant, senior
partner of the well known firm of N. Sturtevant & Co. of this city,

was accidentally killed at the Eastern Railroad crossing at North Chelsea on Wednesday. His carriage was backed directly on the track and was struck by the engine; and Mr. Sturtevant fell upon the track and was so crushed that he died almost instantly. He was identified by one of the passengers on the train. His body was taken to the Massachusetts General Hospital, and notice of the accident was sent to his family in East Boston. The flags at East Boston were flying at half-mast yesterday, as a token of respect to him. He leaves a wife and a large family.

That the carriage was "backed" onto the track suggests that Sturtevant had but to order his horse forward to avoid the locomotive; with this arrangement the horse was presumably not injured. The *Transcript*'s readers would have accepted as plausible the suggestion that Sturtevant had killed himself because of "business reverses," as will be seen in Chapter 6.[30]

Trains also took their toll of the unwary:

FATAL RAILROAD ACCIDENT. This morning, as the nine o'clock outward Brookline train was passing through West Orange street, the cowcatcher attached to the engine struck a little boy of 7 years, son of Mr. *Richard D. Childs, who resides in West Orange street, and threw him with great violence against the brick wall at the side of the track, fracturing his skull and otherwise seriously injuring him, so that he died in half an hour after the accident. The child was playing upon the track.[31]

People seemed to be in a hurry to catch departing trains or to descend from arriving ones. Occasionally they fell beneath, sustaining horrific injuries.[32] Fortunately for the survival of Bostonians, no major railroad's tracks extended through the downtown: each had its own terminal at the edge of the city core. Nevertheless, some people found ways to be run down by locomotives. Usually the victims proved later to have been drunk or sometimes deaf. They were almost always foreign-born.

After the surge of railroad building centered on Boston was virtually completed in 1851 (and commemorated by a Railroad Jubilee[33]), the city had a hiatus of only five years before the first tracks of its horse railroads were laid in the streets, the horsecars replacing the slower but less dangerous omnibuses.[34]

Accidents involving horse railroads were usually more severe than had been those involving omnibuses: an omnibus wheel, after all, might crush or break a person's leg, but a horsecar's flanged wheel amputated the limb, usually causing death from shock or "exsanguination." Horsecars did offer the advantage of a precisely delineated route. Once past the tracks, the pedestrian was safe—from the horsecars at least. Not so the carriage driver. In the winter the horsecar lines plowed their tracks much more promptly than the city cleared the rest of the street (if it bothered to do so). Carriage drivers found this a tempting convenience because, of course, other parts of the streets were blocked. Unfortunately, sometimes it turned out that the distance between a carriage's wheels equaled that between the tracks, and the carriage became "engaged" in the tracks. Not all engaged carriage drivers were headed in the same direction as the horsecars on their temporarily shared track. The most common incident involved someone's attempting to board or leave a moving horsecar and falling beneath it. The *Transcript* ascribed most such mishaps to people's newfound desire to "save time."[35]

A minor variant of the theme of rushing to catch the horsecar involved the city's ferries to East Boston and Chelsea. Sometimes a late passenger attempted to leap aboard a ferry just leaving the slip; the most usual reward was a good soaking, a penalty the editor thought suited the offense.

Crime

Boston suffered a crime wave in the 1850s, brought on by the presence of a large underclass and a supply of prosperous potential victims. The city seemed to seethe with petty pickpockets, coshmen, garroters, and vicious drunks. The level of fatalities among the middle and upper classes caused by crime appears to have been low; most deaths resulted from drunken brawls or domestic disputes among the recent arrivals. Criminals of the 1850s appear to have had a certain panache sadly lacking among today's miscreants:

POCKET PICKED.—A lady residing in Melville, while watching
the parade of the Cavalry Regiment on Thursday, had her pocket
picked of a wallet containing $30 in money and other articles of
value. The thief, after appropriating the money, put the purse,
containing two pieces of gold and some papers, into the pocket
of Mr. *Edward Perkins.[36]

Prosperous Bostonians could always anticipate that criminals might
strike against their places of business, even when those businesses
would seem to have been as unpromising a prospect as a lard oil
factory:

A TOLERABLY CANDID SHOPBREAKER. The Lard Oil factory
of *W. B. Callender, Jr, No 72 Atkinson street, was broken into
on Saturday night, and the rogue, after forcing the desk and
finding no booty, left on a card the following declaration, written
with a gold pen that was on the desk: "I do not want anything but
money." As proof of his asservation he did not carry off the valuable and useful pen, but it has appeared that about 50 cigars were
taken to minister to his taste for the "luxuries of life."[37]

Most of these break-ins occurred at night; the *Transcript* reported
them under the heading "shopbreaking" and usually noted that little
cash was taken because shop owners presumably did not leave much
of it around overnight. As thieves began to realize that pickings could
be easier in the city's outlying areas, where there was no watch patrol-
ling the streets and there were often decent intervals between houses,
they increasingly turned their attention to burglarizing private homes.
Most thieves took care to break into apparently empty houses, as offering them greater opportunities to select and carry off their plun-
der unnoticed. There were strange contrasts in what thieves stole, as
witness this report from the *Transcript*'s owner:

HOUSE BREAKING. The dwelling house of *H. W. Dutton, 524
Washington street, was entered on Saturday night, and sundry
articles carried away. The robbers first entered the yard by climb-
ing over a fence nine feet high, from a passage-way in the rear,
leading from Pine street, and unbolted the gate. From the yard

they passed into the back kitchen by the window, and entering the pantry took a portion of a choice tub of butter, a bucket of brown sugar, and a bucket of white sugar, and some other articles. They then entered the cellar, from the yard, and took a basket of eggs and another of apples and some other articles, and in their retreat left the cellar door, the back kitchen door, which they unbolted, and the gate, open, without disturbing anyone in the family. The robbers were probably boys. They will meet a reception they little think of should they attempt a repetition of the operation.[38]

The criminals could be much more dangerous and more nearly professional:

A BOLD ROBBERY. The dwelling house of Mr *William H. Barnes, Warren street, Roxbury, about a fourth of a mile the other side of Grove Hall, was entered on Thursday night last, about 1 o'clock, and robbed of upwards of $400 worth of silver plate. The robbers came in their stocking feet, and tried several doors and windows to effect an entrance; they finally forced a door in one of the out-houses, and finding some tools, they cut the fastening from an inner door, when the whole house was free for their operations. They first went to the cellar and collected the iron pokers of the furnace for weapons; they then visited the china closets and collected the silver, a tea-pot, water-pot, large and small spoons, wrenched the silver tops from the castor, and took other articles. They then passed upstairs, went into the chamber where Mr Barnes and his wife were asleep, with a lamp burning, took a gold watch from the table and some other articles, and Mr Barnes's pantaloons, and in passing out, the suspender buckle or a button of the pantaloons struck the bedstead, which awoke Mr B., who instantly sprung up, and discovered that his pantaloons were gone. He seized the lamp suddenly, which put it out, and while he was relighting it the robbers passed down stairs, and went off with their plunder. They were tracked some distance in the road, when they struck off across a field, being alarmed by the violent barking of a neighbor's dog. This was one of the most daring robberies we have recently been called upon to record, and it is to be hoped that the villains will be arrested and punished as they deserve.[39]

Who was to defend the homeowner against these invasions? The *Transcript* did not call for increasing watch patrols in residential areas; homeowners were supposed to defend their property with fences, bolts, and locks. Their implied civic duty was to seize the evildoer and detain him for the watch:

AN ESCAPING ROBBER CAUGHT BY A LADY. A bold piece of roguery, which was promptly discovered and quickly brought to an end by a courageous lady, took place in Dover street last night. About 10 o'clock the house of *Stephen Tilton, Jr., No. 29, was stealthily entered through the front door by a man, who stole a valuable coat from the entry. Just as he left the house, Mrs. Tilton discovered the theft and immediately followed and overtook the robber, whom she seized by his coat, and giving the alarm, retained her hold, notwithstanding his efforts to escape, until Messrs. Wheeler and *Richardson relieved her by taking the fellow into their custody.

The culprit being seized by Mrs. Tilton, threw the stolen coat away from him, but it was secured and identified in the Police Court this morning, and the prisoner was committed for trial in default of bail of $200. He gives his name as Thomas F. Davis, and is recognized as having previously been seen lurking about the vicinity.

The greatest credit is due to Mrs. Tilton for her spirited and chivalrous action in thus promptly arresting at her personal peril, and bringing to justice, one of those prowling thieves who are a constant source of annoyance to all housekeepers [homeowners].[40]

Sometimes the robber was already familiar with the house:

HOUSEBREAKING BY AN OLD ROGUE. The house of Deacon *Henry Safford, E street, South Boston, was entered yesterday afternoon, while the family were at church, by John Licett, a State Prison bird, who was set at liberty a few months since. Mrs. Safford on returning home with her son, found Licett in her chamber ransacking a desk. She locked him in, and sent for help. The rogue pushed up the window, jumped a distance of sixteen feet, and ran. He had in his pocket two purses, a Franklin medal belonging to Mr. Safford's son, and a number of other articles of value. While in the house he defaced in a most outrageous manner, the carpet in the parlor. Officer Sleeper took him in charge and committed him to jail. What renders Licett's case more aggravated, says the [Boston] Traveller, is that Mr. Safford assisted him when he came out of prison, furnished him with clothes, obtained for him a good situation, and treated him with the greatest kindness.[41]

Crimes against property seem to have been much more prevalent among members of the samples than were assaults (presumably as prelude to robbery). I located but two cases, of which only one appeared in detail:

GARROTING RECORD.... Mr. *Gilman Page, residing on Pleasant street, was recently met by a couple of members of the garroting profession. He, having more strength than his assailants, seized them, and bumped their heads together with such force that they lustily cried quarter. Quarter they got, but not until their pates were somewhat bruised.[42]

One should not assume that members of the samples necessarily led blameless lives, though they were more sinned against than sinners. At least three of them, *Andrew H. Adams, *Dr. Charles C. Beers, and *Lot Boody, spent some time in state penitentiaries. Adams served in Wisconsin, his crime forgery, Dr. Beers expiated theft in the Connecticut State Prison, and Boody assault in Massachusetts's institution in Charlestown; Adams by then had already removed to Milwaukee, but Dr. Beers came to Boston after his term. Lot Boody remained in the city for some thirty years after his prison term, working variously as a barber, trader, hairdresser, or real estate agent and left for Nashua, New Hampshire, in 1880.[43]

*Spencer R. Brown almost joined this unhappy trio of convicts:

On Saturday evening about half-past 7 o'clock, Mr. John P. Averill, principal of the Chapman School, while on his way to East

Boston, where he resides, was violently assaulted near the ferry
landing by a man named *Spencer R. Brown. In the struggle Mr.
Averill was felled to the earth by a blow from his antagonist
[Brown was a stevedore]. The circumstances which led to the
committal of this outrage are related to us as follows: Brown had
a boy in the Chapman School, and for impudent conduct he had
been punished by Averill. Yesterday, Brown endeavored to get
Judge Russell to issue a warrant for the arrest of the teacher, but
there not being sufficient cause to justify such a proceeding, the
warrant was refused. Not obtaining redress by fair means, Brown
resorted to foul ones, and committed the unmanly act recorded
above. Late on Saturday night he was arrested by Constable
Henry C. Stratton, on a warrant issued by Judge Russell. The
case will undergo a rigid examination, and if the facts are as we
have been led to believe, Brown deserves to be treated with the
full rigor of the law. [Atlas.][44]

Eventually, a judge sentenced Brown "to pay a fine of $75 and
costs—amounting in all to $142.91—and to give bonds in $200 to
keep the peace for six months."[45] This was a stiff punishment for
someone hired by the day who in 1854 was supporting a wife, five
sons, and a daughter.[46] No other crimes were reported as having been
committed by sample members, except for one.

Fittingly, this chronicle of disasters concludes with the ultimate
crime, homicide. Just a few days before the Great Fire, in November
1872, on election day, occurred one of the city's more shocking homicides of the century. The next day a small-time moneylender and
minor property owner, *Abijah Ellis, was discovered to have been
killed, dismembered, packed into two barrels, and thrown into the
Charles River. One barrel grounded in Boston, the other in Cambridge; this had the makings of an interesting jurisdictional dispute,
but Cambridge deferred to the Boston police when the victim's iden-
tity and the likelihood that the crime was committed in Boston became apparent.

Details of the investigation are almost nonexistent and may be inferred from the trial report only with difficulty. The principal inves-
tigator seems to have been Police Chief Edward H. Savage. He did

not reveal how he fastened upon his suspect, *Leavitt Alley, a teamster originally from Eaton, New Hampshire, but there was testimony that the barrels containing the victim also held wood shavings and an invoice from a firm manufacturing billiard tables that allowed Alley to haul away its shavings to use as bedding for his horses.

The trial, which by modern standards seems hopelessly bungled, was notable as the first in American jurisprudential history in which the prosecution offered in evidence microscopic tests of blood (found in Alley's stable and alleged by the prosecution to have come from Ellis, by the defense to have come from a horse treated by having been bled). Whether in reaction to the confusing presentation and sloppy work of the prosecution, or in opposition to accepting the word of "experts" that the blood spots were human in origin, or on yet other grounds, the jury found Alley not guilty. (The prosecution, for example, never suggested that Alley, as a teamster with his own wagon, had ample means to deliver the barreled remains of Ellis to a bridge over the river and dump them in. Who would have thought twice about a teamster dumping trash in the river?) Even twelve years later, Chief Savage still believed Alley was guilty; there were no indications that, after Alley's acquittal, the Boston police sought elsewhere for Ellis's killer. Alley remained in Boston but died in 1876 of lung cancer.[47]

At about the midcentury in Boston, opportunities for members of Boston's Yankee middle and upper classes to be victimized by crime or to be injured otherwise would appear to have been increasing. If one goes by numbers of reports alone, the odds of suffering loss through fire or break-in seem to have been about equal. Because the newspapers' reportorial staffs were minuscule, coverage in outlying areas probably depended on readers' submitting items. In any event, three times as many fires and break-ins were reported as having occurred at sample members' business locations as at their homes; traffic accidents were about one-third as frequently reported as were incidents occurring in homes. Actual assaults on sample members were very rare, only two instances having been found, and only four sample members appear to have committed serious crimes. Finally, it looks as though only one sample member was a homicide victim—perhaps at the hands of another member of the study.

These events were concentrated geographically and by occupation as well. Prosperous shopowners, such as jewelers, were much more likely to have their stores invaded than were, say, carpenters. Carpenters, planing-mill proprietors, wood-wharf owners, and foundry owners, however, suffered fires at their establishments disproportionate to their numbers because those workplaces were crammed with flammable materials.

Should the *Transcript* be faulted for needlessly alarming its readers about the possibility of suffering from fire or burglary? I would argue that, at least concerning fire, it should not. During the inquiry into Boston's Great Fire of 1872, the shopowner in whose store the fire began was asked if he had been "burned out" before; "Never but once. . . . in 1864," was his reply.[48] This suggests that being burned out was not uncommon for a merchant. If the ratio of stories about burglaries to those about fires (roughly one to one) is correct, then break-ins were also a usual part of mercantile life.

In reporting the many cases of personal injury suffered by members of the recently arrived Irish, the *Transcript* probably did exaggerate the dangers to those of native-born ancestry. After all, starting in the late 1840s the better-off Yankees began removing their families from close contact with the Irish masses, while continuing to retain Irish servants. The Yankees' businesses, however, remained vulnerable.

If the Yankees were not generally burned, beaten, or mangled—as one might suppose from newspaper reports—how did they die? Fortunately, one can answer with some precision, as we shall see in Chapter 6, after looking at less final kinds of out-migration.

Leaving
Boston

At the present moment, when emigration offers rare hopes and inducements, there is scarcely to be found in New England a village so insignificant, or so secluded, that there is not there some mother's heart bleeding at the perhaps life-long separation from a darling son.

–[*Maria Susanna Cummins*], The Lamplighter, *1854*

RESIGNATION. *Mr. Moses F. Page, for three years past a faithful and efficient member of the Police Department of this city, has resigned his office. He has gone West to engage in farming.*

–Boston Evening Transcript, *17 March 1856, 2/4*

RESIGNED.—**Alexander Hanscom, esq., for many years an officer in the Custom House, has resigned the office of Auditor, to accept the same position in the New York Custom House.*

–Boston Daily Advertiser, *26 October 1865, 1/6*

Possible Problems in Analyzing Out-Migration

In considering out-migration from Boston, one should keep in mind that when this study's subjects were selected systematically from the manuscript population census, the vast majority was *already* married heads of household: only 33 of the 2,808 men in the study remained single. Based on their experience, Chapter 2 suggested that about half of the male native-born in-migrants to Boston were single, but that may be a low estimate. Since it is difficult to trace unmarried men and even more difficult to trace unmarried women in nineteenth-century records (and since successful linkages are often unsatisfying), the principal outflow from Boston at midcentury may have consisted of single young men and women whose brief stay in Boston made little or no impress on the historical record. Further very sophisticated research (perhaps impossible, given available records) would be required to specify the makeup of this exodus.

Long-Term Persistence

The senior member of the samples, *Rev. Charles Cleveland, born in 1772, also lived the longest, dying just 16 days short of his hundredth birthday.[1] *Erastus E. Jeffery survived until 1933. The men in this study spanned with their lives the period from the establishment of the Massachusetts Committee of Correspondence to the first year of the New Deal. They persisted in Boston for well over a century. In the 1860 sample, the oldest native Bostonian, *John Gair, a prosperous mast maker, was born in 1778; his counterpart in the 1870 sample, the noted attorney *Samuel D. Parker, was born in 1781. *John G. Moseley, a wholesale boot and shoe dealer born in Sullivan, Maine, was the last member of the 1860 sample to die within Boston, in 1923; the last 1870 sample member to die in the city (in 1928) was a well-to-do dry-goods dealer, *Frank W. Wildes, a native of Northborough, Massachusetts. Men of the 1860 sample were thus resident in Boston as early as 1778 and as late as 1923, some 145 years. For 1870 sample members, the corresponding dates were 1781 and 1928, or 147 years.

If we consider only in-migrants and out-migrants, the span of residence is still over a century: the first member of the 1860 sample to
arrive was *Samuel Payson, born in 1777 in Wayland, Massachusetts,
who was living in Roxbury as early as the 1790s. *John P. Bigelow,
born in 1797 in Groton, Massachusetts, came with his family to Boston at the age of ten; he later served as mayor, 1849–51.[2] Of the 1860
sample, *Charles A. Burditt, a millionaire hardware dealer, was the
oldest member to leave Boston, departing in 1922 at the age of 86.
Five years later, *Erastus E. Jeffrey, a retired mason and an 1870
sample member, moved out. Aged 93, he was the second-oldest out-
migrant in the samples (he survived until 1933). Accordingly, in- and
out-migrants were present from the 1860 sample between the 1790s
and 1922, or for about a century and a quarter, and from the 1870
sample between 1797 and 1927, some thirteen decades.

Thus some members of the samples were present in Boston as early
as 85 years before 1860 or 1870 and as late as 60 years thereafter. Of
course, the great mass of sample members did not remain in Boston
as long as did these extreme exemplars, but nevertheless the persistence of these men was unusual. The Yankees of mid-nineteenth-century Boston may be unique among the major urban ethnic groups of
that era in that most of them persisted in Boston in each decade from
the 1830s through the 1870s, except for the 1850s.[3] Their lifetime
persistence (a lifetime persister is one who dies in a community, usually, but not necessarily, after a lengthy residence) was also surprisingly high, as Table 5.1 suggests. As one would anticipate, Boston
natives, because of their family and personal connections, were likely
to spend their whole lives in the city: five out of seven of them, but
only about four out of seven native-born in-migrants, eventually died
in Boston. Nevertheless, among the entire group, three out of five
died in the city. Out-migration was, therefore, not typical behavior
for these men. Today it seems highly unlikely that, of the hundreds
of thousands of people who move to any large North American city,
four out of seven will eventually die residents of that city (and if one
includes Boston's nearby commuter suburbs, its retention rate would
rise to about five out of seven). People today tend to leave cities once
their working years are over. In the mid-nineteenth century, how-

Table 5.1

Lifetime Persistence Rates in Boston of In-Migrants and of Boston Natives

Migration status	Out-migrants (left Boston)		Lifetime persisters (died in Boston)		Totals
	N	%	N	%	
In-migrant	933	43.1	1,232	56.9	2,165
Boston native	185	28.8	458	71.2	643
Totals	1,118	39.8	1,690	60.2	2,808

Percentages sum horizontally.

ever, the demarcation between employed and unemployed was indistinct because the paucity of formal social support mechanisms made each man the master (or victim) of his own fate. If (like *Silas S. Putnam) one could accumulate a "competence" and retire on it, well and good. If not, perhaps one's family, friends, or work associates would help out.[4] And without some such help, leaving Boston was not advisable.

Fortunately, there seem to be strong relationships between some characteristics of these Yankees and their likelihood of leaving Boston. Prominent among these relationships are those of family completion, age, loss of one's wife, ill health, and the classic standby, prosperity or lack thereof.

Family Completion and Out-Migration

There was a strong connection between completing one's family and leaving Boston. Fully 90.1 percent of those couples who had any children and who quit the city had finished producing children before they left. As Table 5.2 indicates, persistence increased with family size. Because determining the exact number of children ever born to

Table 5.2

Lifetime Persistence in or Departure from Boston, by Number of Children Ever Born in First Marriage (In-Migrants Only)

Number of children ever born in first marriage	Sample members			Out-migrants as % of total
	Total	Persisting	Leaving	
None	331	182	149	45.0
1	366	179	187	51.1
2	408	241	167	40.9
3	380	196	184	48.4
4	234	142	92	39.3
5	166	106	60	36.1
6	112	72	40	35.1
More than 6	154	102	52	33.8
Totals	2,151	1,220	931	43.3

"Children" is more precisely defined as "completed pregnancies." Fourteen bachelor out-migrants excluded.

sample members is difficult, the true numbers are probably greater than appear in the table and would display a smoother distribution than is suggested there, where the departure rate for those households with two children appears inconsistent with that for other households. Possibly the actual state of affairs is also obscured by the high levels of infant mortality prevalent at the midcentury; quite a few families listed as having had three or four children may have had only one or two who survived beyond, say, the age of six. The pattern, however, is clear: the more children one had, the less likely one was to leave Boston. Because prosperous sample members had more children (as discussed in Chapter 2) and better-off people tended to persist, this finding is appealing.

Table 5.3

Distribution of Age at Departure from Boston of In-Migrants

Age at departure of in-migrants (male household heads) with children	Number of in-migrants departing Boston				
	Total couples	Total as % of 782	Average no. of children[a]	N	Childless couples as % of cohort
21–30	42	5.4	2.40	10	19.2
31–40	131	16.8	2.43	29	18.1
41–50	164	21.0	2.91	36	18.0
51–60	143	18.3	3.43	27	15.9
61–70	163	20.8	3.27	23	12.4
71–80	104	13.3	3.33	22	17.5
Over 80	35	4.5	3.66	2	5.4
Totals	782	100.0	3.06	149	16.0

[a]For couples who produced children; total number of couples, 931 (782 with children, 149 without); one bachelor excluded.

Age at Departure

Having spent two or three decades, on average, working in Boston, most in-migrants who left were middle-aged (see Table 5.3). Only 44 percent, or about three-sevenths, of the men who left did so before their fifty-first birthday, with about another 18 percent departing in their fifties, leaving yet another three-eighths to quit the city after the age of 61; this last contingent probably should be viewed as retirees in the modern sense, in that their contemporaries would have perceived them as well off. For them, leaving Boston was presumably more a matter of comfort or convenience than necessity, as a glance at their wealthholdings, summarized in Table 5.4, demonstrates. Here the poor financial showing before their departure of most of the

Table 5.4

Average Wealthholding (at Time of Being Sampled) for Out-Migrants from Boston Who Were Also In-Migrants, by Age Cohort

Age at departure of in-migrants (male household heads)	Number of in-migrants departing Boston					
	Total in cohort	Assessed		Average wealth assessed ($)[a]	Zero assessment	
		N	as % of 336		N	% of cohort
21–30	52	6	1.8	3,650	46	88.5
31–40	161	36	10.7	7,771	125	77.6
41–50	200	58	17.3	3,610	142	71.0
51–60	170	66	19.6	6,756	104	61.2
61–70	186	80	23.8	11,530	106	57.0
71–80	126	71	21.1	20,321	55	43.7
Over 80	37	19	5.7	54,842	18	48.6
Totals	932	336	100.0	$12,989	596	63.9

[a]For assessed sample members only (336 were assessed for some wealth, 596 assessed for poll tax only).

younger out-migrants is evident, with about four-fifths of those under the age of 41 at departure not having been assessed for more than a poll tax. Only above the age of 71 did the proportion of nonassessed out-migrants drop below one-half.

Thus, just as there were two primary streams of in-migrants to Boston, single young men and married men in their early thirties, there were also sharply differentiated outflows. Length of stay varied with an individual's age at departure, but, as Table 5.5 indicates, even very young out-migrants had already spent about half their adult working lives in Boston.

Table 5.5

Average Length of Stay in Boston and Average Age at Arrival for Out-Migrants from Boston Who Were Also In-Migrants, by Age Cohort

Age at departure of in-migrants (male household heads)	In-migrants departing Boston				
	Total for whom length of stay is known	Total as % of 896	Average length of stay (years)	Total in cohort	Average age at arrival (years)
21–30	52	5.8	5.9	52	23.1
31–40	151	16.9	11.3	161	25.5
41–50	189	21.1	16.9	200	29.8
51–60	164	18.3	25.6	170	31.1
61–70	179	20.0	33.6	186	32.7
71–80	125	14.0	43.4	126	32.5
Over 80	36	4.0	56.1	37	30.0
Totals	896	100.0	25.5	932	29.9

Regression equation for length of stay (-0.577 times [entry age] plus 42.8 years) is significant at the 0.00001 level.

Other Possible Reasons for Departure

Because few community studies have gathered information on the marriages of their subjects, they may have overlooked a possible reason for the departure of some of those subjects from the community: the loss of their spouses (as occurred to *Silas D. Bryant, cited in Chapter 3). Most of the men who moved to Boston and then left were widowers when their first marriage ended (see Table 5.6). Of course, this tells little about the men's marital status when they removed from Boston, for they could have remarried before departing, but fortunately it is possible to recover some of the desired information. Of

Table 5.6

Marital versus Migration Status, All In-Migrants

Did in-migrant leave Boston?	Migrant's status at end of first marriage		
	Dead	Widower	
	N	N	Totals
No	682	525	1,207
Yes	389	464	853
Totals	1,071	989	2,060

Chi-square significance > 0.0001.

Table 5.7

Age at Departure from Boston, Compared with Marital Status at Departure, All Out-Migrants

Age at departure	Marital status at departure			Marital status unknown
	Married	Widower	Totals	
21–30	52	3	55	3
31–40	163	14	178	16
41–50	196	27	223	15
51–60	148	47	195	13
61–70	142	54	196	16
71–80	70	70	140	12
Over 80	10	31	41	3
Totals	781	246	1,027	78

Chi-square significance > 0.0001.

1,105 sample members who left Boston, Table 5.7 suggests that at least 246 were widowers when they left.

The phenomenon of quick departure after losing one's wife is well illustrated by the experience of *Joseph L. Farley. He was born late in 1822 in Amherst, Massachusetts, but for our purposes first surfaces in the 1850 census of Salem, Massachusetts, as a cooper, aged 32 [*sic*], residing with his widowed mother, Rebecca, and his younger siblings, Henry (also a cooper) and Rebecca. The family claimed no real estate value. Joseph did not move to Boston until after 1861; the 1861 Salem city directory still lists him at his mother's address, but she is alone in that census. She claimed no real or personal estate. Sometime between 1850 and 1870 Joseph married Sarah Smith, a native of Salem, who was born about 1815. Their 1870 census listing in Boston shows them as aged 50 and 45, with $400 in personal estate (he was nevertheless assessed for only a poll tax). On August 9, 1876, Mrs. Sarah Farley died in Boston, "cause unknown," aged 61. Joseph Farley remained in Boston through the following spring, then returned to Salem, where in December 1878 he married his late wife's younger sister Susan, aged 58. The 1880 census found him once again in Salem, continuing his wonted trade of cooper. He died in 1896 in Salem, aged 73.[5] His first wife's death preceded his departure from Boston by less than a year, and his response was to leave Boston for the more familiar precincts of Salem.

Dying to Leave—Leaving to Die

Significant numbers of sample members left Boston because they were in poor health. Certainly quite a few of them died soon after they moved away. The possibilities were limited: if one's children had grown up and moved from Boston and if few other family members lived nearby, it made sense to return to one's hometown, perhaps to the "old homestead," where other family members could care for the invalid. Some 80 sample members (of 933 who both entered and left) died in their town of birth; the figure would be greater if one included men such as *Joseph L. Farley or *Ruel K. Conant (soon to be profiled), who returned to communities where they had lived in their youth. Returning to one's birthplace or to the community of one's youth seems to have been more usual for elderly widowers than for elderly widows, who appear to have moved in with their children more often than did the widowers, perhaps trading light housework and child care for terminal care. The question of return will be discussed in Chapter 6.

Sample Members' Destinations

WHERE THE BOYS GO TO. *The daring and enterprising character of the population of New England carries our young men wherever the spirit of commerce penetrates. The great extent to which the young men of what may be termed the middle class of society are scattered abroad, is hardly known. Distant places attract the attention of our youth.*
—Boston Evening Transcript, *7 April 1855, 2/1*

IMMEDIATE DESTINATIONS AND COMMUTATION

Most of the men who left Boston did not go very far. As one might guess, as time passed, they continued to disperse geographically. Ten years after being sampled, members of the two samples were distributed as Table 5.8 indicates. This table is rendered visually in Maps 5.1 and 5.2, which show the 1870 and 1880 residences, respectively, of the 1860 and 1870 sample members outside Boston but within the northeastern United States.

Glancing (in Table 5.9) at those who were commuting to and from Boston in 1870 and 1880 reveals that commutation was a phenomenon of the more prosperous sample members or of those who could keep reasonable working hours. Intriguingly, the highest proportions of commuters appear among the members of the 1860 sample as of 1880, men who were then on average in their early sixties. Presumably commutation rates declined among yet older men. In no case did the proportion of commuters exceed a seventh of the membership of any occupation group.

Commutation to other towns was thus not a very usual phenomenon, and most sample members who commuted to and from the sub-

Table 5.8

Locations and Conditions of Sample Members Ten Years after Being Sampled

Status	1860 sample as of 1870		%	1870 sample as of 1880		%
Total still alive	1,130	80.4%		1,090	77.7%	
Residing in Boston		858	75.9		832	76.3
Commuting to Boston		74	6.5		71	6.5
Within Massachusetts but beyond commuting distance		102	9.0		108	9.9
Outside Massachusetts		96	8.5		79	7.2
Total who had died	253	18.0%		246	17.5%	
In Boston		217	85.8		214	87.0
In commuting area		4	1.6		9	3.7
In Massachusetts beyond commuting area		13	5.1		13	5.3
Outside Massachusetts		19	7.5		10	4.1
Unknown	22	1.6%		67	4.8%	
Totals	1,405	100.0%		1,403	100.0%	

The two samples are significantly different at beyond the .001 level according to the chi-square test, but removing the "unknowns" makes the difference nonsignificant.

MAP 5.1
Places of Residence in 1870 of Out-Migrants from Boston, 1860 Sample Members

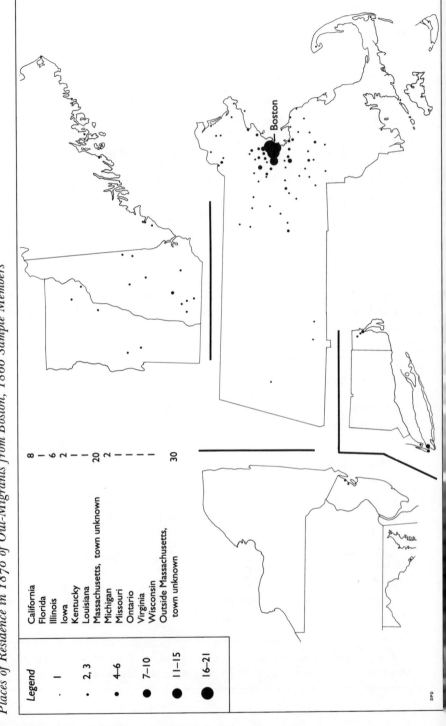

Legend

.	1
•	2, 3
●	4–6
⬤	7–10
⬤	11–15
⬤	16–21

California	8
Florida	1
Illinois	6
Iowa	2
Kentucky	1
Louisiana	1
Massachusetts, town unknown	20
Michigan	2
Missouri	1
Ontario	1
Virginia	1
Wisconsin	1
Outside Massachusetts, town unknown	30

Boston

MAP 5.2
Places of Residence in 1880 of Out-Migrants from Boston, 1870 Sample Members

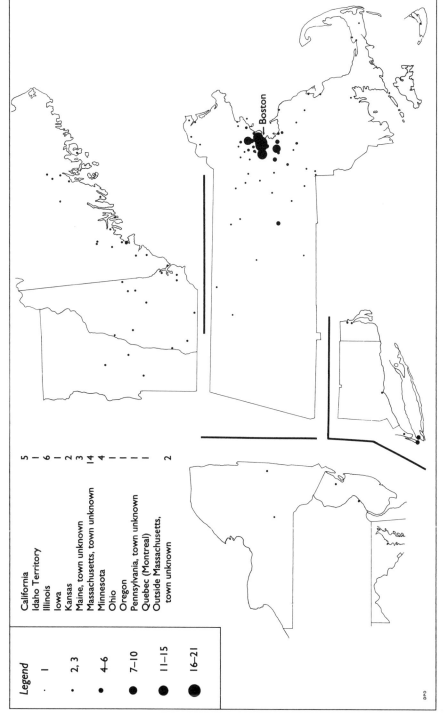

Legend

·	1
•	2, 3
●	4–6
⬤	7–10
⬤	11–15
⬤	16–21

California	5
Idaho Territory	1
Illinois	6
Iowa	1
Kansas	2
Maine, town unknown	3
Massachusetts, town unknown	14
Minnesota	4
Ohio	1
Oregon	1
Pennsylvania, town unknown	1
Quebec (Montreal)	1
Outside Massachusetts, town unknown	2

Boston

DPO

Table 5.9

Distribution of Occupation Groups among Commuters, 1870 and 1880

| Occupation group | 1860 sample | | | | 1870 sample | |
| | in 1870 | | in 1880 | | in 1880 | |
	N	% of group still alive	N	% of group still alive	N	% of group still alive
Unskilled & Menial	2	8.3	1	7.7	1	7.1
Semiskilled & Service	7	4.7	6	5.4	5	3.1
Skilled	33	6.9	26	7.4	19	4.2
Clerical & Sales	11	9.6	12	14.6	15	10.8
Proprietors, Managers, & Officials	21	7.1	21	9.6	26	9.9
Professionals	0	0.0	3	6.5	5	10.6
Totals	74	6.5	69	8.4	71	6.5

There were no commuters among the small Semiprofessional group. The table is interpreted thus: of the 1860 sample members still alive in 1870, two of the Unskilled and Menial were commuters; they made up 8.3 percent of the 24 Unskilled and Menial sample members then still alive. The respective totals still alive were 1,130, 821, and 1,090.

urbs did not do so for extended periods. This suggests that by far the most commutation occurred within the city; even as early as 1850 the number of workers who resided at their workplaces was minuscule.

Wealth, of course, influenced residential decisions. There were also marked differences in how the men moved during those first ten years, according to their wealth. The wealthier sample members tended, as one might anticipate and as Table 5.10 shows, to stay closer to Boston than did the less well off. Men who were assessed for poll tax only (wealth group 0) tended to remove farther from Boston, and to do so more quickly, than did those with some wealth. Fully 139 of the 1,516 men in this group (9.2 percent) were either residing outside Massachusetts ten years after being sampled or had already died outside the commonwealth. It is likely that most, if not all, of the 65 "unknowns" in this group were also outside Massachusetts or had died there because no traces of them remain in state records. They would raise the total of interstate out-migrants during the first decade after the samples were drawn to 204 out of 1,516, or 13.5 percent. Thus about a tenth to an eighth of the poorest men in the samples had departed Massachusetts, and probably New England, within ten years after being sampled.

Among members of the more prosperous wealth groups, the proportions moving to "exurban" Massachusetts, beyond commuting distance, within ten years of being sampled, were much lower than among the poorest sample members: 43 of 409 in group 1 (10.5 percent), only 29 of 458 in group 2 (6.3 percent), and a lowly 2.6 percent (11 out of 425) among the very wealthiest sample members. Given the greater ages of the wealthier sample members, their few such moves likely represented retirement, whereas the less successful men moved to new positions in small towns in the commonwealth.

Some long moves among the more affluent probably exploited even better chances elsewhere. Careful readers of the *Boston Daily Advertiser* during the Civil War probably noted that "Mr. *Samuel S. Stevens, for several years receiving teller of the Globe Bank of this city, has been appointed agent for the New England Mutual Life Insurance Company of Boston, at New York, to fill the vacancy caused by the death of Isaac Hoppen, esq." The Stevenses removed to Brooklyn. Their 1860 census return in Boston had showed $7,000 in real and $1,500 in personal estate, with two domestic servants, but the 1870 listing in Brooklyn revealed $25,000 in personal estate for Mr. Stevens, $10,000 in real and $2,000 in personal estate for Mrs. Stevens, and three servants. They eventually moved to Babylon, on Long Island, remaining New York residents until their deaths.[6]

Likely more typical was the experience of *Ruel K. Conant, a native

Table 5.10

Locations and Conditions of All Sample Members Ten Years after Being
Sampled, by Wealth Group, by Percent

	Wealth Group			
	0 poorest	1	2	3 richest
Total still alive	1,203	325	376	316
	%	%	%	%
Residing in Boston	72.5	74.5	80.3	86.7
Commuting to Boston	6.1	7.4	8.0	5.7
Within Massachusetts but beyond commuting distance	11.6	10.1	7.2	3.2
Outside Massachusetts	9.8	8.0	4.5	4.4
Total who had died	248	71	76	104
	%	%	%	%
In Boston	84.7	78.9	89.5	93.3
In commuting area	1.6	4.2	3.9	2.9
In Massachusetts beyond commuting area	5.2	14.1	2.6	1.0
Outside Massachusetts	8.5	2.8	3.9	2.9
Unknown	65	13	6	5
Totals in groups	1,516	409	458	425

Differences are significant beyond the 0.001 level by chi-square test.

of Stoddard, New Hampshire, who early on began a lifelong association with the transportation industry: at age 25 in 1850, he was a
brakeman for the Boston & Worcester Railroad and boarding in a
large hotel in Springfield, Massachusetts. In 1851 he married Julia A.
Curtis of Antrim, New Hampshire, and by 1855 they had removed to
Boston, where Ruel was a baggage master (railroad not stated) and
their three children were born. The Conants claimed $1,000 in real
and $200 in personal estate in the 1860 census, but he was assessed
for poll tax only (wealth group 0). The family (numbering five when
they left) moved to Springfield in 1862, and Ruel continued as a baggage master, this time for the Hartford & New Haven Railroad; their
1870 census listing shows no real estate but $2,500 in personal estate.
By 1880 Ruel had organized Conant & Co., a parcel express service;
this business may not have succeeded because by 1887 he had re-
verted to being a railroad conductor. His occupation at his death in
Springfield in 1894 was listed as "retired baggage master."[7]

LONGER-TERM DESTINATIONS

Except for those who had removed to the suburban commuting
area by ten years after being sampled, about three-quarters of the men
in the samples had also by then reached the places where they would
die. This held for those who yet remained in Boston, for those still in
Massachusetts but beyond commuting distance, for those within New
England outside Massachusetts, and for those outside New England.
The men residing in Boston's commuting areas ten years after being
sampled tended to move yet again before dying: about half of them
moved farther out into Massachusetts, about one-fifth returned to
Boston to die, and only slightly less than one-fifth died in the commuting area. Sample members may have regarded the nearby suburbs as pleasant places to live in but not to retire to, in that other
members of their families tended either still to reside in small exurban towns or to have remained behind in Boston. The patterns in
their final moves will be treated in the discussion of their deaths.

By 1900, about three-quarters of the men in the samples had died;
their status then is suggested in Table 5.11. There were about 168
men in the 1860 sample and about 121 in the 1870, who, as of 1900,
could be considered interstate out-migrants from Boston, either be-

Table 5.11

Locations and Conditions of Sample Members as of 1900

Status of sample members	1860 sample as of 1900 ("40 years on")	%	1870 sample as of 1900 ("30 years on")	%
Total still alive	223	15.9%	521	37.1%
Residing in Boston	120	53.8	237	45.5
Commuting to Boston	31	13.9	46	8.8
Within Massachusetts but beyond commuting distance	54	24.2	114	21.9
Outside Massachusetts	48	21.5	62	11.9
Total who had died	1,106	78.7%	862	61.4%
In Boston	785	71.0	624	72.4
In commuting area	63	5.7	44	5.1
In Massachusetts beyond commuting area	138	12.5	135	15.7
Outside Massachusetts	120	10.8	59	6.8
Unknown	46	3.3%	82	5.8%
Totals	1,405	100.0%	1,403	100.0%

The two samples are significantly different at beyond the .001 level according to the chi-square test.

cause they resided outside the state or because they had died outside Massachusetts. Because about half of the interstate out-migrants died in New England, however, the true size of the interstate out-migrant group was about 145, or just 5 percent of the whole.

Most of these men sought urban, not rural, locations. As one might guess, those men who left Boston young tended to die farther away (see Table 5.12). The distorting effect of averages is seen in this instance, as including in Table 5.12 the figures for the 106 men who died more than 250 miles from Boston approximately triples the average distances shown there. Presenting the really long-distance out-migrants by themselves, as in Table 5.13, is safer. These men died in communities in California, Colorado, the District of Columbia, England (London), Florida, Illinois, Iowa, Italy (Florence), Kansas, Louisiana, Maine (Eastport and Lubec, both over 300 miles from Boston), Michigan, Minnesota, Missouri, Nebraska, New Jersey, New York, Ohio, Pennsylvania, Tennessee, Vermont (Highgate, almost 300 miles from Boston), Virginia, Washington, Wisconsin, and Wyoming.

Even though metropolitan New York City was not considered a long-distance destination (240 miles), that area should be mentioned because it contained the death locations of some 27 sample members (Manhattan, 14; Brooklyn, 9; Yonkers, 2; and Bronx and Jamaica, 1 each). The most popular long-distance death locations proved to be Chicago (15) and San Francisco (11, together with Oakland and Berkeley, 2 each). Other cities were much less popular: Minneapolis and Philadelphia tied with 3 deaths each, and Atlantic City, Aurora (Illinois), Los Angeles, and Seattle each were the site of 2 sample members' deaths. All other communities were the last homes of 1 sample member each; among this group were such cities as Camden, Chattanooga, Denver, Detroit, Jacksonville (Florida), Kansas City (Missouri), New Orleans, Orlando, Portland (Oregon), Richmond, St. Louis, St. Paul, San Diego, Santa Barbara, Tacoma, Toledo, and Washington, D.C.

One such out-migrant to a faraway city was *Nathaniel P. Conant, a very distant relation of *Ruel K., born in Topsfield, Massachusetts, late in 1819; in his youth his parents moved to Portsmouth, New Hampshire, then returned to Danvers, Massachusetts, and Lowell. Nathaniel married Sophronia Thompson Hartford, a native of New

Table 5.12

Age Cohort at Departure from Boston by Average Distance from Boston at Which "Short-Distance" Out-Migrants Died

Age at departure from Boston	Average distance from Boston at which "short-distance"[a] out-migrants died (miles)	N
21–30	82	33
31–40	71	129
41–50	53	169
51–60	41	159
61–70	34	183
71–80	26	130
Over 80	11	41
Totals	44	844

Distances for 92 of 1,042 men not known.

[a] "Short-distance" out-migrants died less than 251 miles from Boston (New York City was taken to be 240 miles distant). The regression equation relating age at departure from Boston to the distance from Boston at which an out-migrant died, -5.5 times (age at departure) plus 517.6, was significant beyond the 0.001 level (N was 938).

London, New Hampshire, in Newburyport, Massachusetts, in 1844. He was 25, she 19. He worked as a watchmaker and jeweler. Our first glimpse of their household, in 1850, finds them in Danvers; their only children, Emma F. and Eliza O., were aged four and two, respectively. Conant claimed no real estate. Possibly seeking wider scope for his talents, the Conants moved to Boston in 1857; the household remained the same in 1860: four members, no real or personal estate. But in 1868 Mrs. Conant replaced her husband in the Boston city directory. She lived with their younger daughter, Eliza, according to the 1870 census of Boston, still claiming no real or personal estate. Conant had removed to Council Bluffs, Iowa, where his 1870 census

Table 5.13

Age Cohort at Departure from Boston by Average Distance from Boston at
Which "Long-Distance" Out-Migrants Died

Age at departure from Boston	Average distance from Boston at which "long-distance"[a] out-migrants died (miles)	N
21–30	1,677	8
31–40	1,230	25
41–50	1,571	30
51–60	1,590	26
61–70	2,084	11
71–80	1,336	5
Over 80	820	1
Totals	1,538	106

Distances for 92 of 1,042 men not known.

[a] "Long-distance" out-migrants died more than 250 miles from Boston (New York City was taken to be 240 miles distant).

listing showed that he lived alone, worked as a jeweler, but claimed $2,000 in personal estate. There was a happy ending: by 1880 Mrs. Conant also resided in Council Bluffs. She died between 1880 and 1900; he survived until 1902.[8]

The Conants were separated for at least three years before Mrs. Conant moved to Council Bluffs. In most other cases of sample members who moved long distances, the household appears to have shifted as a unit, in that Boston records do not indicate that the wife stayed behind for any length of time. Of course, the principal source for making such an observation, the city directory, often listed sample members for a year or two after they had died, so it is likely none too reliable in this regard.[9]

Mrs. *Seth Wentworth's experience resembled Mrs. Conant's, up to
a point. Seth's father, Isaac, was a carpenter in Milton, New Hampshire, where Seth was born in 1835. Presumably having learned his
trade at home, Seth came to Boston young, and there, in 1857, he
married Mary Jane Keating, a 22-year-old native of Augusta, Maine;
they also had two daughters, Lucy, in 1857 (243 days after their marriage), and Arvilla, in 1864. The 1860 census indicates that Seth
worked as a stair builder, a Skilled occupation, and that he claimed
$200 in personal estate (the assessors rated him for poll tax only). The
1870 census of the household listed no wealth claimed; Seth was still
listed as a stair builder. In 1874 the Wentworths moved out to Somerville, three miles west of Boston. In 1880 Seth was still listed as a
stair builder, while Lucy E., 20 (actually 22), was a store cashier, and
Arvilla, 15, remained at school. The 1881 Somerville city directory
listed Seth Wentworth as "stairbuilder (Cal.), h. 94 Concord Ave.,"
and this was repeated in the 1883 and 1885 directories. The 1889
directory listed "Mrs. Mary J. Wentworth, h. 9 Ivanhoe." Seth Wentworth may have moved to "Cal.," but there are no obvious traces of
him there. Perhaps he did die there in the late 1880s, or he may have
found other places to build stairs. Mrs. Wentworth remained in Somerville, dying there in 1922 at the age of 90, recorded in death as
"widow of Seth." But her grave in Cambridge Cemetery is solitary.[10]

Likely the number of reasons for sample members to depart from
Boston was about the same as the number of sample members departing from Boston. After more than a century, it is scarcely likely
that any comprehensive evidence about the motivations of sample
members for any action, much less that of out-migration, will show
up. This forces modern observers to infer from shaky evidence,
modified by their experience of geographical mobility.

Without torturing the evidence unduly, it does seem safe to conclude that out-migration from Boston was related not only to the individual's wealth, as has long been suspected, but also to his position
along the path of his life. Especially suggestive is that over 90 percent
of those sample members who both had children and departed from
Boston had no more children after that departure. Since many of
these couples were still of child-producing age when they left, they

may well have coordinated their procreative activity with their departure.

Other changes and crises in the family seem also to have been associated with out-migration: illness, the loss of a spouse, perhaps the departure from the household of the last child to marry. Since adverse occurrences were common, perhaps it would be more realistic to suggest that the connection between low socioeconomic status and out-migration was not one of cause and effect, but rather that low socioeconomic status made a household particularly susceptible to being destabilized by serious illness of a spouse or by his or her death. Lacking an economic cushion in the form of savings or property to fall back on in such an emergency, the household had to turn to friends or (preferably) relatives for help. When relatives had not also moved to Boston, or had themselves left, and could not send money, then one had to go to them. Hence the shifts of some sample members to their hometowns or to exurban Massachusetts late in life and the instances of widows moving in with their children. After the death of a spouse, remarriage was also an option but not an immediate solution. For those sample members who remarried after the death of their first wife, the average interval of widowerhood proved to be about 3.1 years (based on 341 of the 536 sample members [63.5 percent] in that situation), with half of the men remarrying within two years. The interval was not significantly related to the number of children produced in the sample member's first marriage, seemingly excluding as a motivation for quick remarriage the need to find someone to care for those children. The most rapid adjustment among the sample members was made by *Sidney Smith, a carpenter-turned-trader-turned-produce dealer, whose wife, Mary T., died 8 December 1852, aged 43, of inflammation of the lungs. On 27 January 1853, he married Eliza Ann Anders, a 29-year-old widow; together they had at least six children to add to the five from his first marriage and at least one from her first marriage. (Unfortunately for this large group, Smith, who had turned to farming, froze to death in a snowbank in Wrentham in December 1869.)[11] No figures on the rapidity of remarriage among widows of sample members were collected (this phenomenon appears not to have been examined at all), so it is impossible to tell whether they waited as long before remarrying. The average age of 907 sample members whose first wives predeceased them was 55.0, but the average age of 1,185 wives whose husbands died first was 61.4, presumably largely removing the widows from the marriage market unless they were well off. Because these widows' economic situations usually would have been worse than those of the widowers, one suspects that the pressure on them to remarry quickly would have been greater than on the widowers but that their ability to remarry would have been less.

There remains to be considered the ultimate out-migration, death.

Death

If they had been allowed to choose, most sample members probably would have died in bed at home, surrounded by supportive relatives, having attained a great age. Most of them did so; only a tiny minority died in hospitals, cared for by strangers, and most who did die in institutions were said to have been insane. Let us triage the topic of death into when, where, and how. Of these, the first two are much easier to specify than the third, for medicine was still an inexact science in the late nineteenth century, and most stated causes of death were little better than guesses.[2]

Length of Life

Today we learn that an individual's life expectancy is 70, 75, or even 80 years—understood as expectation of life at birth. Estimates for the mid-nineteenth century suggest that the expectation of life at, say, age 40 in Massachusetts as of 1850 was 27.9 years for men and 29.8 years for women. By 1949–51, these figures had risen to only 30.7 and 35.2, respectively. Corresponding figures for age 0 (at birth) were 38.3 and 40.5 in 1850, but 66.7 and 72.1 in 1949–51.[3] A century's progress in medicine had succeeded in prolonging the expected lives of middle-aged adults by only 10 to 15 percent but those of newborn infants by about 75 percent, eloquent testimony to the pervasiveness of childhood disease and mortality during much of that century. People who survived to early adulthood during most of the nineteenth century thus had life expectancies approaching those of today's adults. Some of the men in this study threatened to live on indefinitely, but eventually, the deaths of 2,738 (97.5 percent), or all but 70 of them, were found in a wide variety of records (those men still outstanding are listed in Appendix C).

Members of the 1870 sample tended to live to greater ages than did members of the 1860 sample, but, as Table 6.1 demonstrates, the average intervals they survived after their sample years were virtually the same. Since averages in this instance mask fairly diverse mortality experience, the decadal distribution of ages at death, shown in Table 6.2, may be more revealing. Part of the reason for the slightly shorter average remaining lengths of lives among the 1860 sample members was that 102 of them had participated in the Civil War, of whom 12 died in battle or from disease during the conflict and another 10 died before 1870 or within a decade after their sample year. Of the 197 Civil War veterans in the 1870 sample, by contrast, all had to survive for at least five years after the war just to be in the 1870 sample. Only 17 of them died between 1870 and 1880, the decade following their sample year. Although few of the samples' soldiers died in battle or from disease, their lives, as compared with nonveterans of the same ages, were shorter.[4] Members of both samples survived, again on average, their year of being sampled by about 25 years.

Predicting Age at Death: Destiny Not Shaping Their Ends

The number of characteristics of the sample members significantly associated with their ages at death was rather large. In addition to those one would expect, such as age at being sampled or age at marriage, even the number of children produced in the sample member's first marriage (for couples with children) led to regression equations with significance levels nearing .0001. Likely the most unexpected,

Table 6.1

Average Ages at Time of Being Sampled, at Death, and Interval between, by Sample

	Sample			
	1860	N	1870	N
Average age at time of sample	43.2	1,405	45.6	1,403
Average age at death	68.9	1,365	70.7	1,373
Average interval between sample year and death	25.6	1,365	24.9	1,373

Sample means for age at death differ statistically at beyond the .001 level.

but also the strongest, predictor of how long a sample member had left to live after his year of being sampled was the year of birth of his mother, rivaled closely by that of his father, as indicated in Table 6.3. Very often in both historical and genealogical research, the years of birth of nineteenth-century individuals' parent(s) are much easier to determine than are many other characteristics of those individuals, particularly their dates of death. In dealing with large numbers of adults whose dates of death are unknown, but whose parents' birth dates are known, knowledge of this relationship could prove useful. It also suggests that, at least among the members of the samples, parents who were born later produced sons who survived longer, or, as an actuary would put it, as time passed, mortality experience improved. Some may find this depressing or think that it smacks of predestination or fate, but this does not alter the fact that many of the sample members' characteristics *were* significantly related to the lengths of their lives. Perhaps most surprising is that, as we know that so many of their other attributes were related to other facets of their existence, it should occasion comment that the ends of those existences were also connected. Since economic characteristics have

Table 6.2

Age at Death of Sample Members, by Decade, by Sample

Age cohorts at death	1860 sample N	1860 sample %	1870 sample N	1870 sample %
21–30	5[a]	0.4	0	0.0
31–40	48[b]	3.4	30[c]	2.1
41–50	101	7.2	73	5.2
51–60	171	12.2	163	11.6
61–70	335	23.8	318	22.7
71–80	416	29.6	461	32.9
81–90	243	17.3	287	20.5
91–100	46	3.3	41	2.9
Unknown	40	2.8	30	2.1
Totals	1,405		1,403	

Most of the "unknowns" attained at least the age of 50 before vanishing. The samples are significantly different at the 0.005 level by the chi-square test.

[a]Includes 2 Civil War participants.
[b]Includes 8 Civil War participants.
[c]Includes 9 Civil War participants.

proved such accurate augurs of the sample members' lives, it is worth appealing to them again for circumstances of the sample members' deaths.

The Economics of Death

Various characteristics of the sample members were associated, to varying degrees of statistical significance, with the lengths of their lives. Each of the four wealth groups, as shown in Table 6.4, was significantly related to a mortality rate slightly different from the others. Although it helped overall to be well off, in that well-off sample mem-

Table 6.3

Regression Equations for Interval to Death from Sample Year as Predicted by Parent's Year of Birth, by Sample

Sample and parent	N	Parent's average year of birth	Coefficient	Constant	Average interval to death (years)	*t*
1860						
Father	973	1784.367	0.4306	−741.55	26.72	13.971
Mother	852	1789.379	0.4828	−836.24	27.67	14.201
1870						
Father	1,040	1792.913	0.4671	−811.22	26.29	18.090
Mother	936	1797.813	0.5092	−888.39	27.02	17.214

One may derive estimates from this table by multiplying the parent's year of birth by the coefficient and adding to the product the constant, to obtain the estimated remaining life span of the sample member.

bers tended to live longer, since they were older they did not survive as long after their sample year as did the younger members of poorer wealth groups. The connections between relative wealth and notional cause of death will be explored later.

The amounts of assessed wealth for all sample members also provided grist for regression equations that predicted age at death with significance levels hovering around .001. As one might anticipate, given the strong relationship between age and wealth, there were also striking connections between an individual's wealth and his location of death.

The Geography of Death

When they died, on average about 25 years after their sample year, the men in the study were distributed as shown in Table 6.5.

A considerable shift in favor of more distant suburban locations as

Table 6.4

Average Ages at Time of Being Sampled and at Death, by Wealth Group, for Both Samples

Wealth group	Average age at being sampled	N	Average age at death	N	Interval (years)
3 (richest)**	53.2	425	73.8	425	20.6
2	47.5	458	72.0	455	24.5
1 (poorest)	44.0	409	69.5	403	25.5
0 (no wealth)	41.1	1,516	68.0	1,455	26.9

**Differences between wealth group 3 and the other groups are significant beyond the .001 level; others are not. All four regression equations for age at death as predicted by age at being sampled were, however, significant at beyond the 0.00001 level.

final residences had occurred by the time the men in the 1870 sample were dying in quantity. This reflects the process of population succession operating in Boston in the last decades of the nineteenth century, by which the city's ethnic characteristics began to approach those of the twentieth century.[5] Even if one assumes that all of the "unknown" group died outside New England, out-migration to more distant locations still declined from the 1860 to the 1870 sample. Final moves to more distant locales within New England also decreased, albeit slightly.

Why were the suburbs unpopular as a place to die? Perhaps sample members viewed them as primarily areas for commuter residents, not fit for those of advanced age. The suburbs tended to fall between two stools: usually they were too expensive a location (mostly because of time lost in commuting) for one's children to have established a home in by the time sample members were elderly. Since fully 90 percent of the in-migrants had entered Boston from towns more than 14 miles away (hence beyond commuting distance), the suburbs were not filled

Table 6.5

Death Locations of Sample Members, by Type of Location

Location of death	1860 sample	%	1870 sample	%
Boston	866	61.6	848	60.4
Commuting area	73	5.2	63	4.5
Within Massachusetts but beyond commuting distance	253	18.0	319	22.7
Outside Massachusetts but within New England	84	6.0	75	5.3
Outside New England[a]	84	6.0	61	4.3
Unknown	45	3.2	37	2.6
Totals	1,405		1,403	

[a]Includes deaths outside the United States. Deaths were credited to an individual's home location (e.g., a Bostonian who died in Nice, France, on vacation was credited to Boston).

Samples are significantly different at the 0.02 level by the chi-square test.

with sample members' families of origin. Sample members who did move to the suburbs usually did not remain there long. In fact, of the 211 sample members who had moved to Boston from towns less than 16 miles away, only 17 or about 8 percent, died in the suburbs—despite having been born and brought up in such communities.

Because of the time required in traveling to and from the suburbs, only men who worked set (and, for those days, short) hours or were self-employed could realistically expect to commute for any extended period. Even those who had their own means of transportation, such as wagoners of the ilk of *Leavitt Alley, seem to have accepted living in the city as a trade-off against the necessary loss of time (and money) involved in traveling to and from the suburbs. Wealthier individuals tended to remain closer to Boston, while those less well off moved farther away, as was pointed out in Chapter 5. Once out-migrants were more than a few miles distant, they effectively severed all physical connections with the city, as was signaled by their being dropped from the Boston city directory. The extensive development of suburban commuting had to await the combination of improved transportation and shorter working hours.

To judge from the experiences of its Yankee inhabitants, Boston sent out a small but steady stream of mature long-distance out-migrants during the mid- and late nineteenth century. Many of its inhabitants came from within New England, and some returned to their native states but not necessarily to their native towns. Among natives of Maine, 43 of 539 (8.0 percent) returned to and died within that state; New Hampshire men were perhaps slightly more loyal: 39 of their 470 in-migrants (8.3 percent) died there. In this instance belying its reputation for strong out-migration, 14 of Vermont's 153 natives (9.2 percent) in the samples returned there to die. Massachusetts's natives apparently had few better places to go to, for 1,358 of their group of 1,520 (89.3 percent) died within the Bay State (the location of death was defined as the individual's residence at death; men on trips or vacations thus were counted at their homes, not abroad). It does not seem likely that many other nineteenth-century locales will display such powerful retention of their adult natives and native-born in-migrants as did Massachusetts; it would be interesting to see similar statistics for California.

Styles of Death: Accidents

Other than in its brief daily "Deaths" listings, the *Boston Evening Transcript* noted the demise of very few of the sample members. Newspaper space went to the prominent, such as former Mayor *John P. Bigelow (mentioned in Chapter 5), millionaire merchant *Gardner Brewer,[6] or to those who died unusually or shockingly. About 1 percent of the sample members died in accidents. These reports were brief, sometimes brutally so, and minced individuals but no words:

LOCAL INTELLIGENCE.
Accidents.

.   .   .

*F. B. Moody Sawyer [sic], residing on Harbor court, South Boston, while at work at Whitcomb's mill, 29 Wareham street, yesterday [Monday] afternoon, was caught in the coupling of the shaft in an attempt to adjust a belt. His left arm was fractured and he was injured internally. He was taken to City Hospital, where the injured limb was amputated. He will probably die.[7]

Another accident report will show the pattern:

FATAL RAILROAD ACCIDENT. Mr. *Isaac N. Farnham, cooper, who resided at No. 11 Central Square, East Boston, met with a sad and sudden death at the Boston and Lowell railroad station, on Causeway street, yesterday [Wednesday] afternoon. He had purchased a ticket for Danforth Corner, N.H., and his baggage being delayed by mistake in arriving at the depot, he was giving directions to the baggage master to have it forwarded, when, during this conversation, the train started. He ran after it, and in endeavoring to step upon the platform, fell under the wheels, and was instantly killed, his head being nearly severed from his body. He leaves a wife and two daughters, and has one son in the [Union] army. His body was taken to the dead house on North Grove street, where an inquest will be held on it.[8]

From such reports the experienced reader could usually deduce the sequel. If the victim were transported to a hospital, one could conclude he was expected to die; if he were taken to his home, someone thought he would survive. Another mark of an anticipated fatal outcome was "internal injuries." Occasionally, however, even these reliable indicators failed:

ACCIDENT IN CITY HALL. *John M. Whorf, the engineer at city hall, entered the elevator way on the basement floor with his son this [Tuesday] forenoon for the purpose of tightening the starting rope. The elevator had been stopped at the first floor, but probably the wheel had been turned over too far, for it immediately began to slide down, unperceived by the workmen below. It touched the lad on the head first, and he sprang out the door; his father attempted to do the same, but struck his head against the casing, and failed to extricate himself from the weight above, which caught his legs, crushing the flesh against the marble step, and otherwise injuring him. The elevator was quickly raised, and Mr. Whorf in an insensible condition was taken into the health department. No bones were broken, and after restoring him to consciousness he was sent to his home at No. 35 Common street.

Likely Whorf's friends who saw this report were surprised to learn of his death at home three days later.[9]

Of the 2,739 sample members' deaths for which sufficient information as to location of death was available, only 144, or 5.3 percent, occurred in institutions such as hospitals or asylums; the other 94.7 percent took place in private homes or at the sites of accidents. If, using Table 6.6, one compares the location of death with the approximate financial standing of the decedent, one observes the operation of the fin-de-siècle medical system. Those who could afford not to use institutional facilities avoided them. The very poorest sample members, numbering just over half of the group, nevertheless accounted for 72.9 percent of the deaths that occurred in hospitals or asylums. Most of the institutional deaths came from degenerative diseases, of which more later. In contrast, most suicides occurred outside institutions.

Styles of Death: Suicides

Another 1 percent or so of the sample members' deaths was reported as suicides. Likely, as in the case of *Noah Sturtevant, mentioned in Chapter 4, more information, or omniscience, would raise this proportion.[10] According to the newspapers, there were several principal

Table 6.6

Institutional or Noninstitutional Location of Sample Members' Deaths,
by Assessment Group (Both Samples)

	Sample member died				
Assessment group	In hospital or asylum		Elsewhere		Totals
	N	%	N	%	
3 (richest)	7	1.6	418	98.4	425
2	17	3.7	438	96.3	455
1 (poorest)	15	3.7	388	96.3	403
0 (no wealth)	105	7.2	1,351	92.8	1,456
Totals	144	5.3	2,595	94.7	2,739

Percentages sum horizontally (chi-square significance > .001).

reasons for suicide: disappointment in love (but this held mostly for the young), temporary aberration, and business reverses. The manuscript population census returns occasionally noted "causes" of individuals' insanity; business reverses was common, so apparently contemporaries thought it a plausible motivation for suicide:

Mysterious Suicide in a Bathtub
at the Quincy House.

The attachés of the barber shop under the Quincy House detected a strong smell of ether about the room this [Thursday] forenoon, but could not tell whence it came; but at length noticing that one of the bathroom doors had not been opened for some time they forced admission.

They were startled by seeing the naked body of a dead man in the bath tub, his head on the bottom of the tub and one foot on the side. A bottle marked "sulphuric ether," and the strong odor before alluded to, was [sic] convincing indication of the cause of death.

From a letter in the coat pocket it appeared that the deceased was *Nathaniel S. Lillie, about forty-seven years of age, and who for about twenty-four years has been a respected and trusted employé of the American Express Company in this city.

It appears that Mr. Lillie's duties have been to deliver money packages in the northern part of the city; but a few days ago the managers, to secure greater safety for the packages and more rapid delivery, supplied the two money messengers with a team for the purpose of sending them together, and they were to make the rounds of the whole city in company.

Mr. Lillie did not enter into the new regulation with spirit, fearing that the work could not be done so well, and at the conclusion of the first day's work, he had some words with the superintendent, at which Mr. Lillie took offence, and announced his intention of leaving.

Mr. *Homer Ashley, the agent, reasoned with Mr. Lillie about the folly of such conduct; offered every inducement for him to remain; promised him another situation with easier work at the same compensation—in fact in his own name and that of the company begged him to remain.

But Mr. Lillie's mind was made up, and yesterday morning he formally left the office, receiving a very strong letter of commendation from Mr. Ashley, and the offer of another situation at any time he should return and ask for it.

The next intelligence the express company officials had of Mr. Lillie was the news of his suicide, communicated by two reporters in search of particulars. The deceased lived on Walnut street, Chelsea, and leaves a wife, two sons and a daughter.[11]

So pervasive was the notion that business reverses could lead to suicide that a merchant's suspicious death could be seen as accidental primarily because his business was prospering:

A Franklin-street Merchant Accidentally Shoots Himself.

About four o'clock yesterday [Wednesday] afternoon, Mr. *Robert W. Dresser, a well-known Franklin-street woollen dealer, shot himself at his residence in Newton Upper Falls, dying shortly after. Mr. Dresser went home early yesterday afternoon, and after making a general inspection of his farm and talking sociably with his employés, returned to the house and proceeded directly to the dining room. A few moments after he had entered the room a shot was heard, and upon opening the door Mr. Dresser was found with a pistol shot through the head, and he expired almost immediately. The pistol with which Mr. Dresser shot himself was presented to him a few days since, and the general opinion seems to be that he was examining it when it went off accidentally, as no reason can be assigned for his committing suicide. His untimely death has thrown a gloom over the community, in which he was much esteemed. A coroner's inquest was held last night, but no verdict has been reached as yet. [News].[12]

Styles of Death: Typical

The vast majority of sample members died at home in bed, presumably tended by family and visited by friends and creditors. Unless one wishes to accept as typical the deathbed scenes limned in contemporary fiction, there were no startling reports in the newspapers. Accounts of individuals' expirations usually stressed that the deceased had professed his or her faith in Christianity, had suffered relevant pain courageously, and had departed peacefully. Our knowledge of the maladies that carried off the sample members would suggest that, at least in some cases, the newspapers sugarcoated their reports so as not to upset their readers. In any event, high infant mortality alone ensured that death was not long a stranger to most households.

Causes of Death

In 1901 the office of the secretary of the Commonwealth of Massachusetts issued the *Fifty-Ninth Report of Births, Marriages and Deaths in*

Massachusetts . . . for the Year 1900, summing up the state's vital events
for the nineteenth century's closing year. The secretary remarked, in
transmitting the report to the Senate and House of Representatives:
"The nosological arrangement in this report is the same as that used
for over fifty years; but inasmuch as other States have adopted what
is known as the Bertillon system, also in use in foreign countries, this
classification will hereafter be used."[13] Using the traditional nosology,
Samuel W. Abbott, M.D., of the Massachusetts State Board of Health
compiled an extensive study, "The Vital Statistics of Massachusetts. A
Forty Years' Summary [1856–1895]," which appeared in 1897.[14]
Combining the information from both sources has permitted a rough
contemporary classification of the great majority of sample members'
causes of death.

According to the medical wisdom of the late nineteenth century, at
least as received in Massachusetts, people died from causes that could
be divided into five grand classifications and a host of subclassifica-
tions. (Keep in mind that this scheme antedated the germ theory of
disease.) Class I, "zymotic" diseases, included "miasmatic" diseases
such as smallpox and typhoid fever, presumably spread by miasmatic
effusions, but also took in carbuncle. "Enthetic" diseases included
syphilis, hydrophobia, and malignant pustule. "Dietic" diseases embraced privation, scurvy, and alcoholism. Last and least, "parasitic"
ailments included "thrush" and "worms, &c." (No sample members
succumbed to any "parasitic" ailments.)

Class II, "constitutional" diseases, was divided into two categories,
"diathetic" and "tubercular." The former took in gout, anemia, cancer, and mortification, while the latter included phthisis ("consumption of lungs") and scrofula.

Class III, "local" diseases, was the most elaborate of all, with eight
subgroups. "Nervous system" diseases varied from cephalitis and apoplexy through paralysis to brain disease. "Organs of circulation" were
the seat of maladies such as pericarditis, aneurism, and "heart diseases, &c." "Respiratory organs" had their problems, too, such as
bronchitis, pleurisy, and pneumonia, while the "digestive organs"
came in for 16 main ailments, including gastritis, hepatitis, and gall-
stones. "Urinary organs" were not neglected, with such headings as
"Bright's Disease," cystitis, and diabetes. Women's diseases appeared

under the heading of "generative organs" and took in ovarian dropsy and diseases of the uterus. Arthritis and joint diseases were the principal "organs of locomotion" diseases, and the eighth subclass, "integumentary system," featured ulcer, eczema, and various skin ailments.

"Developmental diseases" constituted Class IV, with the first subgroup taking in children's diseases and the second, women's (e.g., childbirth). The third group covered "old people" and seemed to be a catch-all for unspecified ailments such as "old age." The last group included "diseases of nutrition" such as atrophy and debility.

Finally, Class V, "Violent deaths," had five subclasses, ranging from "accident or negligence" through "infanticide," "homicide" (among the sample members only *Abijah Ellis, of divided destinations, qualified), and "suicide" to "execution" (none among sample members).

In attempting to make some sense of death returns supposedly presented under the nosological scheme just sketched, it is important to keep in mind that the nineteenth century's attitude toward death differed from today's. Since the vast majority of deaths occurred at home among family members, society viewed death as primarily a private matter between the family and the physician (if any). Presumably, the question of an exact cause of death, such as would be determined today through extensive testing or by an autopsy, seldom arose; a good approximation sufficed: Father was suffering from "catarrh" or "internal obstruction" or "cancer" or "heart disease." Details were unimportant in most cases because the attending physician (if any) never contemplated surgery because it was usually fatal in the days before the germ theory suggested sterile operations. Can one wonder, then, at some of the evasions masquerading as causes of death? "Natural causes" was popular, as were "old age" and "general debility." If greater specificity were desired, the physician could always fall back on "cancer," "heart disease," or "internal obstruction" without additional detail. The upshot is that, though the locations of death of some 2,739 sample members were classified, the causes of death of only 2,550 could be fitted into the nosology (many of the differences were accounted for by "natural causes"). Nevertheless, some interesting patterns emerged.

General classes of diseases were related not only to the sample members' economic standing (as represented by their assessment

Table 6.7
Class of Sample Members' Cause of Death, Compared with Their Assessment Group (Both Samples), and Providing Average Ages at Death

Class of cause of death (average age at death)	Assessment group				
	0 (no wealth)	1 (poorest)	2	3 (richest)	Σ
I-zymotic	81	15	21	23	140
(64.3) (%)	57.9	10.7	15.0	16.4	
II-constitutional	166	48	37	39	290
(63.6) (%)	57.2	16.6	12.8	13.4	
III-local	921	271	300	270	1,762
(70.6) (%)	52.3	15.4	17.0	15.3	
IV-developmental	103	31	54	58	246
(82.2) (%)	41.9	12.6	22.0	23.6	
V-violent	79	11	14	8	112
(60.2) (%)	70.5	9.8	12.5	7.1	
Totals	1,350	376	426	398	2,550
(70.2) (%)	52.9	14.7	16.7	15.6	
Average ages at death for assessment groups	68.0	69.5	72.0	73.8	69.8
N	1,455	403	455	425	2,738

Percentages sum horizontally (chi-square significance >.001).

group) but also to their broad occupational groups, as Tables 6.7 and 6.8 suggest. The concentration of members of the nonassessed wealth group under the "violent deaths" category is striking. Almost as noticeable is their corresponding failure to figure in the "developmental" diseases classification, with its high average age at death and domination by members of the richest wealth group. Because of their lower average age at death, the nonassessed lacked sufficient time to contract many of the age-related diseases under the "developmental" rubric.

There were, as one ought to suspect by now, similar connections among sample members' occupation groups and their causes of death. In Table 6.8 the striking differences among the major occupation groups crop up particularly in the areas of the violent and the "zymotic" classes, reflecting, presumably, the poorer living conditions of the Semiskilled workers, more of whom died of contagious diseases associated with unhealthful locations. The higher incidence of violent (mostly accidental) deaths among the Skilled workers resulted from their greater exposure to machinery, to other unsafe working conditions, and to heights (recall the many carpenters in this group).

By contrast, the members of the Major Proprietors group enjoyed lower rates of violent and "zymotic" deaths than the average but slightly higher "developmental" rates, as befit their high average age at death. Together, these two tables suggest that either higher levels of wealth or higher positions on the occupational hierarchy (which mostly went together) tended to insulate their possessors from some of the more demeaning or uncomfortable ways people died in late nineteenth- or early twentieth-century Boston and its environs.

Probably with a better nosology, one could draw more, and better, conclusions about the relationships between sample members' lives and how they met their deaths. Given today's concern with environmental causation of death, it seems safe to remark that obvious connections between sample members' occupations or work environments and their causes of death did not emerge during the analysis of the death returns. For example, only one hatter became insane,[15] but others who handled chemicals in their work seem to have died from a variety of unrelated causes. Perhaps this preliminary finding

Table 6.8

Class of Sample Members' Cause of Death, Compared with Their Major
Occupation Group (Both Samples), and Providing Average Ages at Death

Class of cause of death (average age at death)	Semi-skilled	Skilled	Clerical & Sales	Pro-prietors, Managers, & Officials	Profes-sionals	Σ
			Major occupational group			
I-zymotic	25	66	12	26	8	137
(64.3) (%)	18.2	48.2	8.8	19.0	5.8	
II-constitutional	45	114	32	69	12	272
(63.6) (%)	16.5	41.9	11.8	25.4	4.4	
III-local	232	726	199	474	89	1,720
(70.6) (%)	13.5	42.2	11.6	27.6	5.2	
IV-developmental	32	110	14	72	12	240
(82.2) (%)	13.3	45.8	5.8	30.0	5.0	
V-violent	21	58	12	16	3	110
(60.2) (%)	19.1	52.7	10.9	14.5	2.7	
Totals	355	1,074	269	657	124	2,479
(70.2) (%)	14.3	43.3	10.9	26.5	5.0	
Average ages at death for major occupation groups	67.6	69.7	68.1	72.0	71.0	69.9
N	380	1,158	291	694	137	2,660

Percentages sum horizontally (chi-square significance >.001).

could be overturned by studying much larger groups of men in occupations specially chosen for high levels of exposure to deleterious
conditions.

The destiny of all these Yankees, then, was death. In death, as in
life, their origins, their families, their jobs, their economic standing,
their persistence, and their health remained unequal but nevertheless
predictable in retrospect. Will the same hold true for us?

Appendix A
Methods and Sources

Here we perform that which cannot be described.
—*Goethe,* Faust

Though this be madness, yet there is method in it.
—*Shakespeare,* Hamlet, *Act II, scene 2*

The sources for a study of a large number of ordinary nineteenth-century people are almost as varied as the people themselves. The principal sources are well known to genealogists but probably less so to many historians.[1] Since it is likely that most readers will be interested in some particular point, rather than in performing a similar study, they will find considerable detail because various of the techniques applied to sources will be unfamiliar to some readers. Recent and impending advances in computer capacity and portability may soon permit many readily to do studies similar to this (the underlying data have been deposited at the University of Michigan Inter-University Consortium for Political and Social Research).[2] The principal technique undergirding this study was records linkage.

Records Linkage: General Considerations

In records linkage the researcher connects scattered or separated records, each referring (one hopes) to a particular individual, with each other and that individual. It occurs all the time. Say that you wish to call John Smith, but that 47 of them are listed in your telephone directory. Fortunately, you know your John Smith resides on Semple Street: looking for that street in the

directory among the addresses of the John Smiths yields the desired
number. In most qualitative historical research, records linkage is limited. Once a document's author or recipient has been identified, the
researcher usually ceases record linkage for that document (unless it
contains references to unknown names or events), and when the materials for the study have been collected, linkage stops; this may occur
rather early. But linkage is the lifeblood of a collective biography or a
population study because the researcher is working in another direction. He or she commences with a large group and must tunnel
through a variety of sources, creating a network of linkages among
members of the study and some of those in the sources being examined. This requires constant shuttling from a list containing information on the study's subjects to the original source and back. There will,
of course, be gaps in the results, as careful comparison of the "N's" in
various tables in this study will show.

Another distinction between population studies or collective biography and ordinary historical studies is that in the former the finding
rate of positive or correct linkages varies enormously. This occurs because of the much larger numbers of searches involved. In the present study, for example, the 2,808 sample members were sought in
three manuscript population censuses (from among the sequence
1850, 1860, 1870, 1880) other than that from which they were drawn.
They could have been found in 7,328 census locations (the difference
between 3 × 2,808, or 8,424, and 7,328 is accounted for by deaths),
but only 6,424 linkages were made (87.7 percent). Estimating conser-
vatively that 3,000 census households had to be examined to locate
one correct household suggests that this part of the study required
searching about 20 million census households to find 6,424, probably
a medium or typical rate of data recovery for this kind of study. (The
increasing availability of census indexes will lower this ratio.)

The most favorable rate of linkage could well occur in a search for
an individual's marriage record in a well-indexed registration system
when the date of marriage is known to within a few years. A less favorable rate would probably result from searching in a long run of
newspapers for mentions of the deaths of a small group of sample
members whose dates of death are unknown. Finally, the least favorable finding rates crop up when the researcher's assignment may be

approximated thus: *Zebina K. Pangborn was associated with the *Jersey City* (N.J.) *Times* in 1880 so he probably resided in that city; he is not listed in the Soundex index to the 1880 census of New Jersey, even though he then had a ten-year-old son. The population of Jersey City was about 120,000, and its schedules are on four reels of microfilm. Find his household. Even a veteran microfilm cranker faces such a search with trepidation. Fortunately, such endless searches are comparatively rare because they are extremely frustrating if the subject is not located; assuming that the subject was notionally a resident of the community being searched in the census, the researcher then does not know whether the subject was missed by the census enumerator(s) or by the researcher. A second search may prove just as barren as the first. (The only locality avoided in such an endless search was New York City [Manhattan] in 1860.) As a rule of thumb, if one is dealing with hundreds of people in a study, it is usually too time-consuming to search more than about 10,000 to 20,000 households in the manuscript census for a particular household or individual (by the way, Pangborn was found). Here are a few other hard-won suggestions.

Rules for Collective Biographies and Population Studies

Proceed through sources hierarchically, from the notionally most complete down to the least complete or most fragmentary. Here is an example to avoid. One of the first sources checked, after drawing a sample member from the population census, was the series of indexes to deaths in Massachusetts, then maintained at the Division of Vital Statistics office in Boston. This mistake consumed much time unnecessarily (although it did not seem so then). The preferable source was the Boston city directory; it would have paid to look up the sample members in that directory at, say, five-year intervals to determine when each vanished, then to have checked within those five-year intervals to learn the last year they were listed. This procedure would have established a "last year known to have been alive" for each sample member and in some cases a good estimate of year of death as well because often a sample member's widow's name would show up a year or two after his death (starting with the 1877 directory, exact dates of death are given for some Bostonians and even a few putative destinations for out-migrants). Second, it would have obviated searching in the death indexes during periods when, from the city directory search, the sample members would have been known to be still alive. Even though one may have access to a potentially very rich and complete source and be extremely eager to search through that source, it is advisable to evaluate it first—as best one can—for hierarchic position. If another source, no matter how humdrum or banal, promises information on a greater proportion of one's subjects, look first at the other source. Enthusiasm is not fatal, merely time-consuming.

Search a source intending never to have to look through it again. Of course, this is almost never feasible, but it is a good attitude to cultivate. Have at hand as complete a list as possible, suitably arranged (alphabetically, chronologically, or numerically), of the study members whom one expects to locate in that source, together with additional information (birth year, occupation, location, spouse's name, and so on), to facilitate positive linkages without entailing transporting excessive bulk to archives, libraries, or other locations (here the new "laptop" computers appear promising). Even though the researcher will eventually achieve "passive recognition" of large numbers of names of those being studied, one should carry as well a master list of them, with identifying characteristics, so that chance encounters with them in various sources may be exploited. This master list may be as uncomplicated as a looseleaf binder containing an alphabetical list or as complex as reams of computer printout. Simplest and most convenient is best; whichever method allows the researcher to process large batches of individuals the fastest through a source is preferable.

It is more efficient to seek first those records that will minimize later searching most effectively. These records locate one's subjects geographically and temporally near the limits of their careers. Probably best for this are city directories and death records, then marriage and (if available) birth records. Why search through a state or a city's marriage records from 1851 to 1870 when a census listing suggests that the subject of the search was still single in 1870? Multiply any such search by a factor of several hundred and see the utility of early circumscription.

Record all the information given in the source being consulted, even if some of it then appears to be of no conceivable use, and note as well the complete bibliographical citation of the source. This will strike many readers as mere plain common sense, but when the frenzy of gathering information strikes, when one hits an unexpected "mother lode" of data on a study's subjects, there is a great temptation to grab the information and leave the details for later. There may be no later. That source may be misplaced, stolen, or sold for scrap paper. As for getting it all, here is another example to avoid. The exact date of first marriage was recovered for some 2,233 of the sample members. In almost all instances in which the marriage occurred in Massachusetts, the record contains the name of the officiating clergyman. Thinking that this name was unimportant, I did not record it. Several hundred marriage records and some years later, I wondered whether the name of the clergyman might not have provided a useful clue to the branch of Protestantism practiced by the individuals being married; the task of checking on nineteenth-century clergymen's denominations is not too onerous.[3] In expiation one may argue that choice of the clergyman was usually up to the bride's family so that his denomination was not necessarily that of the groom, but still. . . .

One should explain to those in charge of one's data sources the unusual nature of one's research. Some administrators appreciated the difference between this project (which was "wholesale," rather than "retail") and the usual historical or genealogical research undertaken at their institutions, and they accommodated its voracious requirements. Such assistance can have positive consequences in libraries or archives, where, for example, only three or four sources may be requested at once and no more may be requested until the first lot has been returned. This is acceptable if one wishes, say, to spend an afternoon consulting three genealogies of a family, but if one arrives with a list of 117 genealogies to look at and plans to spend no more than two or three minutes on any single work (deciding which pages, if any, to photocopy), then restrictions on the volume and frequency of requests for material can be crippling. If one cannot secure some relief from the rules, one should use another library if possible; otherwise one spends much more time waiting for materials to be fetched than is required to obtain the data.

Particular Sources

MANUSCRIPT POPULATION CENSUSES

Some interesting research has been done, and much remains to be done, on this source, especially on its accuracy and comprehensiveness. It is sloppy technique for historians to be less critical of this source than of others they employ. Most would not dream of being handed a strange document, being told, "This document was written by X," and then proceeding as if that statement were true. The conscientious among them would certainly ask, at least, "Is this consistent with other documents known to have been produced by X?" and "Did X have an opportunity to create this document?" Yet how different are most historians' attitudes toward the census. Modern census administrators in sophisticated countries struggle to push underenumeration rates below 5 percent, yet many historians who deal with nineteenth-century censuses (designed by politicians, enumerated by their hack appointees, and hand tallied by bored clerks) seemingly never entertain the thought that many lives slipped through the fingers of those amateur statisticians somewhere along the way. Most inquiries into census accuracy seem to emanate from sociologists.[4]

The attraction and the stumbling block of the census are identical: the manuscript population census is nevertheless the most nearly complete listing of everyone who resided in a given area around census time, but it suffers from unknown (and probably fluctuating) omission rates. Part of the present study involved attempting to locate all surviving sample members in the four midcentury population censuses, 1850–80. The individuals were located in the proportions shown in Table A.1. The proportions of those known to be alive but who were not located in the censuses varied from 11.0 to 14.7 percent. Perhaps there was a slight improvement in completeness of enumeration between 1850 and 1880, but the men in these samples represented a reasonably well-educated portion of society, likely familiar with the purpose of a census, so why should not underenumeration rates among illiterates or newcomers unsure of the object of the census have been much higher? True total undercount rates could be in the 18 to 23 percent range.

There are several ways to check on the extent of underenumera-

Table A.1

Location Status of Members of 1860 and 1870 Samples in Censuses of 1850–1880

Year and status	1860 sample		1870 sample	
Alive in 1850	1,405	%	1,403	%
Located in census	1,241	88.3	1,199	85.6
Not located in census	163	11.7	202	14.4
Outside U.S.	1		2	
Alive in 1860	1,405		1,403	
Located in census	1,405	100.0	1,223	87.2
Not located in census	0		180	12.8
Alive in 1870	1,131		1,403	
Located in census	997	88.2	1,403	100.0
Not located in census	134	11.8	0	
1870 status				
unknown[a]	(28)		0	
Alive in 1880	847		1,139	
Located in census	754	89.0	1,010	88.7
Not located in census	93	11.0	129	11.3
1880 status				
unknown[a]	(27)		(17)	
Outside U.S.	0[b]		1[b]	

[a]Status unknown: individual was not known to be alive or dead.

[b]These figures could be as high as, say, 5 because several well-to-do sample members may have been traveling in Europe.

tion, all by comparing other lists with the manuscript census. This study used the most obvious, one of the most powerful: retrospective searching for individuals known to have been alive, combined with prospective searches for individuals known (or strongly suspected) to be alive. Of course, other approaches are possible. For example, one could select a large group of people listed in a city's directory both for the census year and the subsequent year, then see how many were included in the census.[5] Because of possible omissions in the directory, this method is less conclusive than the first. Alternatively, the list to be compared could come from poll book records, from tax-assessment records, or from registries of members of an association, all lists as of a census year. The prime criterion is that fairly large numbers of names—the more the better—appear in the lists to be checked against the census. For example, in November 1849 the Sons of New Hampshire held a large banquet in Boston and later published a list of those who attended, giving town of residence. When Joseph F. Kett and I searched for these men in the 1850 manuscript census of the Boston area, we located only about 81 percent of them, a figure that has risen only slightly even after intensive searching using an index (published in 1978) to the 1850 population census of Massachusetts.[6] Part of the loss is likely attributable to out-migration by some of the Sons in the nine months between the banquet and the start of enumeration for the 1850 census in Boston (30 July; the last ward was begun 7 September, and the census was completed 11 October).

A promising approach is to compare poll books with the census. Since elections were important locally, lists of potential or actual voters were probably compiled and scrutinized more carefully than were the federal or even state censuses.[7] The poll books' drawback lies in their listing just adult males (usually whites only); other household members' numbers must be estimated. Of course, widespread appreciation of the extent of underenumeration in nineteenth-century censuses must have consequences in areas other than history; political science, which has some interest in historical levels of voter turnout, and economic history, which occasionally studies per capita production levels, spring to mind.[8]

STATE VITAL STATISTICS REGISTRATION SYSTEMS

In Massachusetts the registration of vital events supposedly began in 1841–42, but it was none too good until about 1850.[9] Vital events were usually noted contemporaneously, then compiled annually by the town and city clerks and the results sent to the state registrar's office in Boston for revision and binding into large volumes. These were arranged annually by event (birth, death, marriage) and, within each volume (which contains records of only one type of event), first by county, alphabetically from Berkshire to Worcester. Within each county, the records were arranged, again alphabetically, by community. Within a community's record, the order was roughly chronological.

The events were indexed for five-year periods, following an initial 1841–50 compilation. Thus the events are indexed in three series of volumes corresponding to the events themselves (birth, death, marriage [brides are indexed]), for five-year spans starting with 1851 (e.g., 1851–55, 1856–60, 1861–65, and so on). Recent legislation divided responsibility for housing these records: those over 90 years old are open to the public at the Massachusetts Archives, Columbia Point, Boston, and the newer records (open to the public under certain restrictions) are at 150 Tremont Street in Boston at the Division of Vital Records and Statistics, now part of the state's health department. Because the records are indexed in five-year groups, no transfer of them from Tremont Street to Columbia Point occurs until the most recent year of a five-year period is 90 years past. Thus, as of 1989, records through 1895 had been moved; the 1896–1900 records would presumably be relocated in about 1991.

The records through at least 1900 and the indexes through at least 1970 have been microfilmed by the Church of Jesus Christ of Latter-day Saints, Salt Lake City, Utah. Interested researchers should note that the church will sell copies of these films to approved institutions if the archive holding the original records permits; it does not sell copies to individuals, but one may donate funds to an approved institution for the purchase of microfilms, which may then be used by the donor.

Microfilm copies of those Massachusetts records open to the public are available in Salt Lake City, through the church's many branch libraries, and are also being used for reference both at Columbia Point and at 150 Tremont Street. Early in 1988 the New England Historic Genealogical Society, Boston, obtained a set of the 1841–95 films. Because of the difficulty in gaining use of microfilm readers and the time involved in obtaining, threading, winding, rewinding, and returning the films, it is imperative to follow a strict procedure in consulting these records to minimize multiple usages of the same reels of film (e.g., look up all references first in the indexes, then arrange the listings in order of volume and page number). These records, as well as constituting the longest-running series of vital event records in the United States, appeared to be most useful and complete for those events recording adults—marriages and deaths.

Birth records provide child's name (if one had been chosen; some families waited up to a year to name a child); sex; color; date and location of birth; parents' names and birthplaces (country only if foreign-born); and father's occupation. Records for Catholic births were less likely to appear in the Massachusetts system, so if many Catholics are in a study, one should use diocesan records. Marriage records list names of bride and groom, their ages, color, their communities of residence, the couple's communities of birth (country only if foreign-born), parents' names, date and location of marriage, officiating clergyman, number of marriage for bride and groom (first, second, and so on), and groom's occupation. Late in the century more brides began reporting occupations, but fewer than five brides in this study listed an occupation. Death records contain decedent's name, age at death, location of death, "cause" of death (the nosology sometimes humorous), occupation, birthplace (country only if foreign-born), color, civil status (married, widow/widower, divorced, single [this information not always correct]), and parents' names and birthplaces (country only if foreign-born). Early local records often note location of interment, which inquiry eventually was added to the state records.

The vital records of Maine, New Hampshire, and Vermont, which are variously incomplete for the nineteenth century, have also been microfilmed. Vermont's recorded events are combined into one alphabet, a tremendous convenience (unfortunately, the microfilm copy did not register well the dark-colored cards containing death records; these are to be filmed again). Maine's marriages and deaths were separately filmed. Statewide registration began in 1892, but some earlier events have been added. New Hampshire's records are also segregated by type of event, but family names are indexed by their first and third letter, and within a family name the card images may not be alphabetized. (Except for those of Maine, New Hampshire, and Vermont, which were used in the microfilm version, and except for Boston's, which were employed at the Boston City Archives, other states' and communities' records were consulted by mail.)

LOCAL VITAL EVENTS REGISTRATION SYSTEM (BOSTON)

Boston's vital records are stored at the City Archives in the New City Hall, which, as of late 1989, was open eight hours a week. Probably all of the city's holdings have been filmed by the Church of Jesus Christ of Latter-day Saints, Salt Lake City, Utah. Since the church's reference collection in Salt Lake City is open over 100 hours a week and that collection contains as well microfilms of other New England states' vital records (these films mostly unavailable in Boston), paradoxically, Salt Lake City is the most efficient location at which to pursue studies of Boston, of Massachusetts, and probably of most other areas.

Boston has good marriage records for the nineteenth century, very few birth records for 1800 to 1849, and passable death records for the pre-1850 era.[10] In Boston beginning in 1849 and for many years thereafter the city registrar obtained birth records by having the city canvassed twice yearly; because of population circulation, in-migration, and out-migration, these records are incomplete. For 1849–69 the copies at the Boston City Archives are admirably indexed, with parents' names given in the births index (these records have been filmed by a commercial firm, and anyone may buy copies; they could form the basis of a fertility study). Boston's marriage intentions are indexed with marriages; often such a record points to the location of out-of-city marriages (it is occasionally noted on the intention). Marriage intentions are not included in the state registration system.

CITY DIRECTORIES

Boston's pre-1861 city directories are available on microfiche (unfortunately, for those directories extending over more than one fiche, without indication of which names [if any] are on which fiche). The post-1860 directories have been microfilmed up to at least 1901; both projects were undertaken by Research Publications, Inc., New Haven, Connecticut.[11]

Other cities' pre-1861 directories are also available on those RPI microfiche, but not so the post-1860 directories, which were filmed only for 50 selected, usually large, cities. For nonselected communities, recourse to libraries and secondhand bookstores will be necessary.

The Boston city directories gave the study's subjects impressive coverage with remarkable accuracy. Early on it seemed likely that when a sample member did not appear in a directory he had been missed by the canvassers; it turned out that many such individuals actually had been elsewhere when the directory was compiled. As was noted in *The Plain People of Boston*, the directories largely neglected the less well off.[12] Since the directories were compiled for the use of the better off, who would not have had much contact with the less well off, omissions of the less well off are regrettable but only to be expected. A modern parallel is the telephone directory: not everyone is listed in it, some because of economic circumstances, others by choice, yet it is still of considerable utility. So was the nineteenth-century city directory, for its users.

NEWSPAPERS

Next to looking for no one in particular in large cities in the manuscript population census, reading through a long run of a daily newspaper for mentions of specific individuals must rank as one of the most boring activities imaginable. The reward lies in the newspaper's fascinating reports of everyday life. A variant of the comment on the telephone directory, lots of characters, but not much plot, applies to the nineteenth-century newspaper: lots of characters, lots of plots, few resolutions of those plots. Its very diversity and lack of sustained focus are at once the newspaper's attraction and its repulsion.[13] One working on a systematic study finds that there was no system: events occurred, some were reported, some not; some were followed up, others not. Thus these newspapers started many more hares than they ever ran to ground. Nonetheless, this mélange of events does offer insights into nineteenth-century life (see Chapter 4).

There is no denying that daily newspapers provide a sense of the boundaries of the possible in everyday life and point out those commonplaces (such as scuttle falls) that perplex later generations. But unless they can be shown to contain mentions of unusually large proportions of the subjects of a study, newspapers are the source most easily eliminated from systematic population studies; the payoff is not worth the large investment of time involved. (But they are fascinating.)

The principal newspaper used in this study, the *Boston Evening Transcript*, contained daily listings of marriages and deaths almost from its start in 1830. Its death notices have been indexed in three series, 1830–74, 1875–99, 1900–1930; the first series remains in typescript at the Boston Athenæum Library; the second and third have been photographically reproduced and may be found in some research libraries. Most of the death notices up to the 1880s are just that—notices. Full-fledged obituaries were comparatively rare before then. The 1875–1930 indexes omit listings of some obituaries separate from the usual death notices (they are headed "RECENT DEATHS" and usually appear on page 4 or 5). It was unusual to find a death notice for a sample member's widow, rather more usual to find one for his wife; perhaps 20 percent of the sample members' deaths were noted in the *Transcript*.

GENEALOGIES AND FAMILY HISTORIES

Genealogies are here understood to be compilations of ancestral information providing only skeletal pedigrees necessary to determine relationship and descent of family members. Superior are family histories, which add to the pedigrees substantive information about ancestral lives, often giving brief life sketches, in a few cases photographs. Discussions with genealogists suggest that more osmosis of historical procedures and documentation standards through the boundary between genealogy and history is likely. It would also be desirable for a countercurrent to evolve because genealogists could materially aid historians doing social-historical research; but this seems less likely.

More than 900 genealogies and family histories proved useful in this study, principally by directing the search for specific information on sample members to a proper location.[14] The lack of documentation in most genealogies and many family histories required independent verification of their data when practicable. The rate of incorrect information proved very low, most of it no doubt a result of transcription or typographical errors. The incidence of missing information was likely more troublesome. But good genealogies and family histories can save the researcher a lot of time, especially if they are well indexed. It is probably best to begin using them in a systematic study after one has learned the maiden names of any considerable numbers of women in the study because genealogies and family histories for the families of the women provide just as much information on those women as on the men—for at least one generation. The genealogies and family histories usually do not follow out the descendants of female family members, their compilers reasoning that the genealogists of the families into which the women married will treat of them.[15]

TAX-ASSESSMENT RECORDS

Boston is fortunate to have nearly complete tax-assessment records dating from the 1780s. Some years ago these records, which had been stored in a dank and filthy basement vault of the Old City Hall Annex, were moved to the custody of the Boston Public Library, where they are available through the Rare Books Room. Researchers intending to use them are advised to take along their own sink because the records have been carefully preserved with the filth of over a century intact on every volume, and the nearest washing-up facility is half a block away. The condition of the assessment volumes was in stark contrast to that of the volumes in the Rare Books Room itself. As few individuals are familiar with the organization of these extensive records, a description is in order.

The assessment process began with visits, in May, to every building in Boston by two assessors within each ward. They copied down the information they elicited into so-called "Street" volumes, operating under the instruction that, unless there had been a change to a structure, it was to be assessed for the same amount as in the preceding year. The "Street" volumes give the name, civil status, occupation, address, and real and personal estate assessments for each male of voting age, the name (and, if known, ward of residence) of the property's owner (if not owner-occupied), and any relevant comments. This information was processed forward by clerks to another set of volumes, again one for each ward, called "Transfer" volumes. Their purpose was to arrange the names from the "Street" volumes into quasi-alphabetical order and to consolidate into one location all pieces of property owned by each individual within a ward. The clerks then compiled yet a third set of volumes, called "Ward" volumes, which brought together, again in quasi-alphabetical order, all the various pieces of property owned by individuals anywhere in Boston and credited those pieces to their owners according to the ward in which the owner resided. Last, this information was transferred, in yet a fourth step, to "summary" volumes from which individuals' tax bills were made up, sent out, and marked "paid." In a few cases, individuals' bills were reduced, perhaps because they had sold a property shortly before it was assessed, or maybe because they had appealed the amount of an assessment and gotten it reduced. Men over 70 could also request poll tax rebates, and some appear not to have been charged, their entries being marked "poor." A few entries, usually for those charged for a poll tax only, are marked "g.c.f.," which proved to mean "gone, can't find," suggesting that someone had been out searching for payment. Of course, these summary volumes were used just before elections to determine eligibility to vote (no payment of poll tax, no vote); the summary volumes contain additional lists of men who had been missed by the assessors but who came forward at election time, impelled by civic virtue, paid their $1.50 poll tax, and voted.[16]

The assessment records thus constitute a sort of annual census of many heads of household, except that, as two years' residence in Boston was a prerequisite to voting, the listings necessarily excluded short-term residents. Their organization in quasi-alphabetical order facilitates, after a fashion, their use, but the considerable numbers of duplicated names in the assessment rolls require the application as well of a contemporaneous city directory to help resolve binary pairs (and a few triplets) of like-named men. The conservative approach of retaining the previous year's valuation should help determine who was really advancing on a year-by-year basis, provided that one can make correct linkages. The ease of concealing so-called personal estate, in the form of securities, likely led to wealth underassessment at the top of the heap. Nevertheless, the considerable run of these records would permit extensive long-term analyses. The wealth figures in the 1860 and 1870 manuscript population census returns proved to be excellent estimates of assessment values; the two regression equations were estimated 1860 assessment = 0.776 (total wealth in 1860 census) + \$883 (t = 84.403 with 1,405 observations) and estimated 1870 assessment = 0.898 (total wealth in 1870 census) + \$1,226 (t = 34.699 with 1,403 observations). The assessment records for the annexed communities, Roxbury, Dorchester, and Charlestown, which used to be in the basement vault of the Old City Hall Annex, were supposed to have been moved to the Public Library as well but cannot be located because the spines of many of these volumes have deteriorated. (My offer to assist in this identification was declined.)

CEMETERY RECORDS

Boston witnessed the beginning of the "garden cemetery" movement in the United States.[17] Fortunately, its original large garden cemeteries all still survive; all retain their records (I was shown some of Mount Auburn's burial certificates, permissions from Cambridge for interments to occur, dating from the 1860s; earlier certificates are there, too). All of the major cemeteries cooperated beyond my expectations. The cemeteries proved an unexpected cornucopia of information on out-migrants (see below).

Cemeteries usually maintain files listing those interred, with date of interment, age at death, and sometimes date and cause of death. To use these records most effectively, one must know the complete names of the decedents, so it would be premature to proceed to checking them, assuming one wished to look up wives as well as husbands, without having the wives' full names. It *is* possible to proceed from the husband's name to his lot card, which lists all those interred in his lot but gives no relationship to the lot's owner, so without the wife's name one does not know if a given female sharing the owner's family plot and name was his wife, mother, sister, daughter, or "other."

It is advisable to send a full explanation of one's project to the cemetery involved before descending upon its solitude; its staff is probably small, busy, and so would wish to be assured of the usefulness and legitimacy of one's research.

PROBATE RECORDS

As one might assume in a study more than half of the subjects of which were not assessed for more than a poll tax, few of them possessed enough to necessitate probate. The Suffolk County and Middlesex County probate records were most useful in indicating the destinations of out-migrants (see below). Indexes to the probate records of both counties have been published.

LAND-TRANSFER RECORDS

The principal Massachusetts land-transfer records consulted for this study were those of the counties of Suffolk (located in Boston), Middlesex (Cambridge), Norfolk (Dedham), Plymouth (Plymouth) (only for a handful of records), and Barnstable (Barnstable) (only one or two records). The records for Dorchester and Roxbury, before their annexations by Boston, are in Dedham, while those for Charlestown before its annexation are in Cambridge. The records are all in excellent condition. (In warm weather, the Dedham Courthouse is the most pleasant to work in, Cambridge the least.)

Locating Out-Migrants: General Considerations as to Sources

No general rules will infallibly produce high returns of out-migrants in all possible studies. These procedures worked well with the Yankee Bostonians—a group chosen so as to be easier to trace than would have been a population cross section of midcentury Boston. Given the sources and technology available in 1972, a study of a cross section that sought out-migrants would have been impossible. Even today, with all the considerable assistance computers can offer, it is not to be undertaken lightly; I would still not attempt it.

The basic principle in tracing out-migrants is simple but not appreciated by researchers, or there would be many more studies of out-migration: out-migrants very often left traces of their destinations. These traces remain in varying amounts; let us start small and work up.

LIFE INSURANCE COMPANY RECORDS

Officials of the New England Mutual Life Insurance Company, Boston, kindly provided access to their file of nineteenth-century policies and policy applications (commencing in 1844); only one fugitive out-migrant was flushed out of concealment. Too few sample members had purchased life insurance from New England Life for a survey to be worth the effort of an extensive check of the company's policies, but these contain a wealth of economic and medical data (including results of physical examinations) that should be exploited. Early on the company was writing policies in Europe so international comparisons are possible.

NEWSPAPERS

In an article about out-migration from Schoharie County, New York, David P. Davenport reports tracing some interstate out-migrants, using references in the local newspapers to their new locations.[18] Probably for rural populations this is a more fruitful source than it was in Boston, where the departure of only two sample members, with new locations, was noted in the period for which the *Boston Evening Transcript* was checked daily.

Since about a dozen out-migrants had moved to San Francisco and that city's pre-1906 vital records were largely destroyed by its great earthquake, I searched the vital announcements, 1870–86 and 1891–92, of the *San Francisco Evening Bulletin* for notices of the out-migrants' deaths, finding all but one of them (*Abram Rich, supposed to have died in 1891). If one determines not to be distracted by reports of daily events, one can check a year of a four-page daily newspaper's death reports in about an hour and a half. This procedure would be justified only when no local vital events records exist for the period being surveyed. Newspapers' ethnic bias, if any, in reporting deaths may well determine which paper(s) to look at. The *San Francisco Chronicle*, for example, which is also available on microfilm, contained death notices primarily of individuals of Irish and German extraction, hence was useless for my purposes.

Supposedly, all manuscript population censuses before 1860 have been indexed, mostly by Accelerated Indexing Systems (AIS) of North Salt Lake City, Utah, but their quality is nothing to write home about, and, as David P. Davenport has pointed out in a cogent critique, they must be used with great care.[19]

Several indexes to the 1860 census are available; AIS promises to cover the entire country and has already completed a few of the smaller states; for Ohio there are two independent compilations. Theoretically, linkages between people drawn from the 1850 census and followed into the 1860 enumeration will be simplified by the appearance of these volumes.[20] (Given the problems connected with the AIS 1850 indexes, this is unlikely without a radical improvement in the compiling process—the elimination or at least minimization of impossible or garbled names.) Indexes to New Hampshire and Vermont for 1860 were available by summer 1987 but helped locate only three sample members from the 1870 sample who were on their way to Boston. Probably the critical limiting factor of these indexes is not their garbling but census underenumeration.

Researchers should also be aware that censuses of many individual counties of the various states have been indexed, usually by genealogists. Some of these indexes are available in larger research collections.

The 1870 census had not been indexed for any states useful to this study, except Rhode Island, as of summer 1989.

The Soundex index to the 1880 census could be very helpful if it were more nearly complete; it was disturbing to learn, in a few instances (including that of *Zebina K. Pangborn), that sample members who had children under the age of ten as of 1880 and who had been located in the manuscript population census were seemingly not indexed in the Soundex. (Similar results, with probably a higher rate of omissions, emanated from the 1900 Soundex index.) Unless one chooses the individuals to be searched so as to ensure that all of them ought to be in the Soundex index for 1880 (as, for instance, in the Stephenson and Jensen retrospective linkage study[21]), one should not

rely greatly on the Soundex index. Notionally, of course, it does permit searching the whole country, if one does not mind threading,
winding, and rewinding miles of 16-mm microfilm. Why not a verification study that draws a large sample of households with a child under ten from the 1880 census to see how many of its members are in
the Soundex index?

PROBATE RECORDS

Probate records proved only slightly useful in locating out-migrants.
A few had left behind a savings account or a life insurance policy that
had to be transferred to heirs; the file contained a notation of date of
death and, later in the century, of location of death also. A few men
were found by checking the probate files of their fathers or brothers
for addresses of the out-migrants.

GENEALOGIES AND FAMILY HISTORIES

Genealogies and family histories proved of limited utility in tracing
out-migrants, probably because of the works' New England bias. Also,
since many of them appeared during the last quarter of the nineteenth century, my sample members had not yet left Boston when
some of the books were being compiled.[22] Local histories were mar-
ginally superior as a finding source.

CITY DIRECTORIES

Next in ascending order of usefulness would be city directories of
localities other than Boston. Armed with an alphabetized list of suspected out-migrants, the researcher may rapidly check census-year
directories of a multitude of communities for names on that list. The
necessary census search of those localities, to verify that correct
matches have been achieved, takes longer but usually guarantees positive linkages. After census verification one may then return to the
directories to obtain migrants' arrival and departure years for the cities in question.

LAND-TRANSFER RECORDS

Land-transfer records proved unexpectedly helpful in finding out-
migrants. The first visit to the Suffolk County records to see if some

out-migrants waited until they reached their destinations before sell-
ing their property in Boston produced the new locations of 24 long-
distance out-migrants. But that first day's bonanza virtually exhausted
the lode.

CIVIL WAR PENSION FILES

Some 299 sample members served in the Civil War, and most of
them, or their widows, applied for and received pensions from the
federal government. Most of the veterans, 168, left Boston; of these
12 died in the city's suburbs, 66 elsewhere in Massachusetts, 30 elsewhere in New England, and 33 outside New England (6 others died
in unknown locations and the remaining 21 out-migrants returned to
Boston to die). If the veteran's wife predeceased him, information on
his death, except for an approximate date, does not appear in his file
(or no one applied for a pension). But when the veteran died first, his
widow was very likely, unless she were well provided for, to apply for
a pension (or a continuation of his pension) and thus to generate (or
fatten) a file, which then had to include proof of the veteran's death.
As of summer 1989, the fee for obtaining extracts from a Civil War
veteran's pension file from the National Archives was but $5, well
worth the expense. One could exploit the potential of these files by
performing very interesting studies of the later careers of Civil War
soldiers. Is my impression correct that veterans were much more mobile than were nonveterans of their age? One might choose a company from some regiment and write a collective biography of its members, following them throughout their lives.[23]

CEMETERY INTERMENT RECORDS

The most productive source of information on out-migrants was
cemetery interment records. Surprisingly many men who left Boston
were returned for burial in one of its major cemeteries. It would
probably pay to check such records early in the search for deaths in
general. The interment information must usually be supplemented
by a check into the cemetery's other records to produce information
on the place of decedent's demise.

OTHER

Somewhere in this catalog of sources should appear serendipity—
the chance encounter in a newspaper report or in the index to *New
York Times* obituaries, perhaps in a local history one was checking for
information on another subject. The incidence of this benison was
low, but the effect on morale was usually disproportionately high.

Locating Out-Migrants: Procedures

One cannot estimate in advance which sources will yield the most out-
migrants, but one can use the guidelines above, modified for local
conditions. For instance, in states where death registration began late
in the nineteenth century or was not extended statewide until rather
late, the researcher may wish to proceed from a city directory search
to local death records, then to the local cemetery records. Or it may
be advisable to change the time span of the study, looking at people
sufficiently late in the nineteenth century or early in the twentieth so
that statewide death registration becomes available—in other words,
to tailor the study to fit the constraints of the records. Here the 1920
federal population census manuscript schedules, soon to be released,
should be most helpful. (Since some of the 1890 census returns of
Jersey City survived the 1921 Commerce Department fire, it may be
possible to examine at least part of that city right through from 1850
to 1920.)

The most important step in finding out-migrants is the most ele-
mentary: determine soon which of the study's subjects were out-
migrants and approximately when they left the community. This is
needful because tracing them, even though they may represent a minority of the individuals in the study, will demand time and resources
grossly disproportionate to their numbers. Thus they must be tar-
geted early. It is also desirable to have a complete list of them early
on so as to achieve economy of effort in checking sources outside the
community of origin, in line with the rules of delimitation and concentration of effort suggested above.

Destinations of the out-migrants also depended, it would seem, on
their experiences in the community of departure. Men who had

stayed in Boston only a few years were apparently able to return to rural areas, and even to farming, much more readily than were those who had given the city their best years. Young men in business were also likely to remove to other cities, where in another urban milieu they could apply lessons hard won in their formative years in Boston. Older out-migrants, already out of the labor force, tended to favor returning to their home areas in preparation for death. (If husband and wife were both alive at out-migration, though getting on in years, consider the wife's hometown as a possible destination.)

General Procedure

The research operations involved in a collective biography or population study like this one include: (1) choosing whom to study, (2) determining the order of checking sources, (3) searching, (4) establishing routines for "looping" (repeating) searches, and (5) analyzing the information.

The principal fact to keep in mind about a study like this is that it can get complicated. There were 2,808 men in this study, of whom 2,775 married at least once, producing a total of 5,583 primary individuals to be concerned about; second, third, fourth, and fifth wives added another 560 or so. These people produced, in turn, at least 7,830 children, about whom the dates of birth of the earliest and latest from first marriages were desired, so add in another possible 5,550 (2 × 2,775) people about whom some information was sought. Information on sample members' parents (birth date, birthplace, marriage date, father's occupation, father's census wealth in 1850) meant looking for data on yet another 5,616 (2 × 2,808) people. (The total is approaching 24,000.) Each decision to gather an additional datum meant multiplying that datum by 2,808 (assuming that one could obtain 100 percent returns) and the time to gather it for the whole group by a factor of, say, 4,000 (since some data were less accessible than others). Thus one's list of data to be sought should not be extended without an acute appreciation that each additional datum, retrieved for the whole group, will cost.

Another complication is that not all data about the study's subjects were available simultaneously. For example, the wife appearing in the 1860 census listing might turn out, much later, to have been the sample member's second wife; similarly the census or other source may present incomplete lists of children (hence the need to look at newspaper death notices to pick up their deaths). This drawback necessitates "looping": allowing for repeating some of one's procedures to take into account more recent developments. The researcher must process large numbers of individuals, in batches, through various sources, yet also allow for the fact that additional information gained about a subject may require returning to a source already checked, to obtain data previously blocked because of lack of linking information.

An example of looping that cropped up fairly often involved children's births. Because birth records are indexed by the child's name, one cannot look up a record without that name (except in extraordinary instances like that for Boston births, 1849–69, for which the Boston City Archives index gives parents' names). Apparent records of the first birth in some sample members' households later proved false in that later information (usually a child's death notice in the *Transcript*) revealed an earlier birth. Other researchers may wish to exert special efforts to search for first births in cases when the presumed interval from marriage to the first birth exceeds some arbitrary figure, say 800 to 1,000 days. Similarly, the absence of a Massachusetts marriage record for a couple necessitated checking for that event in other states' records (trying first the native state of the bride), thus introducing yet another loop.

Processing a large number of subjects through various sources is not like grinding sausages; it is more like trying to herd a large flock of fractious sheep across a busy highway, using a sheep dog (this does not refer to my several research assistants). Some of the sheep will insist on going their own way; others (the "unknowns") will escape. Short of shooting them, one can but try to keep them rounded up and headed in the right direction.

CHOOSING WHOM TO STUDY

Remember that the group one chooses will make or break the study; they are also people with whom one must live for some time. It is thus necessary to balance several conflicting considerations: characteristics of the group from whom the sample is drawn, if indeed one draws a sample; size of the group one is researching—large enough to be meaningful, perhaps statistically significant, small enough to be "doable" within one's time constraints; availability of records likely to refer to one's subjects, preferably records that have been ordered somehow, even if only alphabetically. Compromises will be needed. Unless one has access to good marriage records, one should not study large numbers of single individuals because poor marriage records render linkages into other records very difficult.

DETERMINING THE ORDER OF CHECKING SOURCES

As was mentioned above, the need to balance the ideal against reality will affect the composition of one's subject group. The same is true for the order of checking sources. If one adheres to the rule of working through the most comprehensive data sources first, a lot of extra work should be eliminated automatically. In the present study, the death records of sample members were checked first, a procedure that seems incorrect (see above). The next step was usually to look for a sample member's marriage, again—and for the same reason—an inappropriate procedure.

Yet another misstep involved using parallel data searches; this occurred when the task of drawing sample members from the manuscript census became too wearisome (because it extended over six years, perhaps I may be forgiven for seeking some diversion). Since there was no way to tell in advance the exact size of the universe from which the samples were to be drawn, the first procedure was to classify all household heads in the 1860 census of Boston plus Dorchester plus Roxbury and in the 1870 census of Boston (which had by then annexed Dorchester and Roxbury), as to sex, race, and nativity. In 1860 there were some 40,538 households in Boston, Dorchester, and Roxbury and another 49,194 in 1870 Boston (see Table 3.17), so this process was slow. But because the sample members were sampled systematically ward by ward, there was a natural temptation to begin looking up some of them in the records as soon as a good batch was drawn. To return to our sheep, the flock was created in many small groups, of 50 or 100, and processing commenced on them. This produced a "pipeline" effect, which was detrimental because it required repeated consultation of the same volumes of records at the Massachusetts Division of Vital Statistics (fortunately, the records were then still accessible in the original volumes). If all the sample members had been drawn before their processing began, drawing the samples would have taken perhaps half or a third of the time actually required. Of course, using a computer for the sample drawing would cut that time to months.

Thus the importance of following strictly the rule of unique processing, of consulting each source with the idea that it will be looked at just once, that all the study's subjects will be run through it, and that one will never revisit it. Naturally, this is not the case. Some sample members will be disqualified; in the present study this was especially likely to occur among those drawn from the 1860 census because it contains no information on parents' nativity. (Foreign names were usually easy to eliminate for by 1860 very few native-born children of Irish parents were old enough to be household heads.) An unexpected problem arose in that the 1870 census information on parentage was not always correct, the most common case being that of an individual with a native-born father but a foreign-born mother. This fact was usually caught either from an individual's death record or his 1880 census listing and required returning to the manuscript census for a replacement—yet another instance of looping, because these "late-joining" sample members had to be brought up to speed with their more advanced fellows.

From the state vital registration system this study spread in several directions at once: into genealogies and family histories, into local histories, and into local published vital records volumes—all to obtain exact birth and marriage data on the sample members and their parents. Since these records were usually available only in Boston, at the New England Historic Genealogical Society, they could be consulted only during summers or leave periods; they were much too numerous to obtain through interlibrary loan. (This suggests the advisability of studying a community to which one has ready access or of moving to Salt Lake City.) Another part of the research, which could be carried on during the academic year, was the search for sample members in censuses other than that from which they were drawn; the necessary films came through interlibrary loan from the Center for Research

Libraries in Chicago. Because many newspapers are available on microfilm, one may wish to relegate their contemplation (if they are used) to times when nothing better offers itself to advance the project. If newspapers are used, they should be consulted last because of their low rate of return for effort invested.

PERFORMING THE SEARCHES

There is little one can profitably add under this heading because everyone's mind works differently. Some people will be able to spend many hours on end patiently cranking reels of microfilm to check vital records; others will want to stop every hour. It is important to find out early one's tolerance for a given activity and then not to exceed it.

In searching various sources, one should always keep in mind the need to economize effort. Approaching a source with a markedly incomplete list of individuals to be checked in it as good as guarantees that one will have to return with more names later. Poor arrangement of names to be checked means having to go back and forth within the source; this too is costly. Every second economized early on probably saves a minute later.

If one is working with nineteenth-century materials, it is useful to become familiar with the kinds of names one may confront, especially in the manuscript census; I have often seen a veteran genealogist glance at what appears to a neophyte an indecipherable scrawl in a census manuscript and say, "Ephraim," or some other biblical name. Many researchers appear to be ignorant of the wide range of given names from that period. The relatively minor variations from today's handwriting (notably the use of "ſ" for "s") are usually easily mastered.

One must also come to terms with the nineteenth century's attitude toward records. Most people then had no need to keep any records whatsoever; probably most families entered births, deaths, and marriages in the family Bible, and some farmers kept rudimentary business records, but only a minority of well-to-do businessmen maintained elaborate books (few of which survive). Most people encountered members of the new bureaucracy only rarely, and they were not, like us, sensitized to the need to know one's Social Security or Social Insurance number, mother's maiden name, and so on. They

considered their affairs private; thus many of them avoided bureaucrats or fobbed them off with incomplete, incorrect, or misleading
responses.[24]

ESTABLISHING ROUTINES FOR LOOPING SEARCHES

Early in a population or community study one may realize that
some sort of records consultation failure is occurring. Perhaps too low
a proportion of marriage records is being recovered. The researcher
suspects that some part of the procedure is defective but cannot
specify it. The remedy may be as simple as cross searching, that is,
looking up every marriage record under both the names of the groom
and the bride, then checking only those records in which the references are identical (a good step when grooms or brides have common
names). Or the problem may be systemic: for religious or other reasons some couples may not have registered. Last, the marriages may
not have occurred in that jurisdiction (because of a delay required
between obtaining a license and going through the ceremony, some
Massachusetts couples in a hurry preferred to marry in New Hampshire or Rhode Island); this necessitates checking adjacent jurisdictions. But one becomes aware of the need for looping searches only
when part of the regular search process fails in quantity. It is worth
thinking about the consequences of search failure before engaging in
large-scale excavation of a new source. One may wish to set advance
parameters: If I find under 75 percent of the marriages I'm looking
for in this source I'm going to have to supplement this part of the
search by going through the local newspaper. In general, one may set
goals proportioned to the finding rates emanating from this study
because few other United States jurisdictions are so bountifully supplied with records as is Massachusetts.

Genealogists constitute an important human resource available to
almost all historical researchers who undertake population or community studies, a resource often overlooked because of the differing
traditions of history and genealogy. Most historical studies are very
much individual efforts, even though some social-science-oriented
historians wish it otherwise. Such research often relies on the slow
accretion of evidence to change the researcher's view of what happened. Population and community studies can profit somewhat from

the fact that, as in genealogy, many of their research tasks permit of subdivision such that one may regard them as having been completed once their implied inquiry has been answered, for example, the question, When did *Lucius P. Barnes die? ordinarily has a unique reply; the question need not be answered twice (the answer: 6 April 1893 and *29 October 1897, the latter date that of the sample member, the former that of an interloper, also a machinist born in Vermont, introduced by fate to confuse historians). Because historians believe that most historical questions have a multitude of answers, it is difficult for them to adjust to situations in which that is true in general but false in particular (and in great quantity). The upshot is that most historians contemplating such a study fail to perceive that they are moving into an area where genealogists have long been at work. Because genealogists have a well-developed tradition of mutual consultation and aid, they are inclined to help the beginner; historians usually are not, because of their individualistic tradition. Genealogists, by contrast, know that much of their research has to be collaborative because they usually cannot visit all repositories of appropriate records. Genealogical research also has an advantage over most historical research in that it is subdivided into discrete parts, each of which may be known to be completed and which then usually does not have to be repeated. Hence in doubtful cases, ask a genealogist. The odds are good that he or she will find the problem familiar. If one is greatly daring, one might even mention the study topic. Don't be surprised by the reply, "Oh, did you know about [source]? I've used it, and it has information on [item]," or "There's a very useful finding aid for [source] that could save you some time; it's on that shelf." If one is fortunate, one may encounter some of those who are attempting to make genealogy a more rigorous discipline (they usually are Fellows of the American Society of Genealogists). I learned more from them about research procedures in this area than could ever have been possible in any graduate seminar. Unfortunately, this occurred only after I had shaken many trees they already knew were fruitless.

ANALYZING THE INFORMATION

One should not contemplate doing a study like this unless one can enter the data directly into a data base or perhaps a spreadsheet program that also has statistical-analysis capabilities. Ideally, it should combine word processing with these; the separation of these three functions during the last phase of the present study led to annoying delays in transferring data from the data base to the statistics package, then printing out any resulting tables so as to get them over to the word-processing program. A combined program, which should certainly hit the market soon, if it has not already done so, is a must.[25] Rather than wondering which trends were developing and being able to determine preliminary results only by laborious hand counting, as was long necessary in the present study (which began with one data card for each sample member), such a program permits one to manipulate the information with impressive rapidity and to minimize paperwork. The possibility of creating specific lists to be checked in any given source, or perhaps even of carrying powerful hand-held computers to various archives, opens the way to much easier collection and analysis of data. If such portable computers possessed sufficient storage capacity (the present study required 4.3 megabytes for the main data file), one could take the entire file to any archive or data source and dispense almost entirely with printed lists; setting search parameters in the data file would automatically present, in any desired order, the names to be checked in that source.

The use of a computer throughout such a study will also enable the researcher to do preliminary data analyses that could spot trends to be followed up, as well as expose those areas of the study where data-recovery rates were insufficient—an automatic "distant early warning" system.

In sum, powerful tools now permit extensive studies of the lives of ordinary people to be undertaken that only a few years ago would have been dismissed out of hand as wishful thinking or as technically impossible. One should also be aware that the subjects of these studies need not necessarily be people: businesses in general or by category would be eligible as well. These population studies are destined, and not only for Yankees—I look forward to them.

Appendix B

Unconsidered Trifles

This ends the lesson. I certify that I have done the best. If I had a chance to do it again I could do it better but as I never shall ask for it I am entirely out of the Road of improvement.
—George B. Randlette, enumerator of District 150, 1880 census of Maine, in a note attached to his returns (microfilm page 181 recto)

THE *numerous customers of H. T. Bonney & Co., Grocers, 456 Washington street, will be happy to learn that they have received another invoice of the Bavarian Co.'s Whiskey.*
—Boston Evening Transcript, 2 May 1862, 2/6

Social history stands at the threshold of tremendous advances. These will become ever more attainable as more and more people gain familiarity with computers and, because of this familiarity, become unwilling (or even unable, at some distant day) to deal with historical records that have not been transferred into media that are accessible electronically. Some optical scanners can already transform printed material into electronic impulses for computer manipulation so it does not seem too farfetched that someday a scanner able to read nineteenth-century handwriting may be unleashed upon manuscript census returns. The possibilities for studies, particularly of internal migration, are unlimited. With sufficient storage capacity and computing power, researchers could eventually link individuals from one household to another in the subsequent census, establishing decadal patterns of net intercensal migration. Historians would also learn, from the computer's failure to create linkages, just how good the nineteenth-century censuses were—or were not. Certainly population figures for that period would have to be raised, as the discussion in Appendix A suggests.

The present study, begun in the "dark ages" of social history (1972), has itself recapitulated centuries of progress in data manipulation, starting with 2,808 5"-×-8" data cards, carefully updated as information on their subjects was quarried out, and progressing to data entry into a personal computer and data manipulation by statistics and word-processing programs.

Just as a microscope can provide only so much magnification, nineteenth-century sources have limits. But as these sources are data-processed, it becomes easier for those who would manipulate them to become, or to remain, ignorant of their fragility and their incompleteness. We of today must keep in mind that people of the nineteenth century mostly did not share our passion for information. Their consumption of it, compared with that of modern individuals, was minuscule. Then only small proportions of the public read a newspaper daily; books were rare in many areas, and the post office handled an average of one letter per household per year.

Today we are saturated with information so that our attitudes toward it are vastly different; it is no longer exotic and expensive but abundant and cheap. We do not hold it in awe, but rather manipulate it readily, whether by watching television (and, increasingly, video-cassettes) or movies, listening to the radio, reading newspapers, magazines, or books, or by pressing on a computer keyboard. The danger lies in projecting our attitudes back into the minds of nineteenth-century people and thinking that, because we have mostly favorable attitudes toward statistical information, or census enumerators, or officials asking personal questions, nineteenth-century people must have shared these attitudes. Thus it is false to think that what they produced in the way of information may be as accurate as what we today produce, except that there was less of it then, and some of it has not survived.

I would suggest that anyone who believes strongly in the willingness or ability of nineteenth-century folk to participate in the great national census diversion has but to compare the information for the same household in successive manuscript population censuses (if indeed one can locate the household) to see that people's names, ages, and states of birth usually vary.[1] In fact, it is an exceptional household that provides consistent information. If this is the problem with such supposedly invariant characteristics as people's names, years of birth, and locations of birth, how much greater errors must lurk in other sources? Let us then be prudent, approaching any nineteenth-century information carefully, especially if it is capable of numerical manipulation, which could invest it with a specious plausibility.

Specifically, there are certain questions that seem worthwhile to have answered, particular research approaches that seem more promising than others, to which, after 23 years' exploration of this area, I would draw the attention of intending investigators.

With increased availability in coming years of death records for individuals who died in, say, the first third of the twentieth century, it should be possible to specify much more exactly the net *lifetime migration* of individuals, given their locales of birth and of death. Probably the most valuable work that could be done along these lines would involve the data-processing of the late nineteenth-century population censuses and their comparison with available mortality records so as to establish age-specific rates of migration and mortality for the period. It has become evident to me, from the examination and casual perusal of thousands of Massachusetts death records, that the patterns both of migration and of mortality, as inferred from general records, are skewed by the presence of minors. Their higher mortality rates, and the fact that they participated in, but presumably did not influence, family migration, are serious confounding factors in our attempts to understand both phenomena. Studies that sort out and differentiate the experiences of the two groups would be most valuable. Similarly, there are very likely considerable differences for the nineteenth century in migration and mortality by gender; here the linkage problems will be daunting, but perhaps computer programs may be devised that will link single women in one census to married women in the next, given common characteristics. Complete accuracy would not be required, provided that, say, a general level of about 75 percent could be reached (i.e., the researcher would be able to say, "The probability is very high that three-quarters of all these single women have been linked to this group of married women, but I can't tell you which links are correct," a sort of Heisenberg Uncer-

tainty Principle applied to linkage). For many purposes, a 75 percent
accuracy level is already pressing nineteenth-century sources close to
their limits.

Household formation, and especially marriage patterns, offer rich
possibilities. When sufficient pairings have been analyzed from a social, occupational, and even economic standpoint, we shall be much
better able to understand the position and function of marriage in the
nineteenth century. (The process of remarriage, by both widowers
and widows, would also amply repay the effort involved in selecting
subjects. It seems probable that widowers' selection criteria, as de-
duced from their choices, would be surprising, to say the least.) Here
again Boston has wonderful records to be analyzed: marriage intentions, beginning with 1849, have been preserved in addition to the
records of marriages. The numbers of intentions not followed by
marriages are striking. In most of these cases, of course, the marriage
occurred outside Boston, usually in the bride's hometown, but a certain proportion probably fell through. What were the characteristics
of these failed arrangements, and what do they reveal about the institution? Incidentally, since most intentions of marriage appear to have
been entered by the potential grooms (the records indicate the initials
of the applicant), one notes that many of them were ignorant of certain information about the women they intended to marry; usually
the most commonly omitted datum about the intended bride was her
town of birth, but I have seen records in which the names of the prospective bride's parents were lacking, others in which the intended
bride's age was absent, and one hilarious record in which her name
was marked (in pencil so as to be corrected later) "can't remember." Of course, this merely reinforces earlier observations about
nineteenth-century attitudes toward which information, if any, was
important.

The debate over *family limitation* suffers from a plethora of gener-
alization and a paucity of specificity. General figures for the numbers
of births in a given year or analysis of ratios of children to mothers in
the census reports are insufficient because the general figures are incomplete, the censuses are incomplete, and the censuses missed those
children who were born and died in the intercensal interval. Social
historians will learn about this phenomenon only by performing

large-scale data linkage, using birth, death, and census records to pick up not only missing births but also, from those birth and death records, households absent entirely from the census. If perhaps 20 percent of the native-born households were omitted from nineteenth-century censuses (as is contended in Appendix A), then should not 20 percent of births also have been missed? The Boston City Archives contains birth records for 1849–69 indexed by name of the child but also giving parents' names; this could be a valuable starting point, which would of course require reinforcement from other sources, such as state records, church records, and newspapers. Since the birth record also gives the birthplaces of the parents, linking them with the census would provide their approximate ages as well, giving insight into the timing and locus (rural or urban) of the onset of family limitation.

Occupation is yet another almost uncharted area deserving exploration. There would appear to be profound connections between men's occupations (especially their earliest occupations) and some of their behavior, connections that this study could only suggest because to have plumbed them would have involved additional years of effort. Which aspects of work—indoor or outdoor, manual or nonmanual, none of the above—were associated with those other activities? More detailed *wealth* data would be desirable in this respect: annual tax assessments would be just the thing, assuming that the researcher can allow for the intracity differences in assessing practices. Perhaps more important than assessment, and certainly easier to deal with, is real estate ownership. A inquiry into this was to feature in the present study, and I began gathering information on all the real estate transactions, during their lives, of the sample members. It rapidly became evident that they were heavily involved in such transactions, and the effort had to be scaled back lest it metastasize and absorb the entire project. Only the activities of the 408 sample members whose names began with "A" and "B" could be checked in the real-estate records of Suffolk, Middlesex, Norfolk, and Plymouth counties between about 1800 and 1910. Even then the process was reduced to a mere count of the numbers and types of transactions, which must have totaled several thousand for just these 408 men. Accordingly, I would urge detailed study of the real estate transactions of ordinary people, suggesting that because most of them were ineligible to use savings banks, mortgages may have provided a relatively safe alternative.

The processes of *death and dying*, especially among adults, need to be looked into carefully, perhaps beginning with large samples drawn from cemetery records so as to assure that correct death dates for husbands, wives, and children are obtained from state sources. Which diseases flourished in different areas? Can historians classify causes of death better than did nineteenth-century physicians? Given descriptions of symptoms, can modern physicians, working with social historians, help revise our understanding of those causes of death? Here again, the considerable differences as between adults and children call for careful separation.

I remain convinced, with no adducible proof, that close study of large numbers of *accidents* and accidental deaths (perhaps based on newspaper reports) would produce interesting information on the rate of integration of various kinds of machinery into American life. For example, was there a time late in the nineteenth century when individuals at last stopped walking down railroad tracks and being run down from behind by locomotives? What of people who, like *Isaac M. Farnham in Chapter 5, fell under trains just starting up? Both types of accidents are rare today, but when did they decline in frequency? Scuttle falls (Chapter 4) do not feature too much in today's news—what happened to them? The scope for a history of accidents, both at work and in the home, is great.

Last, I would warn those tempted to embark upon social-historical research that it can be addicting; whether it is also dangerous to *your* health only time will tell.

Appendix C

Missing Sample Members

The following members of the two population samples are absent from sample without leave. If you encounter any evidence of them (including marriage but especially death), kindly inform the author (Department of History, Vari Hall, York University, Downsview, Ontario M3J 1P3, Canada). They are listed in the format FAMILY NAME, first name, middle name or initial / year of birth / locality or state of birth / occupation(s) / name of first wife / year of birth of first wife / second wife, if known / location and date at which sample member was last known to be alive / other information (if any).

ALLEN, Daniel B. / 1844 / Maine / cabinet-maker / Caroline M. /1845 / San Francisco / 1876 / Caroline M. appears in 1880 San Francisco census as divorced

ATWOOD, Frederick Nelson / 1844 / Province-town, Massachusetts /painter, artist, interior decorator / Catherine N. McDermott / 1842 / Chicago / 1897 / Their children residing with another family in 1900 Chicago census

BAILEY, [Benjamin] Franklin / 1831 / Pittston, Maine / ship chandler / Adelaide S. Cox / 1837 / Boston / 1860 /Adelaide S. died 1896 in Taunton, Massachusetts

BATES, Robert K. / 1834 / New Hampshire / cook / Eliza / 1836 /Boston / 1861

BECKLER, Daniel W. / 1832 / Livermore, Maine / builder and stabler / Julia A. Judkins / 1833 / Boston / 1891 /Julia A. died 1891 in Boston

BECKWITH, Thomas D. / 1831 / Connecticut / laborer / Susan E. / 1832 / Boston / 1860

BLINN, James L. / 1828 / Boston / laborer, clerk, teamster / Elizabeth Lawrence / 1833 / Boston / 1865 / May have removed to Idaho

BOYCE, Sylvanus / 1830 / Vermont / machinist / Phebe Sweetser / 1829 / Springfield (Sangamon County), Illinois / 1870 census

BRYANT, Silas D. / 1820 / Rochester, New Hampshire / harness-maker / Mary J. Pinkham / 1817 / Des Moines, Iowa / 1882 / Mary J. died 1879 in Boston

BURGESS, Cornelius Simmons / 1814 / Little Compton, Rhode Island / carpenter / Susan De Witt / 1823 / Brooklyn, New York / 1866 / Susan listed as "widow" in 1869 Brooklyn city directory

CALEF, James Albert / 1812 / Hampstead, New Hampshire / merchandise weigher / Louisa Heath / 1811 / Boston / 1886

CLEVELAND, Thomas C. / 1830 / Massachusetts / carriage maker / Julia / 1835 / Boston / 1871

COFFIN, Henry J. / 1829 / Cherryfield, Maine / cabinetmaker, farmer / Harriet Merriam / 1834 / Richland, Nebraska / 1880 census / Harriet J. listed as widow in 1900 census of Calamus Precinct (Garfield County), Nebraska

COFFREN, Ariel / 1814 / New Hampshire / porter, store clerk / Hannah D. Cowdin / 1803 / Boston / 1870 / Hannah D. died 1875 in Boston

COLE, Samuel R. / 1818 / Middletown, Connecticut / saloonkeeper, trader / Catherine Welch / 1832 / Boston / 1860 census

COOK, George Dixson / 1825 / Kingston, Massachusetts / mason (brick) / Hannah Elizabeth Vinal / 1824 / Boston / 1880 / Hannah E. died 1878 in Boston

DAY, (Joseph) Addison / 1815 / Rockland, Maine / ship carpenter / Matilda Douglass / 1817 / Boston / 1880 census / Matilda D. died 1884 in Revere, Massachusetts

DEAN, James W. / 1832 / Maine / furniture dealer, laborer / Anna M. / 1832 / Boston / 1874

EATON, Julius C. / about 1837 / Maine / harnessmaker / Abbie / 1840 / Boston / 1873

ELLIS, Frederick A. / 1835 / Fairhaven, Massachusetts / bookkeeper, clerk / Abbie F. Banfield / 1840 / Washington, D. C. / 1907 (clerk in Treasury Department) / Abbie F. died 1913 in Acushnet, Massachusetts

EMERSON, Charles A. / 1830 / Boston / painter / Lucy A. Gardner / 1825 / second wife Ellen Cummings / 1832 / Boston / 1866 / Ellen was born in New York City

EMERSON, David D. / 1801 / Piermont, New Hampshire / pump maker, laborer / Sarah W. / 1808 / Boston / 1875

GETCHELL, Minot D. / 1842 / Wiscasset, Maine / mason (brick) / Celia L. Otis / 1847 / Tremont, Maine / 1880 census / He is buried in Southwest Harbor (Hancock County), Maine

GRIFFIN, Reuben P. / 1800 / Maine / blacksmith / Sally C. Hersey / 1810 / Boston / 1865

HADLEY (sometimes HADLEIGH), John H. / 1832 /Holden, Massachusetts / carpenter, machinist, farmer / Jemima Clampet / 1830 / Burlington, Massachusetts / 1880 census / May have taken a job as machinist in Haiti

HAMBLIN, Albert A. / 1833 / Portland, Maine / painter / Harriet A. Baston / 1837 / Boston / 1879

HARMON, Peter / 1831 / Maine / carpenter / Caroline / 1834 / Boston / 1870

HARRIS, George S. / 1816 / Caldwell, New York / agent of Missouri Land Company / Sarah F. / 1823 / Boston / 1864

HAVENER, Frank W. / 1849 / Rockland, Maine / baker, cook, steward / (Mrs.) Jane N. G. (Smith) Shaw / 1845 / Boston / 1900 census / Jane N. G. died 1884 in Boston

HAYDEN, Aaron B. / 1831 / Jay, Maine / tailor, pressman / Mary H. Orne / 1835 / Boston / 1870

HICKS, Richard C. / 1817 / New Hampshire / teamster / Abby Swain / 1816 / Boston / 1881 / Abbie S. died 1888, location unknown, and is buried in Exeter, New Hampshire

HODGKINS, Hall / 1811 / Damariscotta, Maine / ship carpenter / Mary L. Huse / 1817 / Boston / 1876 / Mary L. died 1906 in Boston

JACKSON, Theodore / 1841 / Plymouth, Massachusetts / bookbinder, ship steward / Mary J. Belknap / 1843 / Boston / 1882 /Mary J. is listed in 1890 Boston city directory as "widow of Theodore"

KIMBALL, John E. / 1805 / Concord, New Hampshire / broker, merchant / Lucy P. Heaton / 1817 / Boston / 1880 census / Lucy P. died 1866 in Boston

LAMBERT, Samuel / 1811 / Maine / laborer / Maria Frazer / 1822 / Boston / 1863

LEAVITT, Isaac / 1822 / Scituate, Massachusetts / printer, bootmaker / Hannah N. Snow / unknown / second wife Betsey A. Hussey / 1834 / Boston / 1871 / Betsey A. died 1886 in Boston

LEONARD, Job / 1824 / Taunton, Massachusetts / dentist / Betsey Ann Cook / 1826 / second wife Clarissa A. E. Furbush / 1831 / Dorchester / 1865 / Clarissa A. E. died 1880 in Boston

LEWIS, Samuel R. / 1837 / New York / chemist / Alwilda Coryell / 1842 / Boston / 1872

LITTLEFIELD, Seth Henry / 1847 / Brooklyn, New York / dry-goods salesman / Anna L. Rust / 1836 / Boston / 1871 / Anna L. died 1927 in Somerville, Massachusetts

MADISON, Otis / 1805 / New Hampshire / tailor / Joan / 1810 / Toronto, Ontario / 1870

MAIR, George H. / 1832 / Boston / bookkeeper / Sarah U. Copeland / 1830 / Salem, Massachusetts / 1876

MANSFIELD, James Bowes / 1817 / Newburyport, Massachusetts / tailor / Amanda J. Benner / 1827 / Boston / 1860 / Amanda J. died 1902 in Boston

MANSFIELD, Willard Lowell / 1841 / Standish, Maine / fresco painter / Susan E. Douglass [?] / 1840 / Boston / 1873 / A Willard L. Mansfield (1842–1916) is buried in West Fryeburg, Maine, together with his (second?) wife, Olive W. Charles (1853–1912), but this couple was not located in the 1880 census, so match, though likely, cannot be confirmed

METCALF, Charles H. / 1832 / Haverhill, New Hampshire / clothing salesman, commercial traveler / Nellie I. West / 1839 / Somerville, Massachusetts / 1881 / Nellie I. died 1915 in Wellesley, Massachusetts

MITCHELL, Horace M. B. / 1818 / Leeds, Maine / carpenter, stationary engineer / Sarah Giles / 1822 / Boston / 1873 / Sarah is listed as "widow" in 1880 Boston city directory; she died 1900 in Boston

MORRILL, Charles A. / 1814 / Canterbury, New Hampshire / schoolteacher / Susan S. Jackson / 1823 / Boston / 1866 / Susan S. J. shown as widow in 1880 Boston census

MORSE, James Anderson / 1814 / Westford, Vermont / teamster, laborer / Elizabeth H. Tucker / 1799 / second wife Lydia V. Tucker / 1810 / 1880 census of Boston (Charlestown Almshouse) / Lydia V.

died 1880 in Charlestown Almshouse / James A. is said to have
died 1889, no location specified

NEWELL, Samuel / 1824 / Sumner, Maine / bootmaker, clerk / Brittania Allen / 1826 / Boston / 1864 / Brittania died 1906 in Rockland, Massachusetts

PAGE, George S. / 1831 / Boston / machinist / Susan Ellen Porter /
1833 / Boston / 1860

PARKER, Jerome Westley / 1830 / Andover, Vermont / clerk, salesman, marketman, meat packer / Ann Eliza Wright / 1831 / Cambridge, Massachusetts / 1882 / Ann Eliza died 1879 in Cambridge, Massachusetts

PHILLIPS, Charles E. / 1836 / Orland, Maine / master mariner /
Mary J. / 1838 / Boston / 1870

QUIMBY, Melvin John (later John Melvin) / 1845 / Worcester, Massachusetts / clerk, waiter, bartender / Ellen E. Coughlan / 1845 /
Boston / 1874

RANDALL, Francis M. / 1820 / Bridgewater, Massachusetts / cook /
Elizabeth P. Waugh / 1821 / Boston / 1865 / Elizabeth P. died 1863
in Boston

RATHBUN, John Avery / 1816 / Charlemont, Massachusetts / machinist / Emily Daniels / 1823 / Roxbury, Massachusetts / 1860 census / See Chapter 4 epigraph

READ, Andrew / 1833 / Massachusetts / barber and hairdresser /
Elizabeth / 1833 / Boston / 1870

RICH, Abram / 1830 / Truro, Massachusetts / grocer, fish and oysters / Adelaide Mallard / 1831 / San Francisco / 1880 census (widower) / He is said to have died in 1891, no location specified

SEYMOUR, Oscar D. / 1830 / New York / jeweler / Sarah / 1835 /
Boston / 1863

SHERMAN, William Connor / 1837 / Belfast, Maine / jeweler / Ann
Frances Garland / 1846 / Boston / 1872 / Ann F. died 1874, no location specified

SIBLEY, Rodney / 1808 / Sutton, Massachusetts / clerk, physician,
boardinghouse proprietor, furniture dealer / Rebecca Avis Benedict / 1812 / Boston / 1871 / Rebecca A. died 1874 in Providence,
Rhode Island, as "widow of Rodney"

SMITH, Robert Rich / 1824 / Wellfleet, Massachusetts / mariner,
    grocer / Tamsin A. / 1825 / Boston / 1891
TRAVIS (also TRAVERSE), William Eldridge / 1832 / Natick, Massa-
    chusetts / teamster / Jane Armstrong / 1831 / Boston / 1880 / Jane
    died 1907 in Boston
VAN BUSKIRK, Daniel / 1823 / New York City / policeman, paper-
    maker / Maria / 1824 / Roxbury, Massachusetts / 1862 / He is listed
    in the 1870 and 1880 New York City directories as a paper dealer
    but was not located in the 1870 or 1880 censuses of that city; he
    appears to have moved to Long Island late in life
WADLEIGH, George Allen / 1820 / Salisbury, Massachusetts / whole-
    sale druggist / Mary Frances Molineaux / 1826 / Brooklyn, New
    York / 1881 / Mary F. died 1876 in Brooklyn
WARREN, John M. / 1835 / Hollis, Maine / painter / Mary A. Flem-
    ing / 1837 / Boston / 1865
WENTWORTH, Frank D. / 1830 / Massachusetts / carpenter / Mary
    F. / 1842 / Boston / 1872 / Mary F. died 1872 in Boston
WENTWORTH, Seth / 1835 / Milton, New Hampshire / stair builder /
    Mary Jane Keating / 1834 / Somerville, Massachusetts / 1885 /
    Mary J. died 1922 in Somerville; Seth was listed in 1885 as "(Cal.)"
WEST, Sidney / 1815 / Jay, Maine / peddler, fancy goods dealer /
    Roxanna McCoy /1802 (?) / Boston / 1861 / Roxanna is listed in the
    1865 Boston city directory
WILD, Washington / 1802 / Massachusetts / farmer, shoemaker /
    Ann B. Haynes / 1808 / Dorchester, Massachusetts / 1860 census /
    Ann B. died 1858 in Dorchester
WILEY, Moses H. / 1835 / Bucksport, Maine / cooper, clerk, cabi-
    net maker, patent agent / Linnie H. Niles / 1842 / Boston / 1872 /
    Linnie H. remarried in Boston, 1875
WOOL, James E. / 1830 / Boston / blacksmith / (Mrs.) Mary A.
    Vaughn / 1838 / Boston / 1872
YOUNG, Enoch B. / 1834 / Chatham, Massachusetts / caulker, mari-
    ner / Lydia A. Kenney / 1838 / Boston / 1860 / Lydia A. remarried
    in Harwich, Massachusetts, 1865
YOUNG, Nelson S. / 1845 / Charleston, Maine / pianomaker / Ade-
    laide Dumas / 1840 / Boston / 1870

Notes

INTRODUCTION

1. Until the advent of widespread immigration into New England after about 1845, the people included in this study were the typical, ordinary, everyday people who permeated the area. Demographic changes beyond their control, chiefly "population succession," rapidly made them atypical in New England's larger urban areas and eventually in many of its rural areas as well. At the midcentury, however, they, and probably everyone else, regarded "Yankees" as the typical people of New England. See chapter 1 of Barbara Miller Solomon's *Ancestors and Immigrants: A Changing New England Tradition* (1956. Reprint. Boston: Northeastern University Press, 1989).

2. About nine years into this study, I learned of Sture Martinius's *Peasant Destinies: The History of 552 Swedes Born 1810–12* (Stockholm: Almqvist & Wiksell International, 1977). Martinius gathered information about only the first 50 years of his subjects' lives; the adoption of half of his book's title, but little of its methodology, ensued, for Sweden's registration system, which began in the early nineteenth century, allows students of its demographic history to begin about where *Yankee Destinies* arrived after 15 years of research: lifetime residential and vital records are notionally available, at the parish level, for all Swedes.

3. Steven E. Kagle, *Late Nineteenth-Century American Diary Literature* (Boston: Twayne, 1988), is a good point of departure. Lewis O. Saum's *The Popular Mood of Pre–Civil War America* (Westport, Conn.: Greenwood Press, 1980), also deserves mention.

4. "We say to our readers, as you value health, life, and happiness, give due attention to thorough and frequent bathing and washing. See that every member of the family attends to it, at least once a month; once a week is better" (*New England Farmer* 1 [6 January 1849]: 29). Of course, few urban homes, even in Boston, possessed bathtubs so total immersion was impractical; for that one had to resort to public "bath rooms." For an unusual usage of such a room, see the newspaper item about *Nathaniel S. Lillie in Chapter 6.

5. *Portsmouth* (N.H.) *Morning Chronicle*, 5 October 1860, 2/1 (page 2, column 1). Perhaps people were putting on weight: "At the late exhibition of the

Franklin Institute [in Philadelphia] there were weighed upon the Fairbanks scales 15,349 men, aggregating 2,314,200 pounds; 17,437 women, aggregating 2,249,370 pounds; making the average weight of each man 149¾ [*sic*; should be 150¾] pounds, and of each woman 129 pounds" (*Boston Evening Transcript*, 21 December 1874, 1/7).

6. Daniel Wait Howe, revised by Gilman B. Howe, *Howe Genealogies . . . Abraham of Roxbury . . .* (Boston: New England Historic Genealogical Society, 1929), 59; 1860 census, Boston, Ward 11, household no. 386, p. 60; 1870 census, Boston, Ward 4, household no. 1311, pp. 229–30; death record of *Anson B. Hardy, 18 May 1876, Newton, Massachusetts Division of Vital Records and Statistics, vol. 284, p. 147. The absence of a child born to the Hardys in 1851–55 suggests that they had, and lost, one in Liverpool; this could be checked in the United Kingdom records.

7. Waldo Lincoln, *History of the Lincoln Family: An Account of the Descendants of Samuel Lincoln of Hingham Massachusetts, 1637–1920* (Worcester, Mass.: Commonwealth Press, 1923), 271–72.

8. Massachusetts Charitable Mechanic Association, *Annals of the Massachusetts Charitable Mechanic Association, 1795–1872, Published by Order of the Association* (Boston: Press of Rockwell & Churchill, 1892), 430.

9. Lincoln, *History of the Lincoln Family*, 272–73.

10. Boston Assessors's records: 1830 Ward 1 Valuation, p. 26; 1840 Ward 1 Transfer, p. 49; 1850 Ward 1 Transfer, p. 69; 1860 Ward 1, p. 117 (amounts for 1830 and 1840 have been doubled to allow for 50 percent valuation in those years); 1870 census, Boston, Ward 2, Part 2, household no. 573, p. 70. The assessment records for Boston are held at the Boston Public Library. The pre-1860 assessments were available since Lincoln, having served in *The Plain People of Boston*, happened to be chosen also for *Yankee Destinies*.

11. *Ephraim H. Hall, 10 March 1915, on Form 3–389 of the Bureau of Pensions; his file no. is WC 500–078, National Archives and Records Service, Washington, D.C.

12. Information from the Civil War pension file, no. WC 500–078, of *Ephraim H. Hall, National Archives and Records Service, Washington, D.C., and from 1850 census, Boston, Ward 11, household no. 988, p. 126, 1860 census, Boston, Ward 11, household no. 3602 (George L. Hall), p. 483, 1870 census, Boston, Ward 12, Part 2, household no. 1841, pp. 233–34, 1880 census, Boston, Ward 23, enumeration district 768, household no. 274, p. 31; Solomon Hall's death, 25 July 1861: Massachusetts Division of Vital Records and Statistics, Boston, vol. 149, p. 95. Civil war records of Edward G. and *Ephraim H. Hall are in Massachusetts Adjutant General, *Massachusetts Soldiers, Sailors, and Marines in the Civil War*, 9 vols. (Norwood/Boston: Norwood Press/Wright & Potter Printing Co., 1931–37), 1:36. (Ephraim's two younger brothers, Nicholas S. and Noah C., also served in the war.)

CHAPTER 1

1. See, for example, Rev. Edwin H. Chapin's *Moral Aspects of City Life. A Series of Lectures* . . . (New York: Henry Lyon, 1853), 97–116. There are also problems involved in specifying the marital characteristics of in- and out-migrants; these will be discussed in Chapter 5.

2. *The Berkshire Jubilee, Celebrated at Pittsfield, Mass. August 22 and 23, 1844* (Albany, N.Y., and Pittsfield, Mass.: Weare C. Little and E. P. Little, 1845), 234–42, lists some out-migrants from western Massachusetts and their residences.

3. Still the standard treatment is Percy W. Bidwell, "Population Growth in Southern New England, 1810–1860," *American Statistical Association Publications* 15 (December 1917): 813–39.

4. Those interested in rural living arrangements should consult Thomas C. Hubka, *Big House, Little House, Back House, Barn: The Connected Farm Buildings of New England* (Hanover, N.H.: University Press of New England, 1984); and Sally Ann McMurry's *Families and Farmhouses in Nineteenth-Century America: Vernacular Design and Social Change* (New York: Oxford University Press, 1988).

5. U.S. Census Office, Eighth Census (1860), *Agriculture of the United States in 1860* . . . (Washington, D.C.: U.S. Government Printing Office, 1864), 222.

6. Lee Soltow, *Men and Wealth in the United States, 1850–1870* (New Haven: Yale University Press, 1975), 41.

7. Soltow describes his selection process, ibid., 4–5. As more film accumulated on the take-up reel of the microfilm reader, toward the end of a reel the men sampled would have been chosen at longer intervals, but Soltow tried to allow for this by sampling from left-hand pages in going forward through the film and right-hand pages coming back. The intervals on the return trip through a reel would start out large, diminishing as the beginning of the film approached so that earlier parts of all reels were oversampled. Where comparisons were possible, his samples stacked up well against the published census results (ibid., 6–7).

8. Ibid., 76. Individuals reporting zero wealth are included in Soltow's averages. In 1850, about 65 percent of native-born farmers reported some real estate (ibid., 33).

9. Ibid., 76–77.

10. Ibid., 33.

11. See the hundreds of short biographies of deceased members in Massachusetts Charitable Mechanic Association, *Annals of the Massachusetts Charitable Mechanic Association, 1795–1892* (Boston: Press of Rockwell and Churchill, 1892), for variations on this central theme.

12. David W. Galenson, "Economic Determinants of the Age at Leaving

Home: Evidence from the Lives of Nineteenth-Century New England Manufacturers," *Social Science History* 11 (Winter 1987): 355–78. The average year
of birth for 290 of the men in the Van Slyck compilation Galenson used was
1815, which would correspond closely with that of the 1860 sample in the
present study.

13. 1850 census, East Livermore, Maine, household no. 18, p. 154, and Jay,
Maine, household no. 213, p. 69. Hayden seems to have been rather mobile;
his daughter Mary was born in Jay, Maine, in 1855, and he is listed in the
1860 Boston city directory as residing at 2 Cherry Street but was enumerated
in Lynn, Massachusetts, in the 1860 census. By 1870 his wife and son had
disappeared from his household (Ward 3, household no. 3135, p. 372). He
left Boston in 1870 or 1871 and could not be traced further.

14. An extended description of working "out" for another family from the
age of just under nine to 15 years, nine months, is in Asa G. Sheldon, *Life of
Asa G. Sheldon: Wilmington Farmer. In Two Arrangements* (Woburn, Mass.: E. T.
Moody, Printer, Journal Press, 1862), 23–71, quotation from p. 23. A reset
edition of this book is available under the title *Yankee Drover: Being the Unpretending Life of Asa Sheldon, Farmer, Trader, and Working Man, 1788–1870* (Hanover, N.H.: University Press of New England, 1988), where the quotation
appears on page 13.

15. Joseph F. Kett, *Rites of Passage: Adolescence in America, 1790 to the Present*
(New York: Basic Books, 1977), 32–33, has also remarked on the career delay
incidental to being a farmer's son.

16. Galenson, "Economic Determinants," 361.

17. This situation is discussed briefly in Clarence A. Day, *A History of Maine
Agriculture, 1604–1860* (Orono: University of Maine Press, 1954), 274; and
in Hal S. Barron, *Those Who Stayed Behind: Rural Society in Nineteenth-Century
New England* (New York: Cambridge University Press, 1984), 94–97. Both
suggest that youngest sons were more likely to take over the farm.

18. Barron states the situation starkly: "The average Chelsea [Vermont]
farmer at midcentury had five children and a farm that was not large enough
to support more than one completed family" (*Those Who Stayed Behind*, 94).

19. Thomas Low Nichols, *Forty Years of American Life, 1821–1861* (New
York: Stackpole Sons, 1937, a resetting of the second, 1874, edition of a work
that appeared first in 1864), 19.

20. Again, that in Barron's *Those Who Stayed Behind* appears to be the only
extended discussion of the problem.

21. "Persistence" measures the proportion (usually expressed as a percent-
age) of members of a group that remains in the same location (usually a community) after the passage of a certain time. In most studies of U.S. communities, the availability of decennial census information has established that
time as ten years, which figure will be understood henceforth.

22. There is ample scope to dig into the New England land-transfer records to learn how property passed from one generation to the next, as well as the extent of the market for farms sold out of a family. The period needed to be covered is later than that treated in Toby L. Ditz's *Property and Kinship: Inheritance in Early Connecticut, 1750–1820* (Princeton: Princeton University Press, 1986).

23. An affecting discussion of this situation by "J.H.D." appears in a letter, "Farmers' Sons," *New England Farmer* 22 (13 March 1844): 292.

24. For a full dose of this nostalgia, see Sons of New Hampshire, *Festival of the Sons of New Hampshire . . . November 7, 1849 . . .* (Boston: James French, 1850); or Sons of Vermont, Worcester, Massachusetts, *First Reunion of the Sons of Vermont, at Worcester, Mass., February 10th, 1874 . . .* (Worcester, Mass.: Charles Hamilton, Palladium Office, 1874). Tamara P. Thornton's *Cultivating Gentlemen: The Meaning of Country Life among Boston's Elite, 1785–1860* (New Haven: Yale University Press, 1989), arrived after my manuscript was completed. It is worthwhile to attempt to determine, perhaps using large-scale national samples from the 1850–80 censuses, whether the majority of young men and women departing the earlier-settled portions of the United States ended up in cities or on (other) farms.

25. U.S. Census Office, Seventh Census, *Statistical View of the United States . . .* (Washington, D.C.: Beverley Tucker, Senate Printer, 1854), 117, 114.

26. Massachusetts Secretary of the Commonwealth, *Abstract of the Census of the Commonwealth of Massachusetts . . . 1855 . . .* (Boston: *William White, 1857), 231–32.

27. Howard S. Russell, *A Long, Deep Furrow: Three Centuries of Farming in New England* (Hanover, N.H.: University Press of New England, 1976), 407.

28. *Boston Evening Transcript*, 27 September 1847, 2/1. See also Dale T. Knobel, *Paddy and the Republic: Ethnicity and Nationality in Antebellum America* (Middletown, Conn.: Wesleyan University Press, 1986).

29. The spread of "improvements" is discussed in chapters 8 and 9 of Clarence H. Danhof, *Change in Agriculture: The Northern United States, 1820–1870* (Cambridge, Mass.: Harvard University Press, 1969).

30. Calculated from U.S. Census Office, Eighth Census (1860), *Agriculture*, 222.

31. For an especially good example, see Charles Oliver Howe, *What I Remember* ([Fort Valley, Ga.?]: Privately published, 1928). Better known, but perhaps exaggerating somewhat the hardscrabble aspects of farm life, is Horace Greeley, *Recollections of a Busy Life: Including Reminiscences of American Politics and Politicians . . .* (New York: J. B. Ford, 1868). One marvels at the *chutzpa* involved in Greeley's later *What I Know of Farming: A Series of Brief and Plain Expositions of Practical Agriculture as an Art Based upon Science . . .* (New York: Tribune Association, 1871).

32. Typical discussions of farm "management" appear in *The American Farmer's New and Universal Hand-book: or, an Improved and Complete Guide . . .* (New York: Livermore, 1851); it was a popular topic in the *New England Farmer*, 1840–60. "L." of Boston's comment is in ibid. 2 (27 April 1850): 140.

33. The sketches in Massachusetts Charitable Mechanic Association, *Annals*, indicate that most of the "mechanics" acquired their initial training in the countryside and likely perfected their skills in Boston.

34. For an earlier period William J. Rorabaugh has remarked in *The Craft Apprentice from Franklin to the Machine Age in America* (New York: Oxford University Press, 1986), 7, that "artisans preferred to apprentice their sons to different trades to increase the possibility of family barter and to decrease family hardship should a particular trade succumb to hard times."

35. See Kett's suggestive discussion of some of these matters in his *Rites of Passage*, 14–36.

36. Harold F. Wilson, *The Hill Country of Northern New England: Its Social and Economic History, 1790–1930* (1936. Reprint. New York: AMS Press, 1967), details this transition.

37. Because I contend in Appendix A that underenumeration in nineteenth-century censuses was considerable, population figures are usually given approximately.

38. Figures for 1830 from Lemuel Shattuck, *Report to the Committee of the City Council Appointed to Obtain the Census of Boston for the Year 1845 . . .* (Boston: John H. Eastburn, City Printer, 1846), 54 (table dd); for 1870, see "Statistics of the City of Boston, Compiled from the Last United States Census, 1873," *Boston City Document* No. 54 (1873), tables XII and V.

39. That even contemporaries found the multiplicity of faiths bewildering is attested to by the publication of John Hayward's *The Book of Religions: Comprising the Views, Creeds, Sentiments, or Opinions, of All the Principal Religious Sects in the World, Particularly of All Christian Denominations in Europe and America . . .* (Boston: John Hayward, 1842). Unfortunately, the U.S. census has never included a question on religious affiliation so church membership estimates from the mid-nineteenth century are based on the number of seats reported in the structures owned by the various sects.

40. For an especially candid admission of the country newspapers' dependence on the Boston papers, albeit from rather late in the period, see *Portsmouth* (N.H.) *Morning Chronicle*, 15 June 1859, 2/2: "The more we clip from them, the more is our appreciation shown; and our adoption of their sentiments, evinces our approval."

41. For lists of expresses and stagecoaches, see Boston city directories, 1800 to 1860. There were also specialty publications aplenty, such as George P. Geer, comp., *Geer's Express Directory, and Railway Forwarder's Guide*, Vol. 1, *Containing the New England States* (Springfield, Mass.: C. R. Chaffee, 1858). A rare editorial page illustration, "An Huge Paw," in the *Boston Evening Transcript* of

25 July 1840 (p. 2, col. 1) suggests the city's early importance in transportation. The "paw"'s fingers were the Providence, Worcester, Lowell, and Eastern railroads and Cunard's line of European steamers, the first of which had docked 19 July.

42. Edward C. Kirkland, *Men, Cities and Transportation*, 2 vols. (Cambridge, Mass.: Harvard University Press, 1948).

43. Winifred J. Rothenberg, "The Market and Massachusetts Farmers, 1750–1855," *Journal of Economic History* 41 (June 1981): 283–314. Daniel Tarbell, who was active in Vermont in the 1840s before the railroad to Boston opened, says he traded actively between Vermont, Nashua, New Hampshire, and Lowell and Boston, dealing in pork, chickens, and butter. See his *Incidents of Real Life* (Montpelier, Vt.: Argus and Patriot Book and Job Printing Co., 1883), 27–29.

44. That this visiting was fairly common is suggested by the frequency with which witnesses in murder trials used relatives' visits to date events. See, e.g., *Leavitt Alley, defendant, Report of the Trial of *Leavitt Alley, Indicted for the Murder of *Abijah Ellis, in the Supreme Judicial Court of Massachusetts. Reported by Franklin Fiske Heard* (Boston: Little, Brown, 1875); and George C. Hersey, defendant, *Report of the Case of Geo. C. Hersey, Indicted for the Murder of Betsy Frances Tirrell, before the Supreme Judicial Court of Massachusetts . . . By James M. W. Yerrinton* (Boston: A. Williams, 1862).

45. This practice was becoming more frequent by 1880, as the manuscript census returns for Boston show. One wonders if the Boston School Committee were aware of it.

46. Here again, scattered bits of testimony from the murder trials are suggestive.

47. Melinde Lutz Sanborn, "The 1860 Census for Ward One, Boston, Massachusetts: Some Special Features and Flaws," *New England Historical and Genealogical Register* 142 (January 1988): 25–28, contains more detail on this ward.

48. Compare the listings in Ward 1 of the 1860 census of Boston with the nativity lists in the 1860 editions of Coolidge and Mansfield. These lists appear in the later single-volume editions, for Maine, New Hampshire, and Vermont, of Austin J. Coolidge and John B. Mansfield, *A History and Description of New England, General and Local . . . in Two Volumes*, Vol. 1, *Maine, New Hampshire, and Vermont* (Boston: Austin J. Coolidge, 1859). Volume 2 apparently never appeared; in 1860, Coolidge and Mansfield brought out individual volumes for the three states, their texts identical to those in the 1859 volume but containing, as appendixes, lists of about 2,600, 1,100, and 660 names, respectively, of natives of those three states residing in Boston and vicinity. Careful perusal of the *Boston Evening Transcript* and the *Boston Daily Advertiser* for late 1859 and early 1860 turned up no mention of the citywide canvass that must have been required to compile the lists.

49. For a typical complaint, see "Benedick," "In Search of Lodging," *Boston Evening Transcript*, 1 June 1850, 1/4.

50. John Modell and Tamara K. Hareven, "Urbanization and the Malleable Household: An Examination of Boarding and Lodging in American Families," in *Family and Kin in Urban Communities, 1700–1930*, ed. Hareven (New York: New Viewpoints, 1977), 164–86, especially 170–75. The observations on marriage patterns derive from my qualitative impressions after having looked through several thousand such records.

51. *Productive* is used here in the sense understood by contemporaries, i.e., as indicating those occupations turning out a tangible product. For examples and further discussion, see Richard P. Horwitz, *Anthropology toward History: Culture and Work in a 19th-Century Maine Town* (Middletown, Conn.: Wesleyan University Press, 1978), 86ff.

52. Coolidge and Mansfield, *History and Description of New England* (1860 editions).

CHAPTER 2

1. This harrowing experience at the age of 30 apparently had no lasting effect on Mrs. Warren, who died of apoplexy at the age of 77 years, 8 months, 13 days, 31 December 1902, in Dorchester (Boston City Archives, death no. 10971 of 1902).

2. These are the figures for Mrs. Hannah Chase of Unity, Maine, who died at the age of 106 (*New York Herald*, 23 July 1845, 3/1, and 26 July 1845, 1/6).

3. Jeremy Atack and Fred Bateman, *To Their Own Soil: Agriculture in the Antebellum North* (Ames: Iowa State University Press, 1987), 64.

4. *Boston Evening Transcript*, 30 September 1851, 2/3. The Flanderses apparently stayed together until 1880, when she died; he died in Boston in 1890. Their relationship would appear to have been stormy; Boston records indicate they were married there 22 January 1841 and 27 January 1856, suggesting that they may have been divorced in the meantime. The second marriage is noted as the second for both.

5. Massachusetts General Court, *The General Statutes of the Commonwealth of Massachusetts: Enacted December 28, 1859, to Take Effect June 1, 1860*, 2d ed. (Boston: Wright & Potter, 1873), 533. Major grounds for divorce included desertion (after five years' absence), adultery, impotence, extreme cruelty, habitual intoxication, and a spouse's being sentenced to serve five years or more in prison (ibid., 532).

6. Ellen K. Rothman, *Hands and Hearts: A History of Courtship in America* (1984. Reprint. Cambridge, Mass.: Harvard University Press, 1987), does not delve into how its subjects met, concentrating instead on analyzing their correspondence. More work on urban social institutions along the lines of Allan

S. Horlick's *Country Boys and Merchant Princes: The Social Control of Young Men in New York* (Lewisburg, Pa.: Bucknell University Press, 1975) is needed.

7. Massachusetts Adjutant-General, *Massachusetts Soldiers, Sailors, and Marines in the Civil War*, 9 vols. (Norwood/Boston: Norwood Press/Wright & Potter Printing Co., 1931–37), 1:385, 4:170. *Brown P. Stowell's Civil War pension file is no. XC-339-400, National Archives and Records Service, Washington, D.C. William H. H. Stowell, *The Stowell Genealogy* . . . (Rutland, Vt.: Charles E. Tuttle Co., 1970), 621–22. The report of *Stowell's fatal fire is in *Boston Evening Transcript*, 27 February 1873, 4/6–4/7, where his name is given as George B. The paper got it right two days later in "The Funeral of Mr. Brown P. Stowell," ibid., 1 March 1873, 8/2.

8. Lee Soltow, *Men and Wealth in the United States, 1850–1870* (New Haven: Yale University Press, 1975), 33, 70.

9. Ibid., 33, 77 (table 3.4).

10. Charles P. Huse, *The Financial History of Boston from May 1, 1822, to January 31, 1909* (Cambridge, Mass.: Harvard University Press, 1916), tabulates the real estate and personal estate valuations for 1822 to 1908 on pages 376–77.

11. For the conditions surrounding incorporation of larger firms before the advent of a general incorporation law, see George Heberton Evans, Jr., *Business Incorporations in the United States, 1800–1943* (New York: National Bureau of Economic Research, 1948). Several of my conclusions about the organization of firms were anticipated by Evans's "A Sketch of American Business Organization, 1832–1900," *Journal of Political Economy* 60 (December 1952): 475–86. Exhaustive detail is in Edwin M. Dodd's *American Business Corporations until 1860 with Special Reference to Massachusetts* (Cambridge, Mass.: Harvard University Press, 1954). Massachusetts's first general incorporation law was passed in 1851 (ibid., 385–87).

12. The Dun credit reports at the Harvard Graduate School of Business Administration, Boston, are depressing in that they reveal mercilessly the undercapitalization of so many entrepreneurs. The first study to quantify the extensive turnover in nineteenth-century businesses (and in partnerships) was Ruth G. Hutchinson, Arthur R. Hutchinson, and Mabel Newcomer, "A Study in Business Mortality: Length of Life of Business Enterprises in Poughkeepsie, New York, 1843–1936," *American Economic Review* 28 (September 1938): 497–514.

13. It has proved difficult to learn when almost half the wives who predeceased their husbands died. Many of them may have returned to their families out of state for care during a terminal illness and died there, thus evading the Massachusetts registration system; hence in Table 2.7 I have resorted to a regression equation.

14. Ruth Schwartz Cowan, *More Work for Mother: The Ironies of Household Technology from the Open Hearth to the Microwave* (New York: Basic Books,

1983), shows in chapter 2 how the preparation of food and the maintenance of a household were so time-consuming that men unversed in household techniques (probably the vast majority) would not have been able to perform their work outside the home and then return home to undertake domestic tasks as well. Thus men were virtually forced to obtain a housekeeper (paid or unpaid) or a maid as soon as their wives died, and if their children were still young, widowers were likely to remarry within a year or two.

15. This compares with an average interval for remarriage of 1.9 years for men (5.6 years for women) in Newburyport during the first decades of the nineteenth century, as reported in Susan Grigg, "Toward a Theory of Remarriage: A Case Study of Newburyport at the Beginning of the Nineteenth Century," *Journal of Interdisciplinary History* 8 (Autumn 1977): 217.

16. To quote from but one of a multitude of advice manuals, William A. Alcott's anonymously published *The Moral Philosophy of Courtship and Marriage. Designed as a Companion to the "Physiology of Marriage." By the Same Author* (Boston: John P. Jewett, 1857), 9: "In matrimonial life we are not only to increase and multiply ourselves by doubling, trebling, and quadrupling our own physical, moral, and intellectual efficiency, but we are also to increase and multiply the race numerically."

17. Contemporary comments were sparse, but the bitter tone of "Babies vs. Houses," *Boston Evening Transcript*, 24 October 1845, 2/4, is outstanding: "Our landlords, it would seem, have commenced a war of extermination against children." This study cannot, of course, determine why couples decided to limit the numbers of their children, but for a suggestive treatment of some of these matters, see Donald H. Parkerson and Jo Ann Parkerson, "'Fewer Children of Greater Spiritual Quality': Religion and the Decline of Fertility in Nineteenth-Century America," *Social Science History* 12 (Spring 1988): 49–70.

18. The earliest reports of the Boston city registrar, which began with that for 1849, treat this topic as already well known.

19. Atack and Bateman, *To Their Own Soil*, 49–50.

20. Carl N. Degler, *At Odds: Women and the Family in America from the Revolution to the Present* (New York: Oxford University Press, 1980), chap. 8, esp. pp. 187–94. The strongest predictor of the interval to first birth was the groom's age at marriage (significant at the 0.003 level); the bride's age was significant only at the 0.249 level. But in analyzing the total number of children produced in fruitful first marriages, the strongest predictor was the wife's age at birth of the first child, as compared with husband's age at that birth. This relationship holds for all sample members' first marriages contracted after 1828; for all first marriages contracted after 1827, 1826, and so on, the husband's age at the birth of the first child is the stronger predictor. This suggests the possible temporal locus of an important change in nineteenth-century marital behavior.

21. Atack and Bateman, *To Their Own Soil*, 63 (table 4.3).

CHAPTER 3

1. In 1860 Solomon Piper was assessed for $158,200 in real and $75,000 in personal property; his firm was assessed for $22,000 in personal property. See Boston Assessors, *List of Persons, Copartnerships, and Corporations, Who Were Taxed on Ten Thousand Dollars and Upwards, in the City of Boston, in the Year 1860 . . .* (Boston: Geo. C. Rand & Avery, City Printers, 1861), 99.

2. Charles P. Huse, *The Financial History of Boston from May 1, 1822, to January 31, 1909* (Cambridge, Mass.: Harvard University Press, 1916), 376, and information from 1860 assessment records. Since the native-born made up about 44 percent of the city's heads of household, or about 14,800 (Peter R. Knights, *The Plain People of Boston, 1830–1860: A Study in City Growth* [New York: Oxford University Press, 1971], 36), 54 percent of that figure would amount to about 8,000, leaving 6,800 native-born heads of household to be taxed for more than a poll tax. Allowing another two or three thousand for sons of these men, it appears that, as late as 1860, well over 90 percent of the men in Boston who were taxed for any property must have been native-born.

3. Boston Assessors, *List of Persons, 1860*. The top 472 taxpaying entities (over $102,199 in valuation) were assessed for $110,674,700, or 46.7 percent, of Boston's total valuation. As a rough approximation, those individuals, groups, and organizations assessed for $100,000 or more accounted for about half the city's valuation as of 1860.

4. The assessment records for Boston for 1860 and 1870 were consulted at the Boston Public Library (details appear in Appendix A). For Roxbury in 1860 the manuscript census returns, supplemented by information in the 1860 Roxbury city directory, were used. For Dorchester the source was Dorchester, Massachusetts, Assessors, *The Taxable Valuation of the Real and Personal Estates, with the Polls and Amount of Tax, in the Town of Dorchester, for the Year 1861* (Boston: David Clapp, Printer, 1861). *Edward Jarvis's "On the System of Taxation Prevailing in the United States, and Especially in Massachusetts," *Journal of the Statistical Society of London* 23 (September 1860): 370–78, was encountered after the manuscript was completed.

5. Manuscript population censuses: 1850, Gardiner, Maine, household no. 306, p. 551; 1860, Gardiner, Maine, household no. 92, p. 12; 1870, Boston, Ward 8, household no. 928, pp. 137–38 of part 2; 1880, Alameda (Alameda County), California, household no. 260, enumeration district 31, p. 24; Massachusetts Division of Vital Records and Statistics: vol. 198, p. 91 (birth of Mary J. Jaquith, 4 December 1867); vol. 483, p. 172 (death of *Silas B. Jaquith, 16 April 1898); George O. Jaquith and Georgetta J. Walker, *The Jaquith Family in America* (Boston: New England Historic Genealogical Society, 1982), 136, 206–7.

6. Manuscript population censuses: 1850, Dover, New Hampshire, household no. 1263, p. 160; 1860, Boston, Ward 2, household no. 2829, p. 350;

1870, Boston, Ward 1, household no. 1171, p. 138 of part 2; 1880, Everett, Massachusetts, household no. 317, enumeration district 389, p. 30; Massachusetts Division of Vital Records and Statistics, vol. 347, p. 89 (death of *Silas Foss, 17 January 1883).

7. Manuscript population censuses: 1850, Boston, Ward 12, household no. 2065, p. 719; 1860, Boston, Ward 12, household no. 729, p. 94; 1870, Boston, Ward 16, household no. 1836, p. 221; Massachusetts Division of Vital Records and Statistics, vol. 312, p. 2 (death of Mrs. Mary J. [Pinkham] Bryant, 2 January 1879). Inquiry to Cedar Grove Cemetery, where Mrs. Bryant is interred, revealed that Silas is not buried there. The purchase of the Clarence Place house is detailed in the land records of Norfolk County, vol. 334, p. 247 (25 August 1865), Norfolk County Courthouse, Dedham.

8. Massachusetts Secretary of the Commonwealth, *Statistical Information Relating to Certain Branches of Industry in Massachusetts, for the Year Ending June 1, 1855* (Boston: *William White, 1856), 455 (blacksmiths), 458 (harnessmakers); Massachusetts Secretary of the Commonwealth, *Abstract of the Census of the Commonwealth of Massachusetts . . . 1855 . . .* (Boston: *William White, 1857), 165 (horses).

9. Massachusetts Secretary of the Commonwealth, *Abstract of the Census, 1855*, 163.

10. Those with strong stomachs and an inquiring disposition may wish to peruse *New England Grocer*, comp., *The Grocer's Companion and Merchant's Hand-Book. Containing a Comprehensive Account of the Growth, Manufacture and Qualities of Every Article Sold by Grocers . . .* (Boston: New England Grocer Office, 1883), to learn what nineteenth-century Bostonians might have ingested.

11. Boston Assessors, *List of Persons, 1860*, 86. The last volume of this useful series seems to be that covering 1865.

12. Unfortunately, the census enumerators were very remiss in collecting wealth statistics in Boston in 1870; several wards are virtually innocent of such data. The last printed assessment report, for 1865, indicates that S. & W. Meriam & Co. was assessed for $30,000 in personal property. Silas P. was not listed on his own, perhaps because the minimum amount required for inclusion had risen to $20,000 (Boston Assessors, *List of Persons, Copartnerships, and Corporations, Who Were Taxed on Twenty Thousand Dollar and Upwards, in the City of Boston, in the Year 1865* [Boston: J. E. Farwell, 1866], 87).

13. Manuscript population censuses: 1850, Boston, Ward 4 (downtown), household no. 697, p. 396; 1860, Boston, Ward 4, household no. 63, p. 14; 1870, Boston, Ward 4, household no. 1060, pp. 167–68; Massachusetts Division of Vital Records and Statistics, vol. 366, p. 69 (death of *Silas P. Meriam, 9 March 1885); Charles Henry Pope, comp., *Merriam Genealogy in England and America . . .* (Boston: The Compiler, 1906), 138, 225–26. Information on assessment of S. P. & W. Meriam & Co. from Boston Assessors, *List of Persons, 1860*, 86. Silas P. Meriam's last daughter did not wed until he was 75 years old.

14. Massachusetts Bureau of Statistics of Labor, *Comparative Wages and Prices: 1860–1883. Massachusetts and Great Britain. [From the Sixteenth Annual Report of the Massachusetts Bureau of Statistics of Labor.]* (Boston: Wright & Potter Printing Co., 1885), 46. The U.S. Bureau of Labor Statistics's "Consumer Prices: All Items" index for 1860 is 27, for 1870, 38 (1967 = 100), suggesting an advance of about 40 percent in the decade. U.S. Bureau of Economic Analysis, *Long Term Economic Growth, 1860–1970* (Washington, D.C.: U.S. Government Printing Office, 1973), 222.

15. Manuscript population censuses: 1850, Boston, Ward 10, household no. 2733, p. 954; 1860, Roxbury, Massachusetts, Ward 5, household no. 1702, p. 209; 1870, Boston, Ward 16, household no. 848, p. 105; 1880, Boston, Ward 24, household no. 238, enumeration district 776 and 777, pp. 23–24; Massachusetts Division of Vital Records and Statistics: vol. 46, p. 200 (marriage of Silas S. Putnam to Anna Maria Whitmarsh, Abington, 19 December 1850); vol. 73, p. 267 (birth of Silas S. Putnam [Jr.], 4 August 1853); vol. 456, p. 231 (death of *Silas S. Putnam, 10 June 1895). Mrs. Anna M. Putnam's parents, Joshua and Harriet Whitmarsh, appear in the 1850 manuscript population census of Abington at household no. 67, p. 354. Joshua Whitmarsh is listed under "boot and shoe manufacturers" in *The New-England Mercantile Union Business Directory . . . for the Year 1849 . . .* (New York: Pratt, 1849), 119.

16. Roger Lane indicates that a policeman's pay in the early 1850s was $2 a day, twice that of a master mason, so if one could remain on the force long enough, one could expect to accumulate (*Policing the City: Boston, 1822–1885* [Cambridge, Mass.: Harvard University Press, 1967], 76).

17. Lee Soltow, *Men and Wealth in the United States, 1850–1870* (New Haven: Yale University Press, 1975), 72. On page 74 he suggests using, as a good approximation, a growth rate for individual wealth of 4.5 percent per year.

18. These successful men's careers are suggested in Robert F. Dalzell, Jr.'s *Enterprising Elite: The Boston Associates and the World They Made* (Cambridge, Mass.: Harvard University Press, 1987).

19. The trends in native-born flight, first from the city's core areas to its periphery in the 1840s and then to the nearer suburbs in the 1850s, have been outlined in Knights, *Plain People of Boston*, 103–18, particularly table VI-6, p. 112.

20. See Charles J. Kennedy, "Commuter Services in the Boston Area, 1835–1860," *Business History Review* 36 (Summer 1962): 153–70. The commuter-oriented railroads also advertised extensively in the *Boston Evening Transcript* and in the *Boston Directory*. Henry C. Binford, *The First Suburbs: Residential Communities on the Boston Periphery, 1815–1860* (Chicago: University of Chicago Press, 1985), is also apposite.

21. Count Adam G. de Gurowski, *America and Europe* (New York: D. Appleton, 1857), 371. One may wonder if the Count knew of the activities of the

Dun credit-reporting agency, dedicated to the proposition that not too many of those who were dusting themselves off would mulct others after so doing.

22. Ezra S. Stearns, *History of Plymouth, New Hampshire* . . . , 2 vols. (Cambridge, Mass.: University Press for the Town, 1906), 2:288. See also Jesse A. Barney, *Rumney, Then and Now History* (Rumney, N.H.: Published by the Town, 1967), 168. The late Mr. Barney offered much encouragement in the early days of this study.

23. Stearns, *History of Plymouth, New Hampshire*, 2:288–89; 1860 census, Roxbury, Massachusetts, Ward 1, household no. 615, p. 73; 1870 census, Plymouth, New Hampshire, household no. 18, p. 2; 1880 census, Rumney, New Hampshire, household no. 199, enumeration district 99, p. 22; New Hampshire Department of Health and Welfare, death certificate of *Asa K. George, Rumney, 23 September 1901. Asa K. George's parents, William and Mary, were enumerated in the 1850 census in Plymouth, New Hampshire, household no. 7, p. 341.

24. Manuscript population censuses: 1850, Lyme, New Hampshire, household no. 926, p. 124 (parents in Norwich, Vermont, household no. 136, p. 242); 1860, Roxbury, Massachusetts, Ward 1, household no. 1191, p. 139 (household no. 1200, p. 140, for William H. Mathews); 1870, Boston, Ward 13, household no. 171, p. 22; 1880, Everett, Massachusetts, household no. 303, enumeration district 388, p. 28. Massachusetts Division of Vital Records and Statistics, 1908, vol. 35, p. 168 (death of *Philander C. Mathews, 28 December 1908); vol. 243, p. 55 (birth of Clara Frances Mathews, 22 August 1872, giving mother's birthplace as Danbury, New Hampshire).

25. R. G. Dun & Co., credit reports, Massachusetts Volume 76, p. 221, R. G. Dun & Co. Collection, Baker Library, Harvard University Graduate School of Business Administration, Boston. Quoted by kind permission of Dun & Bradstreet Co. This is the most scathing credit report I have seen.

26. 1850 census, Barrington, New Hampshire, household no. 756, p. 510; 1860 census, Canton, Massachusetts, household no. 1849, p. 222; 1870 census, Boston, Ward 9, household no. 1665, p. 230; Barrington Historical Society, comp., *Graveyards of Barrington, New Hampshire* (Barrington: Barrington Historical Society, 1976), 25. Chesley is not listed in the Dover, New Hampshire, directories of 1880–92; perhaps he was back in Barrington.

27. A brief history of the early days of the MCMA is in Massachusetts Charitable Mechanic Association, *Annals of the Massachusetts Charitable Mechanic Association, 1795–1892* (Boston: Press of Rockwell and Churchill, 1892), 1–14. The question of masters' decreasing authority over their apprentices is treated in William J. Rorabaugh, *The Craft Apprentice from Franklin to the Machine Age in America* (New York: Oxford University Press, 1986), esp. in chap. 2, "The Master's Authority."

CHAPTER 4

1. *Boston Evening Transcript*, 9 June 1851, 1/5–1/6, and 12 June 1851, 2/3. To complete the tragedy, Dr. *Cummings served in the Civil War as a surgeon with the Forty-second Massachusetts Volunteer Militia, was taken prisoner at Galveston, Texas, in 1863, and died that year in a Confederate prison (Massachusetts Adjutant-General, *Massachusetts Soldiers, Sailors, and Marines in the Civil War*, 9 vols. [Norwood, Mass./Boston: Norwood Press/Wright & Potter Printing Co., 1931–37], 4:153).

2. See "Stealing Dead Bodies," *New York Herald*, 30 April 1845, 1/5. The Luke Hall mentioned there was *Seth's father, "a town pauper." This was ironic in that Seth himself was a sexton.

3. On this topic I wish to acknowledge several illuminating discussions during the summer of 1964 with the late William E. Branen, president-editor of the *Burlington* (Wis.) *Standard-Press*. Richard A. Schwarzlose of the Medill School of Journalism, Northwestern University, has also greatly influenced my thinking on nineteenth-century newspapers and newspapering. His *The Nation's Newsbrokers*, 2 vols. (Evanston, Ill.: Northwestern University Press, 1989–90) represents a quantum advance in U.S. communications history. For a commonsense discussion of some of these matters, Martin Mayer's *Making News* (Garden City, N.Y.: Doubleday, 1987), chap. 2, is helpful.

4. Joseph E. Chamberlin, *The Boston Transcript: A History of Its First Hundred Years* (Boston: Houghton Mifflin, 1930). *Dutton was much more interested in the newspaper side of the business than was Wentworth, who died in 1847 (ibid., p. 106). His heirs sold their interest to Dutton. A brief notice of Wentworth is in Joseph T. Buckingham, comp., *Annals of the Massachusetts Charitable Mechanic Association* (Boston: Press of Crocker and Brewster, 1853), 377n.–378n. Some of the *Transcript*'s business records are at the Baker Library, Harvard Graduate School of Business Administration, Boston, where I spent the summer of 1965 working with them.

5. Chamberlin, *Boston Transcript*, 102, suggests that the *Transcript* was beginning to show some antislavery leanings as early as mid-1849, but the tone of the paper under editor Epes Sargent (1847–53) was antiblack, and reports critical of the antislavery movement were given space. I date the paper's "conversion" as having occurred early in the editorial stint of Daniel N. Haskell (1853–74). For a taste of the contemporary storm in Boston over the Burns incident, see Charles Emery Stevens, *Anthony Burns. A History* . . . (1856. Reprint. Williamstown, Mass.: Corner House Publishers, 1973).

6. They married in Boston 22 September 1847, both aged about 32, and had three children between 1847 and 1853. William Richards, who listed himself in the 1860 census as a "gentleman," with $98,000 in real and $18,000 in personal estate, claimed "no occupation" in the 1870 enumeration but had

moved up to $150,000 in real and $15,000 in personal estate. The household contained two female servants in 1850, 1860, and 1870, another indication of the family's high economic position. Richards died 22 June 1877, aged 61 years, eight months, of inflammation of the liver; his wife survived him. See "A Register of Marriages in Boston from 1800 to 1849," 2:270, in Boston City Archives, Boston City Hall; 1850 census, Boston, Ward 4 (downtown), household no. 152, p. 272; 1860 census, Boston, Ward 6, household no. 307, p. 56; 1870 census, Boston, Ward 6, household no. 279, p. 47; death record of *William Bordman Richards, Boston, Massachusetts Division of Vital Records and Statistics, vol. 294, p. 120.

7. This population shift was real: foreigners made up 5.6 percent of the city's population in 1830, the not naturalized accounted for 10.3 percent in 1835, and foreigners and their children amounted to 32.6 percent in 1845. In 1850, it is estimated that 47.3 percent of the city's households were headed by foreign-born; by 1860 this had advanced to 55.6 percent and by 1870 to 59.6 percent (Peter R. Knights, *The Plain People of Boston, 1830–1860: A Study in City Growth* [New York: Oxford University Press, 1971], 35–36; 1835 figures are from *The Boston Almanac, for the Bissextile Year 1836* . . . [Boston: S. N. Dickinson, 1836] [no pagination]; 1870 estimate from a sample of 386 household heads drawn for, but not used in, Knights, *Plain People of Boston*).

8. *Boston Evening Transcript*, 15 October 1850, 2/4.

9. Gerald N. Grob, *Edward Jarvis and the Medical World of Nineteenth-Century America* (Knoxville: University of Tennessee Press, 1978), chapter 5, sketches the general situation regarding the insane at midcentury. But see also Massachusetts Commission on Lunacy, *Report on Insanity and Idiocy in Massachusetts, by the Commission on Lunacy, under Resolve of the Legislature of 1854* (Boston: *William White, Printer to the State, 1855).

10. The pattern seems similar to that described in Charles E. Rosenberg's *The Cholera Years: The United States in 1832, 1849, and 1866* (Chicago: University of Chicago Press, 1962). See also Charles Francis Adams, Jr., *Notes on Railroad Accidents* (New York: G. P. Putnam's Sons, 1879), and for a completely "modern" approach, including early photographs, Massachusetts Board of Railroad Commissioners, *Special Report by the Massachusetts Board of Railroad Commissioners to the Legislature in Relation to the Disaster on Monday, March 14, 1887 . . . at . . . the Bussey Bridge* (Boston: Wright & Potter Printing Co., 1887). Quotation from Stephen Salsbury, *The State, the Investor, and the Railroad: The Boston & Albany, 1825–1867* (Cambridge, Mass.: Harvard University Press, 1967), 183.

11. *John K. Porter narrowly escaped injury at home one morning when the boiler of his cooking range exploded while a plumber was trying to thaw its frozen pipes; apparently it got chilly at night in his house (*Boston Evening Transcript*, 21 January 1857, 2/7).

12. *Boston Evening Transcript*, 26 July 1867, 1/7. The cause of death was

listed as "paraplegia—7 weeks." See death record of *Thomas Palmer, 24 July 1867, Boston, Massachusetts Division of Vital Records and Statistics, vol. 204, p. 95.

13. *Boston Evening Transcript*, 10 April 1861, 1/8. (Libby lived to be 84 and died in 1903.)

14. *Boston Evening Transcript*, 9 September 1859, 4/3. *Dexter R. Dearing (the correct spelling), a longtime member of the Fire Department (Arthur W. Brayley, *A Complete History of the Boston Fire Department . . . from 1630 to 1888 . . .* [Boston: John P. Dale, 1889], 719–20), seems otherwise to have been a reliable sort (Boston Commissioners Appointed to Investigate the Cause and Management of the Great Fire in Boston, *Report of the Commissioners Appointed to Investigate the Cause and Management of the Great Fire in Boston* [Boston: Rockwell & Churchill, City Printers, 1873], 124–27, 518).

15. See Boston Commissioners Appointed to Investigate the Cause and Management of the Great Fire in Boston, *Report*. Many witnesses testified as to the rapidity with which flames spread through the first building to be consumed (pp. 7, 14, 18, 40, 42, 70–71, etc.).

16. *Boston Evening Transcript*, 27 June 1853, 2/5.

17. Ibid., 29 April 1864, 4/2. Ryerson was to survive another 12 years, dying at home of "many infirmities" and congestive pneumonia on 7 May 1876, at the age of 68 years, 8 months (Massachusetts Division of Vital Records and Statistics, vol. 285, p. 113). He was, by the way, his father's twenty-fourth (and last) child (Albert W. Ryerson, comp., *The Ryerson Genealogy* [Chicago: Privately printed, 1916], 102).

18. *Boston Evening Transcript*, 16 October 1857, 4/2.

19. Ibid., 7 December 1846, 2/3; for examples of camphene-initiated fires, usually causing fatalities, see ibid., 10 March 1852, 1/4; 20 August 1852, 2/1; 26 June 1854, 2/4; 4 October 1856, 1/4; 21 October 1856, 2/4; and *Portsmouth* (N.H.) *Morning Chronicle*, 15 August 1860, 2/3. There is a brief but comprehensive discussion of camphene in Harold F. Williamson and Arnold R. Daum, *The American Petroleum Industry: The Age of Illumination, 1859–1899* (Evanston, Ill.: Northwestern University Press, 1959), 33–37. A fascinating work on safety in the home remains to be written.

20. From the beginning of Boston's electric fire-alarm system, 28 April 1852, through 31 December 1859, 1,304 alarms were sounded, or about 14 per month. This accords well with the impression one gets from reading the newspapers, suggesting that fires too small to require an alarm went unreported in the press. "The larger number of fires occur between six o'clock P.M. and six o'clock A.M. . . . Of the days of the week, the larger number of alarms occur on Tuesdays, and the next in number on Saturdays. This may be accounted for from the fact that Saturday is baking-day, and Tuesday is generally apportioned to ironing,—both requiring more intense fires than upon other days, excepting, perhaps Monday, washing-day, when there is

always plenty of water for subduing any fires which may occur" (George B. Prescott, *History, Theory, and Practice of the Electric Telegraph* [Boston: Ticknor and Fields, 1860], 246–48).

21. For information on the development of the city's water supply, see Nelson M. Blake, *Water for the Cities: A History of the Urban Water Supply Problem in the United States* (Syracuse, N.Y.: Syracuse University Press, 1956), 172–218; and Fern L. Nesson, *Great Waters: A History of Boston's Water Supply* (Hanover, N.H.: University Press of New England for Brandeis University, 1983), 1–14. For the Great Fire of 1872, consult Boston Commissioners Appointed to Investigate the Cause and Management of the Great Fire in Boston, *Report*. Christine M. Rosen has examined the political struggles following that fire in *The Limits of Power: Great Fires and the Process of City Growth in America* (New York: Cambridge University Press, 1986).

22. There are vivid descriptions of Boston's major fires to 1856 in *David D. Dana, *The Fireman: The Fire Departments of the United States, with a Full Account of All Large Fires, Statistics of Losses and Expenses . . .* (Boston: E. O. Libby, 1858), 23–35. The annual *Boston Almanac*s listed major fires as well.

23. *Boston Evening Transcript*, 12 May 1845, 2/2–2/3. The *Seth Hall in this story is the same whose father's body had been disinterred by resurrectionists back in his old hometown only about three weeks previously; 1845 was none too pleasant a year for Seth.

24. Ibid., 30 April 1867, 1/5.

25. *Boston Daily Bee*, 28 June 1856, 2/4. The hackman, Edward L. Dennie, was held in $1,200 bail for trial (*Boston Evening Transcript*, 3 July 1856, 2/3). No report of the outcome was located. It is interesting to contrast this report with modern stories of what happens when moneybags being delivered by armored truck are spilled.

26. *Boston Evening Transcript*, 13 May 1853, 2/3.

27. Edwin T. Freedley, ed., *United States Mercantile Guide. Leading Pursuits and Leading Men. A Treatise on the Principal Trades and Manufactures of the United States . . .* (Philadelphia: Edward Young, 1856), 306–7.

28. Reliable figures are sparse, but "from a record of all the [nation's] railroad and steamboat accidents, for a period of fourteen and a half consecutive months, ending March, 1854, the following results have been obtained: The whole number of railroad accidents was 190; killed, 268; wounded, 624. The whole number of steamboat accidents during the same period was 48; killed, 691; wounded, 225" (David A. Wells, ed., *Annual of Scientific Discovery: or, Yearbook of Facts in Science and Art for 1855 . . .* [Boston: Gould & Lincoln, 1855], 44). This information may have appeared originally in the *New York Herald* of 27 March 1854. For details on railroad accidents, see Robert B. Shaw, *A History of Railroad Accidents, Safety Precautions and Operating Procedures*, 2d ed. (Potsdam, N.Y.: The author, 1978).

29. Wolfgang Schivelbusch, *The Railway Journey: Trains and Travel in the 19th*

Century (1979. Reprint. Berkeley: University of California Press, 1986), contains interesting insights. The philosophy of "preventable accidents" is summed up strongly by *John A. Haven, editor of the (Boston) *American Railway Times*, in "Prevention of Railway Accidents," *American Railway Times* 3 (13 November 1851): 2/1–2/2.

30. *Boston Daily Advertiser*, 6 December 1861, 4/1. Not until just after the end of the Civil War did most readers learn that Sturtevant's business affairs were in disarray all through 1861 and that he was very agitated and concerned about them (ibid., 29 April 1865, 1/6–1/7).

31. *Boston Evening Transcript*, 30 June 1859, 2/4; the family's correct name was Child.

32. See, for example, the case of *Isaac M. Farnham, described in Chapter 6.

33. Boston City Council, *The Railroad Jubilee. An Account of the Celebration Commemorative of the Opening of Railroad Communication between Boston and Canada, September 17th, 18th, and 19th, 1851* (Boston: J. H. Eastburn, City Printer, 1852).

34. Edward H. Savage, comp., *Boston Events. A Brief Mention and the Date of More Than 5,000 Events That Transpired in Boston from 1630 to 1880 . . .* (Boston: Tolman & White, Printers, 1884), 124.

35. See, e.g., "More Accidents," *Boston Evening Transcript*, 2 August 1856, 2/2.

36. *Boston Daily Advertiser*, 21 December 1861, 1/8. Those just starting to read about nineteenth-century criminals may enjoy John B. Lewis and Charles C. Bombaugh, *Remarkable Stratagems and Conspiracies: An Authentic Record of Surprising Attempts to Defraud Life Insurance Companies* (New York: G. W. Carleton, 1878); George S. McWatters, *Knots Untied: or, Ways and By-ways in the Hidden Life of American Detectives* (Hartford, Conn.: J. B. Burr & Hyde, 1872); and George P. Burnham, *Memoirs of the United States Secret Service . . .* (Boston: Laban Heath, 1872).

37. *Boston Evening Transcript*, 21 October 1850, 2/3.

38. Ibid., 12 April 1852, 2/3.

39. Ibid., 21 May 1850, 2/2; one John Connor was later arrested for the crime and held for trial; the outcome is unknown (ibid., 27 May 1850, 2/4).

40. Ibid., 18 May 1853, 2/4.

41. Ibid., 28 March 1853, 2/5. Franklin medals were awarded to the best scholars of Boston Latin [High] School. Licett probably defecated on the Saffords's carpet, behavior sometimes observed among present-day burglars.

42. *Boston Daily Advertiser*, 23 November 1865, 1/6. *Gilman Page, a mason, died, aged 82, in 1881. The other assault occurred, apparently, on *Theodore H. Badlam in the summer of 1854. Its outcome was reported in the *Boston Evening Transcript*, 28 August 1854, 2/5.

43. *Andrew H. Adams was last listed in the Milwaukee city directory in

1869, and his first listing in the Chicago city directory was for 1873. According to his Dun credit report, he spent at least part of the hiatus in Wisconsin's Waupun prison (R. G. Dun & Co., credit reports, Illinois Volume 43 p. 11 [Ottoman Cahvey Co.], R. G. Dun & Co. Collection, Baker Library, Harvard University Graduate School of Business Administration, Boston). *Charles C. Beers is in the 1850 census, Wethersfield, Connecticut, household no. 325 (State Prison), p. 146, line 3. *Lot Boody may be found in the 1850 census for Charlestown, Massachusetts, household no. 3466 (State Prison), p. 442.

44. *Boston Evening Transcript*, 3 July 1854, 1/7.

45. Ibid., 21 November 1854, 2/5.

46. Census listings for *Spencer R. Brown, all in East Boston: 1850, Ward 4, household no. 1248, p. 152; 1860, Ward 2, household no. 1100, pp. 133–34; 1870, Ward 1, part 1, household no. 1937, p. 237; 1880, Ward 1, enumeration district 581, household no. 268, p. 31. Brown was a native of Old Point Comfort, Virginia, and died 5 September 1891, aged 83 years, 11 months (Boston, Massachusetts Division of Vital Records and Statistics vol. 420, p. 306).

47. *Leavitt Alley, defendant, *Report of the Trial of *Leavitt Alley, Indicted for the Murder of *Abijah Ellis, in the Supreme Judicial Court of Massachusetts* (Boston: Little, Brown, 1875); Savage, comp., *Boston Events*, 103. *Leavitt Alley had served during the Civil War in the First New Hampshire Volunteer Heavy Artillery; his widow received a pension from 1890 until her death in 1915 (WC 304–995, National Archives and Records Administration, Washington, D.C.). There would seem to be considerable potential in studying transcripts of nineteenth-century murder trials to determine just which sorts of arguments and evidence juries found convincing and which not; such a study could help construct a "social perception of reality" for the period.

48. Boston Commissioners Appointed to Investigate the Cause and Management of the Great Fire in Boston, *Report*, 2–3.

CHAPTER 5

1. Edmund J. Cleveland and Horace G. Cleveland, *The Genealogy of the Cleveland and Cleaveland Families . . .* , 3 vols. (Hartford, Conn.: Case, Lockwood & Brainard, 1899), 1:110, 227. For an example of Reverend Cleveland's activities as a privately financed missionary, see *Charles Cleveland, *Thirty-Third Annual Report of Rev. Charles Cleveland, Missionary. For the Year Ending June 30, 1866* (Boston: *T. R. Marvin & Son, 1866). For his obituary, see *Boston Evening Transcript*, 5 June 1872, 4/2.

2. Gilman B. Howe, *Genealogy of the Bigelow Family of America, from . . . 1642 . . . to the Year 1890* (Worcester, Mass.: Charles Hamilton, 1890), 267. Bigelow's obituary is in the *Boston Evening Transcript*, 5 July 1872, 2/4.

3. The persistence rate for native-born in the 1850s fell to the low 40 percent range. Peter R. Knights, *The Plain People of Boston, 1830–1860: A Study in City Growth* (New York: Oxford University Press, 1971), table IV-10 (p. 63). (This work proved indispensable to the present study.)

4. Civil War pension files could probably be mined systematically for information on how disabled men got by. Certainly some of them among the 299 Civil War veterans in the study samples relied much more on the kindness of friends than one would suspect. Perhaps employing a wounded or incapacitated veteran gained the employer social merit. Disproportionate numbers of these men appear to have obtained government employment.

5. 1850 census, Salem, Massachusetts, Ward 3, household no. 347, p. 267; 1860 census, Salem, Massachusetts, Ward 5, household no. 3963, p. 1140 (Mrs. Rebecca Farley); 1870 census, Boston, Ward 13, household no. 203, p. 26; 1880 census, Salem, Massachusetts, Ward 5, household no. 272, enumeration district 239, p. 28; death of Sarah (Smith) Farley, 9 August 1876, Boston, Massachusetts Division of Vital Records and Statistics, vol. 285, p. 193; second marriage of Joseph L. Farley, 11 December 1878, Salem, ibid., vol. 298, p. 272; death record of *Joseph L. Farley, 18 March 1896, Salem, ibid., vol. 463, p. 585. (No first-marriage record was located for Farley in Massachusetts after 1850.)

6. *Boston Daily Advertiser*, 18 August 1864, 1/7; 1860 census, Boston, Ward 6, household no. 359, pp. 62–63; 1870 census, Brooklyn, N.Y., Ward 6, household no. 122, p. 236 recto; death record of *Samuel S. Stevens, Boston (resident of Babylon, N.Y.), 30 December 1907, Massachusetts Division of Vital Records and Statistics, 1907, vol. 22, p. 601.

7. Frederick O. Conant, *A History and Genealogy of the Conant Family in England and America* . . . (Portland, Me.: Privately printed, 1887), 381, 479. Census listings: 1850: Springfield, Massachusetts, household no. 388 (New England House, listing 13), p. 44; 1860: Boston, Ward 10, household no. 827, p. 119; 1870: Springfield, Massachusetts, Ward 1, household no. 418, p. 49; 1880: Springfield, Massachusetts, enumeration district 309, p. 26, household no. 316; death record of *Ruel K. Conant, 23 February 1894, Springfield, Massachusetts Division of Vital Records and Statistics, vol. 445, p. 734. (Although the Conants spent only seven or eight years in Boston, like about 90 percent of couples in the study who were both in-migrants and out-migrants, all of their children—three—were born there.)

8. Conant, *History and Genealogy of the Conant Family*, 292–93, 385. Census listings: 1850: Danvers, Massachusetts, household no. 25, p. 4; 1860: Boston, Ward 1, household no. 1471, p. 187; 1870: Boston, Ward 3, household no. 2010 (fourth listing), p. 230 (Mrs. Conant and Eliza); Council Bluffs, Iowa, Ward 2, household no. 42, p. 36 recto (Mr. Conant); 1880: Council Bluffs, Iowa, Ward 4, household no. 302, enumeration district 194, p. 29; 1900: Council Bluffs, Iowa, enumeration district 139, p. 5, line 68 (from Soundex

index); death record of *Nathaniel P. Conant, 27 September 1902, Council Bluffs, State of Iowa Department of Health Certificate no. 78-02-201, filed 1 September 1903. Mrs. Conant was last listed in the 1871 Boston city directory. One assumes she died before Iowa's death registration system began.

9. The modern analogy is the continuation in the telephone directory of a listing under the name of a deceased head of household.

10. John Wentworth, *The Wentworth Genealogy: English and American*, 3 vols. (Boston: Little, Brown, 1878), 2:275–76. Census listings: 1850: Milton, N.H., household no. 179, p. 231; 1860: Boston, Ward 11, household no. 1312, p. 190; 1870: Boston, Ward 9, household no. 289, p. 38; 1880: Somerville, Ward 2, household no. 143, enumeration district 487, p. 334 recto; death record of Mary Jane (Keating) Wentworth, 9 March 1922, Somerville, Massachusetts Division of Vital Records and Statistics, 1922, vol. 72, p. 92, and inquiry to Cambridge (Massachusetts) Cemetery.

11. Death record of Mary T. (Vaughan) Smith, 8 December 1852, Boston City Archives, death no. 3485 of 1852; marriage of *Sidney Smith and Mrs. Eliza Ann Anders, 27 January 1853, Boston, Massachusetts Division of Vital Records and Statistics vol. 71, p. 22; death record of *Sidney Smith, 5 December 1869, Wrentham, ibid., vol. 221, p. 295; census returns: 1850, Farmington, Maine, household no. 346, p. 386; 1860, Boston, Ward 5, household no. 244, pp. 34–35.

CHAPTER 6

1. This motto is usually translated as "The end depends upon the beginning."

2. Relevant studies include John W. Florin, *Death in New England: Regional Variations in Mortality* (Chapel Hill: University of North Carolina Department of Geography, 1971); David E. Stannard, ed., *Death in America* (Philadelphia: University of Pennsylvania Press, 1975); and James J. Farrell, *Inventing the American Way of Death, 1830–1920* (Philadelphia: Temple University Press, 1980).

3. U.S. Bureau of the Census, *Historical Statistics of the United States, Colonial Times to 1970* (Washington, D.C.: U.S. Government Printing Office, 1976), 56.

4. Warren Wilkinson's *Mother, May You Never See the Sights I Have Seen: The Fifty-seventh Massachusetts Veteran Volunteers in the Army of the Potomac 1864–1865* (New York: Harper & Row, 1990), which appeared after this section was completed, contains short biographies of over 1,000 of that regiment's members, including Major *James W. Cushing. The postwar life spans of many of them seem to have been all too short. Growing interest in the demographic aspects of the Civil War is evidenced by Maris A. Vinovskis's

"Have Social Historians Lost the Civil War? Some Preliminary Demographic Speculations," *Journal of American History* 76 (June 1989): 34–58.

5. For a quick overview of this process, see Peter R. Knights, "Ethnic Massachusetts," in *The Commemorative Guide to the Massachusetts Bicentennial* (Boston: Yankee Press, 1974), 74–77. The process of suburbanization is featured in Sam Bass Warner, Jr.'s *Streetcar Suburbs: The Process of Growth in Boston, 1870–1900* (Cambridge, Mass.: Harvard University Press and MIT Press, 1962), a vivid demonstration of how far a historian may advance on the basis of mundane data—in this case, building permits.

6. Obituary of *Gardner Brewer, *Boston Evening Transcript*, 30 September 1874, 4/1; death of *Gardner Brewer, 30 September 1874, cancer, aged 68 years, 5 months, Newport, Rhode Island Division of Vital Statistics, certificate no. 1036, 3 July 1980.

7. *Boston Evening Transcript*, 9 September 1873, 1/6. His correct name was Franklin R. Moody; his occupation was sawyer. Although he came from Vassalborough, Maine, and had married his Boston-born wife in 1853, the Moodys spent most of the late 1850s and all of the 1860s in Illinois and Minnesota, returning to Boston in 1870 (1870 census, Boston, ward 12, part 2, household no. 92, p. 11; death record of *Franklin B. Moody, 9 September 1873, aged 49 years, 5 months, 28 days, of "fracture of arm, leg, etc.," Boston City Hospital, Massachusetts Division of Vital Records and Statistics, vol. 258, p. 193).

8. *Boston Evening Transcript*, 27 August 1863, 4/2. Farnham's correct name was Isaac M. (Death record of *Isaac M. Farnham, 26 August 1863, aged 59 years, 3 months, 21 days, "accidental," Boston, Massachusetts Division of Vital Records and Statistics, vol. 167, p. 114).

9. *Boston Evening Transcript*, 7 November 1876, 8/2; death record of *John M. Whorf, 10 November 1876, aged 53 years, 10 months, of "injury to back and chest," Boston, Massachusetts Division of Vital Records and Statistics, vol. 285, p. 268.

10. See the excellent discussion of deciding when a "suspicious" death was really a suicide in Roger Lane, *Violent Death in the City: Suicide, Accident, and Murder in Nineteenth-Century Philadelphia* (Cambridge, Mass.: Harvard University Press, 1979), 13–21.

11. *Boston Evening Transcript*, 11 May 1876, 4/3; death record of *Nathaniel S. Lillie, 11 May 1876, "suicide at Quincy House," aged 45 years, 9 months, Boston, Massachusetts Division of Vital Records and Statistics, vol. 285, p. 115.

12. *Boston Evening Transcript*, 2 December 1875, 1/4; death record of *Robert W. Dresser, 1 December 1875, "pistol wound," aged 46 years, 10 months, Newton, Massachusetts Division of Vital Records and Statistics, vol. 275, p. 172. In the 1870 census Dresser claimed $50,000 in personal estate but no

real estate (1870 census, Boston, Ward 11, part 1, household no. 92, p. 12).

13. Massachusetts Secretary of the Commonwealth, *Fifty-Ninth Report of Births, Marriages and Deaths in Massachusetts . . . for the Year 1900* (Boston: Wright & Potter Printing Co., 1901), unnumbered page following title page.

14. Massachusetts State Board of Health, *Twenty-Eighth Annual Report of the State Board of Health of Massachusetts* (Boston: Wright & Potter Printing Co., 1897 [pp. 711–829 contain Samuel W. Abbott's "The Vital Statistics of Massachusetts. A Forty Years' Summary {1856–1895}"]). This article is conveniently reprinted in the anonymous compilation *The Demographic History of Massachusetts* (New York: Arno Press, 1976).

15. Death record of *Charles A. Huckins, "exhaustion from chronic dementia," aged 72, 19 November 1901, Medfield Asylum, Massachusetts Division of Vital Records and Statistics, vol. 518, p. 60. Huckins was a native of Ossipee, New Hampshire.

APPENDIX A

1. A recent guide and a good starting point is Ralph J. Crandall, ed., *Genealogical Research in New England* (Baltimore: Genealogical Publishing Co., 1984), which has a chapter on each of the six states.

2. Professor Russell E. Chace of my department has kindly offered advice on personal computer strategy and tactics over the last few years.

3. Boston city directories listed clergymen in a separate table. For the rest of New England, see *The New-England Mercantile Union Business Directory for the Year 1849 . . .* (New York: Pratt, 1849), *The New England Business Directory . . .* (Boston: Adams, Sampson, 1860; Sampson, Davenport, 1871, 1881). There are other *New England Business Directories* for 1856, 1865, 1868, 1873, 1875, 1877, and 1879—at least. For New Hampshire, see Nathan F. Carter, *The Native Ministry of New Hampshire . . .* (Concord, N.H.: Rumford Printing Co., 1906). The names of the clergymen who officiated at the sample members' marriages could probably be recovered by several months' work because I did record date and location of marriage; anyone wishing to salvage these data should apply to me.

4. Caren A. Ginsberg, "Estimates and Correlates of Enumeration Completeness: Censuses and Maps in Nineteenth-Century Massachusetts," *Social Science History* 12 (Spring 1988): 71–86, by comparing county atlases (which presumably listed mostly landowners) with the manuscript census, produces estimates of completeness of enumeration for seven small western Massachusetts towns in 1870 that average to 81.5 percent. For comprehensive evidence of the ad hoc arrangements for the censuses of 1850–80, see Margo J. Anderson, *The American Census: A Social History* (New Haven: Yale University Press, 1988), 32–100. A recent example of failure to criticize the complete-

ness of the manuscript census occurs in the otherwise comprehensive study by Richard G. Lowe and Randolph B. Campbell, *Planters and Plain Folk: Agriculture in Antebellum Texas* (Dallas: Southern Methodist University Press, 1987), which discusses various possible shortcomings of the authors' samples of about 5,000 households each from the 1850 and 1860 population censuses of Texas (pursued, with admirable pertinacity, into the agricultural and slaveholding returns), but does not consider the possibility of underenumeration in those population censuses. Possibly this occurred because the authors drew independent samples and did not attempt linkage from 1850 to 1860 or vice versa. The 1989 Social Science History Association meetings devoted a session to census inadequacies; doubtless some of its papers will be published.

5. My York University colleague Gerald A. Ginsburg has been working on this approach for Buffalo, New York, as of 1855.

6. Ronald Vern Jackson and Gary Ronald Teeples, eds., *Massachusetts 1850 Census Index* (Bountiful, Utah: Accelerated Indexing Systems, 1978). Joseph F. Kett, *Rites of Passage: Adolescence in America, 1790 to the Present* (New York: Basic Books, 1977), 96–102, reports some of his early findings on the Sons of New Hampshire.

7. Paul F. Bourke and Donald A. DeBats of the Flinders University of South Australia are investigating this problem, using a large collection of poll books from several states. See their "The Structures of Political Involvement in the Nineteenth Century: A Frontier Case," *Perspectives in American History*, n.s. 3 (1987): 207–38, which indicates a census undercount for adult (white) males in Washington County, Oregon, of about 15 percent in 1860 (p. 212). A study received during manuscript preparation, Kenneth J. Winkle, *The Politics of Community: Migration and Politics in Antebellum Ohio* (New York: Cambridge University Press, 1988), pursues the matter even further: in Clinton Township, Ohio, the persistence of white adult males, 1850–60, was but 27 percent, and "the U.S. census recorded the addition of only 200 new voters to Clinton Township's electorate between 1850 and 1860. But in fact over 800 new voters arrived and departed during the same decade" (pp. 92–93).

8. Gerald A. Ginsburg, "Computing Antebellum Turnout: Methods and Models," *Journal of Interdisciplinary History* 16 (Spring 1986): 579–611, has attempted to point this out for voter turnout studies. He met a less than enthusiastic reception from Walter Dean Burnham, "Those High Nineteenth-Century American Voting Turnouts: Fact or Fiction?" ibid., 613–44.

9. Robert Gutman, *Birth and Death Registration in Massachusetts, 1639–1900* (New York: Milbank Memorial Fund, 1959), is the basic source. For an example of what clever manipulation of admittedly incomplete and defective statistics can produce, see Maris A. Vinovskis, *Fertility in Massachusetts from the Revolution to the Civil War* (New York: Academic Press, 1981).

10. See Crandall, ed., *Genealogical Research*. Since the appearance of that work, Roger D. Joslyn, FASG, has compiled *Vital Records of Charlestown Mas-*

sachusetts to the Year 1850, Vol. 1 (Boston: New England Historic Genealogical Society, 1984). A second volume is planned. (Boston annexed Charlestown in 1874.)

11. See Dorothea N. Spear, comp., *Bibliography of American Directories through 1860* (Worcester, Mass.: American Antiquarian Society, 1961). A similar listing for 1861 to 1901 would be a boon to researchers.

12. Peter R. Knights, *The Plain People of Boston, 1830–1860: A Study in City Growth* (New York: Oxford University Press, 1971), 127–39.

13. For a comprehensive introduction, see Richard A. Schwarzlose, *Newspapers: A Reference Guide* (Westport, Conn.: Greenwood Press, 1987).

14. Although it is outdated, Library of Congress Catalogue Division, comp., *American and English Genealogies in the Library of Congress: Preliminary Catalogue* (Washington, D.C.: U.S. Government Printing Office, 1910), is handy for checking quickly whether there was then a nineteenth-century genealogy or family history for a specific family. Secondhand copies of this and other editions of this reference work were still cheap at the time of writing.

15. Two outstanding exceptions are Edmund J. Cleveland and Horace G. Cleveland, *The Genealogy of the Cleveland and Cleaveland Families . . .* , 3 vols. (Hartford, Conn.: Case, Lockwood & Brainard, 1899); and Charles H. Farnam, *History of the Descendants of John Whitman of Weymouth, Mass.* (New Haven, Conn.: Tuttle, Morehouse & Taylor, Printers, 1889).

16. This summary is based on my examination and use of these volumes over a two-year period in the late 1960s and further visits to them in their new home during the summers of 1987 and 1988, as well as on the sheets "Directions for Assessing Taxes," found in some of the "Street" volumes.

17. Stanley French, "The Cemetery as Cultural Institution: The Establishment of Mount Auburn and the 'Rural Cemetery' Movement," in David E. Stannard, ed., *Death in America* (Philadelphia: University of Pennsylvania Press, 1975), 69–91.

18. David P. Davenport, "Tracing Rural New York's Out-Migrants, 1855–1860," *Historical Methods* 17 (Spring 1984): 62–65.

19. David P. Davenport, "Census Indexes: Research Boon or Bane?" manuscript, ca. January 1990. Professor Davenport generously sent me a copy.

20. For an example of this approach, see Richard H. Steckel, "Census Matching and Migration: A Research Strategy," *Historical Methods* 21 (Spring 1988): 52–60, which used 1850 census indexes to trace 59 percent of a sample, drawn from the 1860 census, back to the 1850 census, then analyzed the characteristics of the linked and nonlinked households. Given that all of the households being traced backward were in existence as of 1850 and then contained at least one child, the linkage rate seems very low and likely reflects on the poor quality of the 1850 census indexes rather than on the diligent researcher.

21. Charles Stephenson, Richard J. Jensen, and Janice Reiff Webster, "So-

cial Predictors of American Mobility: A Census Capture-Recapture Study of New York and Wisconsin, 1875–1905," 2 vols., mimeographed (Chicago: Newberry Library Family and Community History Center, May 1978).

22. Here one should consult the various articles and the forthcoming book of John W. Adams and Alice B. Kasakoff.

23. See Warren Wilkinson, *Mother, May You Never See the Sights I Have Seen: The Fifty-seventh Massachusetts Veteran Volunteers in the Army of the Potomac, 1864–1865* (New York: Harper & Row, 1990), which is just such a work.

24. There are some amusing cartoons and anecdotes suggesting popular reactions to the census enumerator in U.S. Bureau of the Census, *Twenty Censuses: Population and Housing Questions, 1790–1980* (Washington, D.C.: U.S. Government Printing Office, 1979).

25. Professor J. Morgan Kousser, California Institute of Technology, in his helpful comments on the present study, suggested "Microsoft Works 2.0" as combining word processing, statistics, and a spreadsheet.

APPENDIX B

1. One may also glean some notion of popular attitudes toward the census from press comments about it. Two humorous items, both titled "Taking the Census," appeared in the *New England Farmer* 24 (6 August 1845): 48, and 24 (20 August 1845): 64. The *Boston Evening Transcript* carried a series of letters and complaints about the Boston city census of 1845: 12 June, 2/2–2/3; 13 June, 2/1–2/2; 14 June, 2/1–2/2; 17 June, 2/2–2/3; 20 June, 4/1; 24 June, 2/2–2/3. The newspaper's reaction to the published report appeared 18 May 1846, 2/1. By 1850, fewer humorous items seem to have been published. The *Transcript* of 6 June 1850, 4/2, reprints one. Its editorial comment on the Boston city census of 1855 was favorable (25 April 1855, 2/1). U.S. Bureau of the Census, *Twenty Censuses: Population and Housing Questions, 1790–1980* (Washington, D.C.: U.S. Government Printing Office, 1979), 6, reprints an amusing cartoon from the 18 August 1860 *Saturday Evening Post*. There seem to be no scholarly studies of popular reception of the census in the nineteenth century.

Bibliography

Principal Printed Sources Consulted

The archival and other unpublished materials employed in this study are discussed and summarized in Appendix A. Here are listed nineteenth-century printed works that proved useful. Only a few of the many Massachusetts community vital records volumes and no family histories or genealogies are listed below because they are numerous.

NINETEENTH-CENTURY MATERIALS

(as in the text, members of the samples are marked*)

Abbott, Jacob. *Gentle Measures in the Management and Training of the Young; or, the Principles on Which a Firm Parental Authority May Be Established.* . . . New York: Harper & Brothers, 1871.

Alcott, William A. *The Moral Philosophy of Courtship and Marriage. Designed as a Companion to the "Physiology of Marriage." By the Same Author.* Boston: John P. Jewett, 1857.

———. *The Young House-keeper, or Thoughts on Food and Cookery. By* . . . *Sixth Stereotype Edition.* Boston: Waite, Peirce, 1846.

———. *The Young Woman's Guide to Excellence* . . . *Thirteenth Edition.* Boston: Charles H. Peirce, Binney & Otheman, W. J. Reynolds, 1847.

Alexander, James Waddell. *The Working-man. By Charles Quill, Author of "The American Mechanic."* Philadelphia: Perkins & Purves, 1843.

Allen, Richard L. *The American Farm Book: or Compend of American Agriculture; Being a Practical Treatise on Soils, Manures, Draining, Irrigation, Grasses, Grain, Roots, Fruits* . . . *and Every Staple Product of the United States.* . . . New York: C. M. Saxton, Barker, 1860.

*Alley, Leavitt, defendant. *Report of the Trial of *Leavitt Alley, Indicted for the Murder of *Abijah Ellis, in the Supreme Judicial Court of Massachusetts. Reported by Franklin Fiske Heard.* Boston: Little, Brown, 1875.

The American Farmer's New and Universal Hand-Book: or, an Improved and Complete Guide. . . . New York: Livermore, 1851.

Anspach, Frederick Rinehart. *The Sons of the Sires; A History of the Rise, Prog-ress, and Destiny of the American Party, and Its Probable Influence on the Next Presidential Election.* . . . Philadelphia: Lippincott, Grambo, 1855.

Appletons' Illustrated Hand-Book of American Travel: A Full and Reliable Guide by Railway, Steamboat, and Stage, to . . . *the United States and the British Provinces. By T. Addison Richards. With Careful Maps.* New York: D. Appleton, 1857.

Ayer, James Bourne. **James Ayer In Memoriam: Born October 4, 1815 Died De-cember 31, 1891.* N.p. [Boston?]: Privately printed, 1892.

Baldwin, Thomas, and J. Thomas, comps. *A New and Complete Gazetteer of the United States; Giving a Full and Comprehensive Review of the Present Condition, Industry, and Resources of the American Confederacy.* . . . Philadelphia: Lippin-cott, Grambo, 1854.

Beecher, Catharine E. *A Treatise on Domestic Economy, for the Use of Young La-dies at Home, and at School. By Miss* . . . *Revised Edition, with Numerous Addi-tions and Illustrative Engravings.* Boston: Thomas H. Webb, 1842.

Beecher, Henry Ward. *Norwood; or, Village Life in New England.* New York: Charles Scribner, 1868.

The Berkshire Jubilee, Celebrated at Pittsfield, Mass. August 22 and 23, 1844. Al-bany, N.Y., and Pittsfield, Mass.: Weare C. Little and E. P. Little, 1845.

**Bigelow, Erastus B. *Remarks on the Depressed Condition of Manufactures in Massachusetts, with Suggestions as to Its Cause and Its Remedy.* Boston: Little, Brown, 1858.

Blake, Rev. John L. *The Farmer's Every-Day Book; or, Sketches of Social Life in the Country: With the Popular Elements of Practical and Theoretical Agricul-ture.* . . . New York: Miller, Orton, 1857.

Boston Assessors. *List of Persons, Copartnerships, and Corporations, Who Were Taxed on Ten Thousand Dollars and Upwards, in the City of Boston, in the Year 1860.* . . . Boston: Geo. C. Rand & Avery, City Printers, 1861.

————. *List of Persons, Copartnerships, and Corporations, Who Were Taxed on Twenty Thousand Dollars and Upwards, in the City of Boston, in the Year 1865.* Boston: J. E. Farwell, 1866.

Boston. Baldwin Place Baptist Church. *Catalogue of the Members of the Baldwin Place Baptist Church. Boston, May, 1850.* Boston: Damrell & Moore, 1850.

Boston Board of Street Commissioners. *A Record of the Streets, Alleys, Places, Etc., in the City of Boston. Compiled under the Direction of the Street Commission-ers.* . . . Boston: City of Boston Printing Department, 1910.

Boston Board of Trade. *Second Annual Report of the Government, Presented to the Board at the Annual Meeting, on the 16th of January, 1856.* Boston: Moore & Crosby, 1856.

Boston. Charters. *The Charter and Ordinances of the City of Boston, Together with the Acts of the Legislature Relating to the City. Collated and Revised.* . . . Boston: J. H. Eastburn, City Printer, 1834.

Boston City Clerk, comp. *Members of the School Committee of the Town and City of Boston: Prepared by Wilfred J. Doyle, City Clerk 1942* [Boston City Document No. 53, 1942]. Boston: City of Boston Printing Department, 1942.

Boston City Council. *Fortieth Anniversary of the Election of *Washington Parker Gregg as Clerk of the Common Council of the City of Boston. Celebrated by a Complimentary Banquet.* . . . Boston: Printed by Order of the City Council, 1882.

―――――. *The Railroad Jubilee. An Account of the Celebration Commemorative of the Opening of Railroad Communication between Boston and Canada, September 17th, 18th, and 19th, 1852.* . . . Boston: J. H. Eastburn, City Printer, 1852.

―――――. *Reports in Relation to the Annexation of Roxbury to Boston, and the Act of the Legislature to Unite Said Cities.* Boston: Alfred Mudge & Son, 1867.

―――――. Joint Special Committee on Gas Inspection. *Report of the Evidence and Other Matter Presented before a Joint Committee of the City Council of Boston upon the Subject of Gas.* Boston: Geo. C. Rand & Avery, Printers, 1867.

Boston City Registrar, comp. *The Inaugural Addresses of the Mayors of Boston. Vol. 1. From 1822 to 1851.* Boston: Rockwell & Churchill, 1894.

Boston. Cochituate Water Board. *Report . . .* [for the years 1851–57]. Boston: Various publishers, 1852–58.

Boston Commissioners Appointed to Investigate the Cause and Management of the Great Fire in Boston. *Report of the Commissioners Appointed to Investigate the Cause and Management of the Great Fire in Boston.* Boston: Rockwell & Churchill, City Printers, 1873.

Boston Directory. Boston: Various publishers, 1789–1930.

Boston Marine Society. *Constitution and By-Laws of the Boston Marine Society, Instituted in the Year 1742; Incorporated in the Year 1754. Together with a Brief History of the Society.* . . . Boston: Press of *T. R. Marvin & Son, 1878.

Boston Mercantile Academy. *Annual Catalogue and Circular of the Boston Mercantile Academy, at No. 16 Summer Street. For the Year Ending July 31, 1857.* Boston: *William White, Printer, 1857.

―――――. *First Semi-Annual Catalogue and Circular of the Boston Mercantile Academy, at No. 16 Summer Street. December, 1855.* Boston: McIntire & Moulton, Printers, 1855.

Boston Record Commissioners. *A Catalogue of the City Councils of Boston . . . 1822–1890; Roxbury . . . 1846–1867; Charlestown . . . 1847–1873; and of the Selectmen of Boston, 1634–1822.* . . . Boston: Rockwell & Churchill, City Printers, 1891.

―――――. *A Report of the Record Commissioners of the City of Boston, Containing Boston Births from A.D. 1700 to A.D. 1800.* Boston: Rockwell & Churchill, City Printers, 1894.

―――――. *A Report of the Record Commissioners of the City of Boston, Containing Dorchester Births, Marriages, and Deaths to the End of 1825.* Boston: Rockwell

& Churchill, City Printers, 1891.

————. *Vital Records of the Town of Dorchester, from 1826 to 1849.* Boston: Municipal Printing Office, 1905.

————. *A Volume of Records Relating to the Early History of Boston, Containing Boston Marriages from 1752 to 1809.* Boston: Municipal Printing Office, 1903.

Boston. Rowe Street Baptist Church. *A Brief History of the Rowe Street Baptist Church, Boston; with the Declaration of Faith, the Church Covenant, and List of Members.* Boston: Gould & Lincoln, 1853.

Boston Traveller. *Boston Traveller Extra. Incomes of the Citizens of Boston, and Other Cities and Towns of Massachusetts. Viz: Boston, Roxbury, Cambridge, Charlestown. . . .* Boston: A. Williams, 1866.

Bourne, Ezra A., plaintiff. *Report of the Case of Ezra A. Bourne versus the City of Boston, Tried in the Supreme Judicial Court of Massachusetts, at Dedham, March, 1853.* Boston: Eastburn's Press, 1853.

Boutwell, George S. *Address Delivered at Concord, September 18, 1850, before the Middlesex Society of Husbandmen and Manufacturers. . . .* Boston: Printed by Abner Forbes, 1850.

Bowditch, Vincent Y. *Life and Correspondence of *Henry Ingersoll Bowditch by His Son Vincent Y. Bowditch.* 2 vols. Boston: Houghton Mifflin, 1902.

Bragdon, Joseph H. *Report of the Proceedings, on the Occasion of the Reception of the Sons of Newburyport Resident Abroad, July 4th, 1854, by the City Authorities. . . .* Newburyport, Mass.: Moses H. Sargent, 1854.

Brayley, Arthur W. *A Complete History of the Boston Fire Department . . . from 1630 to 1888. . . .* Boston: John P. Dale, 1889.

Brockett, Linus P. *Asiatic Cholera: Its Origin, History, and Progress. . . .* Hartford, Conn., and Chicago: L. Stebbins & A. Kidder, 1866.

Bromley, George W., and Walter S. Bromley, comps. *Atlas of the City of Boston: City Proper and Roxbury. . . .* Philadelphia: G. W. Bromley, 1890.

Brookes, Richard, comp. *Brookes's Universal Gazetteer, Re-modelled and Brought Down to the Present Time. By John Marshall; with Numerous Additions by the American Editor. . . .* Philadelphia: E. H. Butler, 1843.

————. *Darby's Edition of Brookes' Universal Gazetteer; or, A New Geographical Dictionary . . . The Third American Edition, with Ample Additions and Improvements. . . .* Philadelphia: Bennett & Walton, 1823.

Buckingham, Joseph T., comp. *Annals of the Massachusetts Charitable Mechanic Association.* Boston: Press of Crocker and Brewster, 1853.

Burley, S. W. *Burley's United States Centennial Gazetteer and Guide. 1876 . . . Properly Indexed, Classified and Arranged under the Personal Supervision of the Proprietor. . . .* Philadelphia: S. W. Burley, Proprietor & Publisher, 1876.

Burnham, George P. *Memoirs of the United States Secret Service. . . .* Boston: Laban Heath, 1872.

Cambridge, Massachusetts. *The Cambridge Directory, for 1860; Containing a*

Directory of the Citizens, a Business Directory, and a List of the City Officers. . . . Cambridge, Mass.: Thurston, Miles, & Pritchett, 1860.

————. *The Cambridge Directory, for 1861; Containing a Directory of the Citizens, a Business Directory, a List of the City Officers.* . . . Cambridge, Mass.: Thurston & Miles, Chronicle Office, 1861.

Carlier, Auguste. *Marriage in the United States.* . . . Boston: De Vries, Ibarra, 1867.

Carter, Nathan F. *The Native Ministry of New Hampshire.* . . . Concord, N.H.: Rumford Printing Co., 1906.

Chapin, Rev. Edwin H. *Moral Aspects of City Life. A Series of Lectures by Rev. E. H. Chapin.* New York: Henry Lyon, 1853.

Charlestown, Massachusetts. *The Charlestown Directory, Containing the City Record, the Names of the Citizens, and a Business Directory; with Other Useful Information. By Sampson, Davenport, & Co.* Charlestown, Mass.: Abram E. Cutter, 1870.

————. *Vital Records of Charlestown Massachusetts to the Year 1850.* Vol. 1. Boston: New England Historic Genealogical Society, 1984. Roger D. Joslyn, FASG, has Volume 2 in preparation.

Charlton, Edwin A., comp. *New Hampshire as It Is. In Three Parts. Part I. A Historical Sketch of New Hampshire . . . Part II. A Gazetteer of New Hampshire . . . Part III. A General View.* Claremont, N.H.: A. Kenney, 1857.

Chelsea, Massachusetts. *The Chelsea and Revere Directory for the Year 1880. No. 17. [See Preface.] Compiled for the Publisher by John Sale.* Chelsea, Mass.: Charles L. Sale, 1879.

————. *Chelsea Directory for 1860 and Municipal Register for 1859: and Other Valuable Miscellaneous and Statistical Information. By John Bent.* Chelsea, Mass.: Samuel Orcutt, 1859.

Chickering, Jesse. *Immigration into the United States.* Boston: Charles C. Little & James Brown, 1848.

Clapp, John Bouvé. *A Century of Service, 1815–1915.* Boston: *Silas Peirce, 1915.

*Cleveland, Charles. *Thirty-Third Annual Report of Rev. *Charles Cleveland, Missionary. For the Year Ending June 30, 1866.* Boston: *T. R. Marvin & Son, 1866.

*Cobb, Sylvanus. *Autobiography of the First Forty-One Years of the Life of *Sylvanus Cobb, D.D. to Which Is Added A Memoir by His Eldest Son, Sylvanus Cobb, Jr.* Boston: Universalist Publishing House, 1867.

Colton's General Atlas, Containing One Hundred and Eighty Steel Plate Maps and Plans, on One Hundred and Eight Imperial Folio Sheets. . . . New York: J. H. Colton, 1862.

"Commercial and Industrial Cities of the United States. Number LV. Boston, Massachusetts." *Hunt's Merchants' Magazine and Commercial Review* 39 (July 1858): 41–48.

"Commercial and Industrial Cities of the United States. Number LXXVIII. Boston, Massachusetts." *Hunt's Merchants' Magazine and Commercial Review* 44 (February 1861): 173–84.

Coolidge, Austin J., and John B. Mansfield, *A History and Description of New England, General and Local . . . in Two Volumes.* Vol. 1. *Maine, New Hampshire, and Vermont.* Boston: Austin J. Coolidge, 1859.

Courtney, Wilshire S., revised and enlarged by George E. Waring, Jr. *The Farmers' and Mechanics' Manual. With Many Valuable Tables for Machinists, Manufacturers, Merchants, Builders, Engineers, Masons, Painters, Plumbers. . . .* New York: E. B. Treat, 1878.

*Dana, David D. *The Fireman: The Fire Departments of the United States, with a Full Account of All Large Fires, Statistics of Losses and Expenses. . . .* Boston: E. O. Libby, 1858.

Darby, William, and Theodore Dwight, Jr., comps. *A New Gazetteer of the United States of America; Containing a Copious Description of the States, Territories, Counties, Parishes, Districts, Cities and Towns—Mountains, Lakes, Rivers and Canals—Commerce, Manufactures, Agriculture. . . .* Hartford, Conn.: Edward Hopkins, 1833.

Davenport, Bishop, comp. *A History and New Gazetteer, or Geographical Dictionary, of North America and the West Indies . . . A New and Much Improved Edition.* New York: S. W. Benedict, 1842.

Davies, Thomas A. *How to Make Money, and How to Keep It.* New York: G. W. Carleton, 1867.

The Demographic History of Massachusetts. New York: Arno Press, 1976 [reprints articles from 1882 to 1902 and 1969].

Derby, Elias H. "Commercial Cities and Towns of the U.S. Number XXII. City of Boston," *Hunt's Merchants' Magazine and Commercial Review* 23 (November 1850): 483–97.

De Voe, Thomas F. *The Market Assistant, Containing a Brief Description of Every Article of Human Food Sold in the Public Markets of the Cities of New York, Boston, Philadelphia. . . .* [all published]. New York: Orange Judd, 1866.

Dickerman, Charles W., assisted by Charles L. Flint. *How to Make the Farm Pay; or, the Farmer's Book of Practical Information on Agriculture, Stock Raising, Fruit Culture, Special Crops, Domestic Economy. . . .* Philadelphia: Zengler, McCurdy, 1868.

Dickinson, Rodolphus. *A Geographical and Statistical View of Massachusetts Proper.* Greenfield, Mass.: Denio & Phelps, 1813.

Dorchester, Massachusetts, Assessors. *The Taxable Valuation of the Polls and Estates and Amount of Tax in the Town of Dorchester, for the Year . . . [1850, 1853, 1855, 1861, 1865, 1869].* Boston: Various publishers, 1850–69.

Eastman, Mary F. *The Biography of *Dio Lewis, A.M., M.D.* New York: Fowler & Wells, 1891.

Eddy, Rev. Daniel C. *The Young Man's Friend; Containing Admonitions for the*

Erring, Counsel for the Tempted, Encouragement for the Desponding, Hope for the Fallen. 1855. Reprint. Boston: Wentworth, Hewes, 1859.

Farmer, John, and Jacob B. Moore, comps. *A Gazetteer of the State of New-Hampshire . . . Embellished with an Accurate Map, of the State, and Several Other Engravings: by Abel Bowen.* Concord, N.H.: Jacob B. Moore, 1823.

Fisher, Richard Swainson, comp. *A New and Complete Statistical Gazetteer of the United States of America, Founded on and Compiled from Official Federal and State Returns, and the Seventh National Census.* New York: J. H. Colton, 1853.

Fogg, Alonzo J., comp. *The Statistics and Gazetteer of New-Hampshire. Containing Descriptions of All the Counties, Towns and Villages; Also, Boundaries and Area of the State, and Its Natural Resources, with Over One Hundred Pages of Statistical Tables. . . .* Concord, N.H.: D. L. Guernsey, 1874.

Freedley, Edwin T. *A Practical Treatise on Business: or How To Get, Save, Spend, Give, Lend, and Bequeath Money: With an Inquiry into the Chances of Success and Causes of Failure. . . .* Philadelphia: Lippincott, Grambo, 1853.

———, ed. *United States Mercantile Guide. Leading Pursuits and Leading Men. A Treatise on the Principal Trades and Manufactures of the United States. . . .* Philadelphia: Edward Young, 1856.

French, John Homer, ed. *Gazetteer of the State of New York: Embracing a Comprehensive View of the Geography, Geology, and General History of the State, and a Complete History. . . .* Syracuse, N.Y.: R. Pearsall Smith, 1860.

Geer, George P., comp. *Geer's Express Directory, and Railway Forwarder's Guide.* Vol. 1, *Containing the New England States.* Springfield, Mass.: C. R. Chaffee, 1858.

Gould, Benjamin Apthorp. *Investigations in the Military and Anthropological Statistics of American Soldiers.* New York: Hurd & Houghton, for the U.S. Sanitary Commission, 1869.

Gould, Ralph E. *Yankee Boyhood: My Adventures on a Maine Farm Seventy Years Ago.* New York: W. W. Norton, 1950.

———. *Yankee Storekeeper.* New York: McGraw-Hill, 1946.

Greeley, Horace. *Recollections of a Busy Life: Including Reminiscences of American Politics and Politicians. . . .* New York: J. B. Ford, 1868.

———. *What I Know of Farming: A Series of Brief and Plain Expositions of Practical Agriculture as an Art Based upon Science. . . .* New York: Tribune Association, 1871.

Greenslet, Ferris. *The Life of *Thomas Bailey Aldrich.* Boston: Houghton Mifflin, 1908.

de Gurowski, Count Adam G. *America and Europe.* New York: D. Appleton, 1857.

Hale, Edward Everett. *A New England Boyhood.* 1893. Reprint. New York: Grosset & Dunlap, 1927.

Haskel, Daniel, and J. Calvin Smith, comps. *A Complete Descriptive and Statistical Gazetteer of the United States of America . . . with an Abstract of the Census and Statistics for 1840. . . .* New York: Sherman & Smith, 1844.

Hayward, John. *The Book of Religions: Comprising the Views, Creeds, Sentiments, or Opinions, of All the Principal Religious Sects in the World, Particularly of All Christian Denominations in Europe and America.* . . . Boston: John Hayward, 1842.

————, comp. *A Gazetteer of Massachusetts, Containing Descriptions of All the Counties, Towns and Districts in the Commonwealth.* . . . Boston: John Hayward, 1847.

————. *A Gazetteer of the United States of America: Comprising a Concise General View of the United States . . . to Which Are Added Valuable Statistical Tables.* Philadelphia: James L. Gihon, 1854.

————. *The New England Gazetteer; Containing Descriptions of All the States, Counties and Towns in New England: Also Descriptions of the Principal Mountains, Rivers.* . . . Concord, N.H.: Israel S. Boyd & Wm. White, 1839.

Hazen, Edward. *Popular Technology; or, Professions and Trades.* 2 vols. New York: Harper & Bros., 1842–45.

Hersey, George C., defendant. *Report of the Case of Geo. C. Hersey, Indicted for the Murder of Betsy Frances Tirrell, before the Supreme Judicial Court of Massachusetts . . . By James M. W. Yerrinton.* Boston: A. Williams, 1862.

Howe, Charles Oliver. *What I Remember.* [Fort Valley, Ga.?]: Privately published, 1928.

Hunnewell, Hollis Horatio. *Life Letters and Diary of *Horatio Hollis Hunnewell: Born July 27, 1810; Died May 20, 1902: With a Short History of the Hunnewell and Welles Families* [vol. 2]. Boston: Privately printed, 1906.

Hurd, Duane Hamilton, ed. *History of Norfolk County, Massachusetts, with Biographical Sketches of Many of Its Pioneers and Prominent Men.* Philadelphia: J. W. Lewis, 1884.

*Jarvis, Edward. "On the System of Taxation Prevailing in the United States, and Especially in Massachusetts." *Journal of the Statistical Society of London* 23 (September 1860): 370–78.

Johnson, Alvin J., comp. *Johnson's New Illustrated (Steel Plate) Family Atlas, with Physical Geography, and with Descriptions Geographical, Statistical, and Historical, Including the Latest Federal Census, A Geographical Index, and a Chronological History.* . . . New York: Johnson & Ward, 1864.

*Lewis, Dio. *Our Digestion; or, My Jolly Friend's Secret.* Philadelphia: Geo. Maclean, 1872.

————. *Talks about People's Stomachs.* Boston: Fields, Osgood, 1870.

————. *Weak Lungs, and How to Make Them Strong. Or Diseases of the Organs of the Chest, with Their Home Treatment by the Movement Cure.* Boston: Ticknor & Fields, 1865.

Lewis, John B., and Charles C. Bombaugh. *Remarkable Stratagems and Conspiracies: An Authentic Record of Surprising Attempts to Defraud Life Insurance Companies.* New York: G. W. Carleton, 1878.

*Lincoln, Frederic Walker. *In Memoriam *Frederic Walker Lincoln.* Boston: Privately printed, 1899.

Lippincott's Pronouncing Gazetteer. A Complete Pronouncing Gazetteer, or Geographical Dictionary of the World. . . . Philadelphia: J. B. Lippincott, 1856.

Loring, James Spear. *The Hundred Boston Orators Appointed by the Municipal Authorities . . . from 1770 to 1852.* . . . Boston: John P. Jewett, 1854.

Lynn, Massachusetts. *The Lynn Directory, Containing the City Record, the Names of the Citizens, and a Business Directory. With an Almanac for 1860. Number VII. By Adams, Sampson, & Co., Publishers.* . . . Lynn, Mass.: James M. Munroe/Thomas Herbert, 1859.

McWatters, George S. *Knots Untied: or, Ways and By-ways in the Hidden Life of American Detectives.* Hartford, Conn.: J. B. Burr & Hyde, 1872.

Maine Adjutant-General. *Report of the Adjutant General of the State of Maine, for the Years 1864 and 1865.* Augusta, Me.: Stevens & Sayward, Printers to the State, 1866.

———. *Supplement to the Annual Reports of the Adjutant General of the State of Maine, for the Years 1861, '62, '63, '64, '65 and 1866.* Augusta, Me.: Stevens & Sayward, Printers to the State, 1867.

Massachusetts Adjutant-General. *Massachusetts Soldiers, Sailors, and Marines in the Civil War.* 9 vols. Norwood, Mass./Boston: Norwood Press/Wright & Potter Printing Co., 1931–37.

Massachusetts Board of Railroad Commissioners. *Special Report by the Massachusetts Board of Railroad Commissioners to the Legislature in Relation to the Disaster on Monday, March 14, 1887 . . . at . . . the Bussey Bridge.* Boston: Wright & Potter Printing Co., 1887.

Massachusetts Bureau of Statistics of Labor. *Comparative Wages and Prices: 1860–1883. Massachusetts and Great Britain. [From the Sixteenth Annual Report of the Massachusetts Bureau of Statistics of Labor.]* Boston: Wright & Potter Printing Co., 1885.

———. *A Compendium of the Census of Massachusetts: 1875. Prepared by Carroll D. Wright, Chief of the Bureau of Statistics of Labor.* Boston: Albert J. Wright, 1877.

———. *The Census of Massachusetts: 1875. Prepared under the Direction of Carroll D. Wright.* . . . Vol. 1. *Population and Social Statistics.* 3d ed. Boston: Albert J. Wright, 1877.

———. *The Census of Massachusetts: 1875. Prepared under the Direction of Carroll D. Wright.* . . . Vol. 2. *Manufactures and Occupations.* 3d ed. Boston: Albert J. Wright, 1877.

———. *The Census of Massachusetts: 1875. Prepared under the Direction of Carroll D. Wright.* . . . Vol. 3. *Agricultural Products and Property.* 1st ed. Boston: Albert J. Wright, 1877.

———. *The Census of Massachusetts: 1880. Compiled by Authority of the Legislature . . . from the Returns of the Tenth Census of the United States. By Carroll D.*

Wright. . . . Boston: Wright & Potter Printing Co., 1883.

———. *History of Wages and Prices in Massachusetts: 1752–1883 . . . [Being Parts III. and IV. of the Sixteenth Annual Report . . .] by Carroll D. Wright. . . .* Boston: Wright & Potter Printing Co., 1885.

Massachusetts Charitable Mechanic Association. *Annals of the Massachusetts Charitable Mechanic Association, 1795–1892.* Boston: Press of Rockwell and Churchill, 1892.

Massachusetts Cities Directory, for 1881, Comprising a Business Directory of Twenty-One Cities . . . Also a Business Directory of All Towns. . . . Boston: W. A. Greenough, 1881.

Massachusetts Commission on Lunacy. *Report on Insanity and Idiocy in Massachusetts, by the Commission on Lunacy, under Resolve of the Legislature of 1854.* Boston: *William White, Printer to the State, 1855.

Massachusetts General Court. *The General Statutes of the Commonwealth of Massachusetts: Enacted December 28, 1859, to Take Effect June 1, 1860.* 2d ed. Boston: Wright & Potter, 1873.

———. Committee on Valuation, 1850. *Documents Printed by Order of the Valuation Committee, during Their Session in 1850.* Boston: *Dutton & Wentworth, State Printers, 1850.

———. Committee on Valuation, 1860. *Journal and Documents of the Valuation Committee of the Year 1860: Together with Acts of 1861, to Secure a Uniform Description and Appraisal of Estates. . . .* Boston: *William White, 1861.

———. Special Joint Committee Appointed to Investigate the Whole System of the Public Charitable Institutions of the Commonwealth. *Report of the Special Joint Committee Appointed to Investigate the Whole System of the Public Charitable Institutions of the Commonwealth . . . 1858.* Boston: *William White, Printer to the State, 1859.

Massachusetts Secretary of the Commonwealth. *Abstract of the Census of Massachusetts, 1860, from the Eighth U.S. Census, with Remarks on the Same. Prepared under the Direction of *Oliver Warner, Secretary of the Commonwealth.* Boston: Wright & Potter, 1863.

———. *Abstract of the Census of Massachusetts, 1865: With Remarks on the Same, and Supplementary Tables. Prepared under the Direction of *Oliver Warner, Secretary of the Commonwealth.* Boston: Wright & Potter, 1867.

———. *Abstract of the Census of the Commonwealth of Massachusetts . . . 1855. With Remarks on the Same. Prepared under the direction of Francis DeWitt, Secretary of the Commonwealth.* Boston: *William White, 1857.

———. *Fifty-Ninth Report of Births, Marriages and Deaths in Massachusetts . . . for the Year 1900.* Boston: Wright & Potter Printing Co., 1901.

———. *Historical Data Relating to Counties, Cities and Towns in Massachusetts.* Boston: Commonwealth of Massachusetts, 1966.

———. *. . . List of Persons Whose Names Have Been Changed in Massachusetts, 1780–1883.* Boston: Wright & Potter Printing Co., 1885.

————. *Statistical Information Relating to Certain Branches of Industry in Massachusetts, for the Year Ending June 1, 1855.* Boston: *William White, 1855.

————. *Statistical Information Relating to Certain Branches of Industry in Massachusetts, for the Year Ending May 1, 1865. Prepared . . . by *Oliver Warner, Secretary of the Commonwealth.* Boston: Wright & Potter, 1866.

————. *Statistical Tables: Exhibiting the Condition and Products of Certain Branches of Industry in Massachusetts, for the Year Ending April 1, 1837.* . . . Boston: *Dutton & Wentworth, State Printers, 1838.

Massachusetts State Board of Health. *Twenty-Eighth Annual Report of the State Board of Health of Massachusetts.* Boston: Wright & Potter Printing Co., 1897 (pp. 711–829 contain Samuel W. Abbott's "The Vital Statistics of Massachusetts. A Forty Years' Summary [1856–1895]").

Mitchell's New General Atlas, Containing Maps of the Various Countries of the World, Plans of Cities, Etc. Embraced in Ninety-Three Quarto Maps. . . . Philadelphia: Wm. M. Bradley & Bro., 1884.

Mitchell's New General Atlas, Containing Maps of the Various Countries of the World, Plans of Cities, Etc. Embraced in Sixty-Three Quarto Maps. . . . Philadelphia: S. Augustus Mitchell, 1872.

Mitchell, Samuel Augustus, Jr., comp. *An Accompaniment to Mitchell's Reference and Distance Map of the United States.* . . . Philadelphia: S. Augustus Mitchell, 1843.

Morrison, Leonard A. *The History of Windham in New Hampshire (Rockingham County), 1719–1883.* . . . 1883. Reprint. Canaan, N.H.: Phoenix Publishing, 1975.

Nason, Rev. Elias, comp. *A Gazetteer of the State of Massachusetts; with Numerous Illustrations on Wood and Steel.* Boston: B. B. Russell, 1874.

The New England Business Directory. Boston: Adams, Sampson, & Co., 1860; Sampson, Davenport, & Co., 1871, 1881.

The New England Gazetteer, Comprising a Concise description of the Cities, Towns, County Seats, Villages, and Post-offices, with their location, and Population. . . . Boston: Sampson, Davenport, 1884.

New England Grocer, comp. *The Grocer's Companion and Merchant's Hand-Book. Containing a Comprehensive Account of the Growth, Manufacture and Qualities of Every Article Sold by Grocers.* . . . Boston: New England Grocer Office, 1883.

The New-England Mercantile Union Business Directory . . . for the Year 1849. . . . New York: Pratt, 1849.

New Hampshire Adjutant-General. *Revised Roster of the Soldiers and Sailors of New Hampshire in the War of the Rebellion, 1861–1866. Prepared and Published by Authority of the Legislature.* Concord, N.H.: Ira C. Evans, Public Printer, 1895.

New York Adjutant-General. *New York in the War of the Rebellion, 1861–1865 . . . Third Edition.* 6 vols. Albany: J. B. Lyon Co., State Printers, 1912.

Nichols, Thomas Low. *Forty Years of American Life, 1821–1861.* 1st ed. 1864; 2d ed. 1874. New York: Stackpole Sons Publishers, 1937.

Portsmouth, New Hampshire. *A Directory Containing the Names, Occupations & Residence of the Inhabitants of the City of Portsmouth: Also a Street Directory. . . .* Portsmouth, N.H.: Charles W. Brewster, 1851.

———. *1860–61. The Portsmouth Directory: Containing the Names, Occupations and Residences of the Inhabitants of the City of Portsmouth N.H. Incorporated 1849.* Portsmouth, N.H.: Charles W. Brewster & Son, 1860.

———. *The Portsmouth Jubilee. The Reception of the Sons of Portsmouth Resident Abroad, July 4th, 1853, by the City Authorities and the Citizens of Portsmouth.* Portsmouth, N.H.: C. W. Brewster & Son, 1853.

Prescott, George B. *History, Theory, and Practice of the Electric Telegraph.* Boston: Ticknor and Fields, 1860.

Providence, Rhode Island. *The Providence Directory . . . for the Year Commencing June 1, 1861. "What Cheer."* Providence, R.I.: Adams, Sampson, 1861.

*Pulsifer, David, comp. *Guide to Boston and Vicinity, with Maps and Engravings. By *David Pulsifer.* Boston: A. Williams, 1871.

Reid's and Price, Lee & Co.'s Consolidated Railroad Guide Containing the Official Time-Tables of all Railroads and Steamships in New England, New York. . . . Providence, R.I.: J. A. & R. A. Reid, 1886.

Robinson, Solon. *Facts for Farmers; also for the Family Circle. A Compost of Rich Materials for All Land-Owners, about Domestic Animals and Domestic Economy. . . .* 2 vols. New York and Cleveland: A. J. Johnson/F. G. & A. C. Rowe, 1867.

Roxbury, Massachusetts. *The Roxbury Directory, Containing the City Record, the Names of the Citizens, and a Business Directory, with an Almanac for 1860. Number VII.* Boston: Adams, Sampson, 1860.

———. *Vital Records of Roxbury, Massachusetts to the End of the Year 1849* Vol. 1, *Births*; Vol. 2, *Marriages and Deaths.* 2 vols. Salem, Mass.: Essex Institute, 1925–26.

Russell, Charles Theodore. *Agricultural Progress in Massachusetts for the Last Half Century. An Address Delivered before the Agricultural Society of Westborough and Vicinity. . . .* Boston: Chas. C. P. Moody, 1850.

Safford, Nathaniel F. *Argument of Nathaniel F. Safford, Esq., in the Matter of the Petition for the Annexation of Boston and Roxbury.* Boston: Alfred Mudge & Son, Printers, 1865.

Salem, Massachusetts. *The Salem Directory. Containing the Names of the Citizens, City Officers, a Business Directory, and an Almanac for 1861. Also, a Business Directory. . . .* Salem, Mass.: G. M. Whipple & A. A. Smith, 1861.

———. *The Salem Directory: Containing the City Record, Banks, Insurance Companies, Churches, and Societies. Names and Business of the Citizens, an Almanac. . . .* Salem, Mass.: Henry Whipple, 1851.

Savage, Edward Hartwell. *A Chronological History of the Boston Watch and Po-*

lice, from 1631 to 1865; Together with the Recollections of a Boston Police Officer. . . . Boston: Published and sold by the author, 1865.

―――, comp. *Boston Events. A Brief Mention and the Date of More Than 5,000 Events That Transpired in Boston from 1630 to 1880, Covering a Period of 250 Years, Together with Other Occurrences of Interest, Arranged in Alphabetical Order.* Boston: Tolman & White, Printers, 1884.

Shattuck, Lemuel. *Report to the Committee of the City Council Appointed to Obtain the Census of Boston for the Year 1845, Embracing Collateral Facts and Statistical Researches.* . . . Boston: John H. Eastburn, City Printer, 1846.

Sheldon, Asa G. *Life of Asa G. Sheldon: Wilmington Farmer. In Two Arrangements.* Woburn, Mass.: E. T. Moody, Printer, Journal Press, 1862. Available in a reset edition retitled *Yankee Drover: Being the Unpretending Life of Asa Sheldon, Farmer, Trader, and Working Man, 1788–1870.* Hanover, N.H.: University Press of New England, 1988.

Sizer, Nelson. *Choice of Pursuits; or, What to Do, and Why, Describing Seventy-Five Trades and Professions, and the Talents and Temperaments Required for Each.* . . . 1876. Reprint. New York: Fowler & Wells, 1883.

Sons of New Hampshire. *Festival of the Sons of New Hampshire: With the Speeches of Messrs. Webster, Woodbury, Wilder, Bigelow . . . Celebrated in Boston, November 7, 1849.* . . . Boston: James French, 1850.

―――. *Second Festival of the Sons of New Hampshire, Celebrated in Boston, November 2, 1853; Including Also an Account of the Proceedings in Boston.* . . . Boston: James French, 1854.

Sons of Vermont, Worcester, Massachusetts. *First Reunion of the Sons of Vermont, at Worcester, Mass., February 10th, 1874. Address of Hon. Clark Jillson; Together with Toasts, Sentiments, Speeches.* . . . Worcester, Mass.: Charles Hamilton, Palladium Office, 1874.

Spofford, Jeremiah, comp. *A Gazetteer of Massachusetts: Containing a General View of the State, with an Historical Sketch of the Principal Events from Its Settlement to the Present Time, and Notices of the Several Towns Alphabetically Arranged.* Newburyport, Mass.: Charles Whipple, 1828.

―――. comp. *A Historical and Statistical Gazetteer of Massachusetts, with Sketches of the Principal Events from Its Settlement . . . with a New Map of the State . . . Second Edition—Revised, Corrected, and a Large Part Re-written.* Haverhill, Mass.: E. G. Frothingham, 1860.

Spring, James W. *Boston and the *Parker House: A Chronicle of Those Who Have Lived on That Historic Spot Where the New Parker House Now Stands in Boston.* Boston: Privately printed for J. R. Whipple Corp., 1927.

Steinwehr, Adolf Wilhelm August Friedrich, Baron von, comp. *The Centennial Gazetteer of the United States. A Geographical and Statistical Encyclopaedia of the . . . American Union.* . . . Philadelphia: J. C. McCurdy, 1876.

Stevens, Charles Emery. *Anthony Burns. A History.* . . . 1856. Reprint. Williamstown, Mass.: Corner House Publishers, 1973.

Stockbridge, John C. *The Model Pastor. A Memoir of the Life and Correspondence of Rev. *Baron Stow, D.D., Late Pastor of the Rowe Street Baptist Church, Boston.* Boston: Lee & Shepard, 1871.

Sweetser, Moses F., ed. *New England: A Handbook for Travellers. A Guide.* . . . 7th ed. Boston: James R. Osgood, 1883.

Tarbell, Daniel. *Incidents of Real Life.* Montpelier, Vt.: Argus and Patriot Book and Job Printing Co., 1883.

Trollope, Anthony. *North America by Anthony Trollope: Edited with an Introduction, Notes and New Materials by Donald Smalley and Bradford Allen Booth.* 1951. Reprint. New York: Da Capo Press, 1986.

U.S. Census Office. Seventh Census (1850). *Statistical View of the United States, Embracing its Territory, Population—White, Free Colored, and Slave—Moral and Social Condition, Industry, Property.* . . . Washington, D.C.: Beverley Tucker, Senate Printer, 1854.

———. Seventh Census (1850). *The Seventh Census of the United States: 1850. Embracing a Statistical View of Each of the States and Territories, Arranged by Counties, Towns, etc.* . . . Washington, D.C.: Robert Armstrong, Public Printer, 1853.

———. Eighth Census (1860). *Agriculture of the United States in 1860; Compiled from the Original Returns of the Eighth Census, under the Direction of the Secretary of the Interior.* . . . Washington, D.C.: U.S. Government Printing Office, 1864.

———. Eighth Census (1860). *Manufactures of the United States in 1860; Compiled from the Original Returns of the Eighth Census, under the Direction of the Secretary of the Interior.* Washington, D.C.: U.S. Government Printing Office, 1865.

———. Eighth Census (1860). *Population of the United States in 1860; Compiled from the Original Returns of the Eighth Census, under the Direction of the Secretary of the Interior.* . . . Washington, D.C.: U.S. Government Printing Office, 1864.

———. Eighth Census (1860). *Statistics of the United States (Including Mortality, Property, &c.,) in 1860; Compiled from the Original Returns and Being the Final Exhibit of the Eighth Census.* . . . Washington, D.C.: U.S. Government Printing Office, 1866.

———. Ninth Census (1870). *Statistical Atlas of the United States Based on the Results of the Ninth Census 1870 with Contributions from Many Eminent Men of Science.* . . . New York: Julius Bien, Lith., 1874.

———. Ninth Census (1870). *The Statistics of the Population of the United States, Embracing the Tables of Race, Nationality, Sex, Selected Ages, and Occupations.* . . . Washington, D.C.: U.S. Government Printing Office, 1872.

———. Ninth Census (1870). *The Statistics of the Wealth and Industry of the United States, Embracing the Tables of Wealth, Taxation, and Public Indebtedness;*

of Agriculture; Manufactures. . . . Washington, D.C.: U.S. Government
Printing Office, 1872.

———. Tenth Census (1880). *Report on the Productions of Agriculture as Returned at the Tenth Census (June 1, 1880), Embracing General Statistics and
Monographs.* . . . Washington, D.C.: U.S. Government Printing Office,
1883.

———. Tenth Census (1880). *Statistics of the Population of the United States at
the Tenth Census (June 1, 1880), Embracing Extended Tables of the Population of
States, Counties.* . . . Washington, D.C.: U.S. Government Printing Office,
1883.

U.S. Secretary of the Treasury. *Annual Report of the Chief of the Bureau of Statistics on the Commerce and Navigation of the United States for the Fiscal Year
Ended June 30, 1870.* Washington, D.C.: U.S. Government Printing Office,
1871.

———. *. . . Report of the Secretary of the Treasury, Transmitting a Report . . .
Commerce and Navigation of the United States for the year Ending . . . 30th June,
1850.* . . . Washington, D.C.: Gideon & Co., Printers, 1851.

———. *Report of the Secretary of the Treasury, Transmitting a Report . . . Commerce and Navigation of the United States, for the Year Ending June 30, 1860.*
Washington, D.C.: Geo. W. Bowman, Printer, 1860.

Varney, George J., comp. *A Gazetteer of the State of Maine with Numerous Illustrations.* Boston: B. B. Russell, 1881.

Vermont Adjutant-General. *Revised Roster of Vermont Volunteers and Lists of
Vermonters Who Served in the Army and Navy of the United States during the War
of the Rebellion, 1861–66.* Montpelier, Vt.: Press of the Watchman Publishing Co., 1892.

Walling, Henry F., and Ormando W. Gray, comps. *Official Topographical Atlas
of Massachusetts, from Astronomical, Trigonometrical and Various Local Surveys;
Compiled and Corrected.* . . . Philadelphia: Stedman, Brown & Lyon, 1871.

Webster, John White, defendant. *Report of the Case of John W. Webster . . . Indicted for the Murder of George Parkman . . . Before the Supreme Judicial Court
of Massachusetts.* . . . Boston: Charles C. Little & James Brown, 1850.

Webster, Noah, comp. *An American Dictionary of the English Language; Exhibit-
ing the Origin, Orthography, Pronunciation, and Definitions of Words. By Noah
Webster, LL.D. Abridged from the Quarto Edition of the Author to Which Are
Added a Synopsis of Words.* . . . New York: Harper & Bros., 1845.

Winslow, Rev. Hubbard. *The Young Man's Aid to Knowledge, Virtue, and Happiness.* 1st ed. 1837; 6th ed. 1856. Boston: Crocker & Brewster, 1856.

Winsor, Justin, ed. *The Memorial History of Boston, Including Suffolk County,
Massachusetts, 1630–1880.* 4 vols. Boston: Ticknor, 1880–81.

Wise, Rev. Daniel. *The Young Man's Counsellor; or, Sketches and Illustrations of
the Duties and Dangers of Young Men. Designed to Be a Guide to Success in This
Life.* . . . Boston: C. H. Peirce, 1851.

Worcester, Joseph E., comp. *A Gazetteer of the United States Abstracted from the Universal Gazetteer of the Author; With Enlargement of the Principal Articles.* Andover, Mass.: Flagg & Gould, 1818.

Wright, Carroll D., comp. *The Social, Commercial, and Manufacturing Statistics of the City of Boston, (Massachusetts, U.S.A.) from the United States Census Returns for 1880, and from Original Sources, with an Account of the Railroad and Shipping Facilities of the City. . . .* Boston: Rockwell & Churchill, City Printers, 1882.

The Young Mechanic: By the Author of the Young Merchant. 5th ed. New York: Saxton & Miles, 1844.

The Young Merchant. 1st ed. 1839; 2d stereotype ed. Boston: George W. Light, 1840.

TWENTIETH-CENTURY AND/OR ANALYTICAL MATERIALS

Adams, Charles Francis, Jr. *Notes on Railroad Accidents.* New York: G. P. Putnam's Sons, 1879.

Adams, John W., and Alice Bee Kasakoff. "Migration and the Family in Colonial New England: The View from Genealogies." *Journal of Family History* 9 (Spring 1984): 24–43.

Allen, Frederick J. *A Guide to the Study of Occupations: A Selected Critical Bibliography of the Common Occupations with Specific References for Their Study. . . .* Rev. ed. Cambridge, Mass.: Harvard University Press, 1925.

Allen, James P. "Changes in the American Propensity to Migrate." *American Association of Geographers Annals* 67 (December 1977): 577–87.

Anderson, Margo J. *The American Census: A Social History.* New Haven: Yale University Press, 1988.

Anderton, Douglas L., and Lee L. Bean. "Birth Spacing and Fertility Limitation: A Behavioral Analysis of a Nineteenth-Century Frontier Population." *Demography* 22 (May 1985): 169–83.

Atack, Jeremy, and Fred Bateman. *To Their Own Soil: Agriculture in the Antebellum North.* Ames: Iowa State University Press, 1987.

Bailey, William B. *Modern Social Conditions: A Statistical Study of Birth, Marriage, Divorce, Death, Disease, Suicide, Immigration, etc., with Special Reference to the United States.* New York: Century, 1906.

Barron, Hal S. *Those Who Stayed Behind: Rural Society in Nineteenth-Century New England.* New York: Cambridge University Press, 1984.

Bidwell, Percy W. "Population Growth in Southern New England, 1810–1860." *American Statistical Association Publications* 15 (December 1917): 813–39.

———. *Rural Economy in New England at the Beginning of the 19th Century.* Clifton, N.J.: Augustus M. Kelley Publishers, 1972. Originally in *Connecticut*

Academy of Arts and Sciences Transactions 20 (April 1916): 241–399.

———, and John I. Falconer. *History of Agriculture in the Northern United States, 1620–1860.* 1925. Reprint. New York: Peter Smith, 1941.

Binford, Henry C. *The First Suburbs: Residential Communities on the Boston Periphery, 1815–1860.* Chicago: University of Chicago Press, 1985.

Blake, Nelson M. *Water for the Cities: A History of the Urban Water Supply Problem in the United States.* Syracuse, N.Y.: Syracuse University Press, 1956.

Blouin, Francis X., Jr. *The Boston Region, 1810–1850: A Study of Urbanization.* Ann Arbor, Mich.: UMI Research Press, 1980.

Bode, Frederick A., and Donald E. Ginter. *Farm Tenancy and the Census in Antebellum Georgia.* Athens: University of Georgia Press, 1986.

Bourke, Paul F., and Donald A. DeBats. "The Structures of Political Involvement in the Nineteenth Century: A Frontier Case." *Perspectives in American History,* n.s. 3 (1987): 207–38.

Burnham, Walter Dean. "Those High Nineteenth-Century American Voting Turnouts: Fact or Fiction?" *Journal of Interdisciplinary History* 16 (Spring 1986): 613–44.

Bushman, Claudia L. *"A Good Poor Man's Wife": Being a Chronicle of Harriet Hanson Robinson and Her Family in Nineteenth-Century New England.* Hanover, N.H.: University Press of New England, 1981.

Bushée, Frederick A. *Ethnic Factors in the Population of Boston.* New York: Arno Press, 1970. Originally in *American Economic Association Publications,* 3d ser. 4 (May 1903): 299–477.

Chamberlin, Joseph E. *The Boston Transcript: A History of Its First Hundred Years.* Boston: Houghton Mifflin, 1930.

Coale, Ansley J., and Paul George Demeny, comps. *Regional Model Life Tables and Stable Populations.* Princeton: Princeton University Press, 1966.

Coale, Ansley J., and Melvin Zelnik. *New Estimates of Fertility and Population in the United States: A Study of Annual White Births from 1855 to 1960 and of Completeness of Enumeration in the Censuses from 1880 to 1960.* Princeton: Princeton University Press, 1963.

Conference on Research in Income and Wealth (of the National Bureau of Economic Research). *Long-Term Factors in American Economic Growth.* Edited by Stanley L. Engerman and Robert E. Gallman. Studies in Income and Wealth, 51. Chicago: University of Chicago Press for NBER, 1986.

Cowan, Ruth Schwartz. *More Work for Mother: The Ironies of Household Technology from the Open Hearth to the Microwave.* New York: Basic Books, 1983.

Crandall, Ralph J., ed. *Genealogical Research in New England.* Baltimore: Genealogical Publishing Co., 1984.

Dalzell, Robert F., Jr. *Enterprising Elite: The Boston Associates and the World They Made.* Cambridge, Mass.: Harvard University Press, 1987.

Danhof, Clarence H. *Change in Agriculture: The Northern United States,*

1820–1870. Cambridge, Mass.: Harvard University Press, 1969.

Davenport, David P. "Census Indexes: Research Boon or Bane?" Undated manuscript [ca. January 1990].

——. "Duration of Residence in the 1855 Census of New York State." *Historical Methods* 18 (Winter 1985): 5–12.

——. "Tracing Rural New York's Out-Migrants, 1855–1860." *Historical Methods* 17 (Spring 1984): 59–67.

Day, Clarence A. *A History of Maine Agriculture, 1604–1860.* Orono: University of Maine Press, 1954.

Degler, Carl N. *At Odds: Women and the Family in America from the Revolution to the Present.* New York: Oxford University Press, 1980.

The Demographic History of Massachusetts. New York: Arno Press, 1976.

Demos, John P. *Past, Present, and Personal: The Family and the Life Course in American History.* New York: Oxford University Press, 1986.

Ditz, Toby L. *Property and Kinship: Inheritance in Early Connecticut, 1750–1820.* Princeton: Princeton University Press, 1986.

Dodd, Edwin M. *American Business Corporations until 1860 with Special Reference to Massachusetts.* Cambridge, Mass.: Harvard University Press, 1954.

Doherty, Robert W. *Society and Power: Five New England Towns, 1800–1860.* Amherst: University of Massachusetts Press, 1977.

Dublin, Thomas L. "Rural-Urban Migrants in Industrial New England: The Case of Lynn, Massachusetts, in the Mid-Nineteenth Century." *Journal of American History* 73 (December 1986): 623–44.

——. *Women at Work: The Transformation of Work and Community in Lowell, Massachusetts, 1826–1860.* New York: Columbia University Press, 1979.

——, ed. *Farm to Factory: Women's Letters, 1830–1860.* New York: Columbia University Press, 1981.

Dyke, Bennett, and Warren T. Morrill, eds. *Genealogical Demography.* New York: Academic Press, 1980.

Edel, Matthew, Elliott D. Sclar, and Daniel Luria. *Shaky Palaces: Homeownership and Social Mobility in Boston's Suburbanization.* New York: Columbia University Press, 1984.

Evans, George Heberton, Jr. *Business Incorporations in the United States, 1800–1943.* New York: National Bureau of Economic Research, 1948.

——. "A Sketch of American Business Organization, 1832–1900." *Journal of Political Economy* 60 (December 1952): 475–86.

Farrell, James J. *Inventing the American Way of Death, 1830–1920.* Philadelphia: Temple University Press, 1980.

Florin, John W. *Death in New England: Regional Variations in Mortality.* Chapel Hill: University of North Carolina Department of Geography, 1971.

Forster, Colin, and G. S. L. Tucker. *Economic Opportunity and White American Fertility Ratios, 1800–1860.* New Haven: Yale University Press, 1972.

Furstenberg, Frank F., Jr., Douglas Strong, and Albert G. Crawford. "What

Happened When the Census Was Redone: An Analysis of the Recount of 1870 in Philadelphia." *Sociology and Social Research* 63 (April 1979): 475–505.

Galenson, David W. "Economic Determinants of the Age at Leaving Home: Evidence from the Lives of Nineteenth-Century New England Manufacturers." *Social Science History* 11 (Winter 1987): 355–78.

Ginsberg, Caren A. "Estimates and Correlates of Enumeration Completeness: Censuses and Maps in Nineteenth-Century Massachusetts." *Social Science History* 12 (Spring 1988): 71–86.

Ginsburg, Gerald A. "Computing Antebellum Turnout: Methods and Models." *Journal of Interdisciplinary History* 16 (Spring 1986): 579–611.

Griffen, Clyde, and Sally Griffen. *Natives and Newcomers: The Ordering of Opportunity in Mid-Nineteenth-Century Poughkeepsie.* Cambridge, Mass.: Harvard University Press, 1978.

Grigg, Susan. "Toward a Theory of Remarriage: A Case Study of Newburyport at the Beginning of the Nineteenth Century." *Journal of Interdisciplinary History* 8 (Autumn 1977): 183–220.

Grob, Gerald N. *Edward Jarvis and the Medical World of Nineteenth-Century America.* Knoxville: University of Tennessee Press, 1978.

Gutman, Robert. *Birth and Death Registration in Massachusetts, 1639–1900.* New York: Milbank Memorial Fund, 1959.

Hahn, Steven, and Jonathan Prude, eds. *The Countryside in the Age of Capitalist Transformation: Essays in the Social History of Rural America.* Chapel Hill: University of North Carolina Press, 1985.

Hasse, Adelaide R., comp. *Index of Economic Material in Documents of the States of the United States: Massachusetts, 1789–1904, Prepared for the Department of Economics and Sociology of the Carnegie Institution of Washington.* 1908. Reprint. New York: Kraus Reprint Corp., 1965.

Hoffert, Sylvia D. *Private Matters: American Attitudes toward Childbearing and Infant Nurture in the Urban North, 1800–1860.* Urbana: University of Illinois Press, 1989.

Horlick, Allan S. *Country Boys and Merchant Princes: The Social Control of Young Men in New York.* Lewisburg, Pa.: Bucknell University Press, 1975.

Horwitz, Richard P. *Anthropology toward History: Culture and Work in a 19th-Century Maine Town.* Middletown, Conn.: Wesleyan University Press, 1978.

Hubka, Thomas C. *Big House, Little House, Back House, Barn: The Connected Farm Buildings of New England.* Hanover, N.H.: University Press of New England, 1984.

Huntington, Ellsworth, and Martha Ragsdale. *After Three Centuries: A Typical New England Family.* Baltimore: Williams & Wilkins, 1935.

Huse, Charles P. *The Financial History of Boston from May 1, 1822, to January 31, 1909.* Cambridge, Mass.: Harvard University Press, 1916.

Hutchinson, Ruth G., Arthur R. Hutchinson, and Mabel Newcomer. "A

Study in Business Mortality: Length of Life of Business Enterprises in Poughkeepsie, New York, 1843–1936." *American Economic Review* 28 (September 1938): 497–514.

Jackson, Ronald Vern, David Schaefermeyer, and Gary Ronald Teeples, eds. *Rhode Island 1850 Census Index.* Bountiful, Utah: Accelerated Indexing Systems, 1976.

Jackson, Ronald Vern, and Gary Ronald Teeples, eds. *Maine 1850 Census Index.* Salt Lake City, Utah: Accelerated Indexing Systems, 1978.

———. *Massachusetts 1850 Census Index.* Bountiful, Utah: Accelerated Indexing Systems, 1978.

———. *New Hampshire 1850 Census Index.* Bountiful, Utah: Accelerated Indexing Systems, 1978.

———. *Vermont 1850 Census Index.* Bountiful, Utah: Accelerated Indexing Systems, 1978.

Jones, Douglas Lamar. *Village and Seaport: Migration and Society in Eighteenth-Century Massachusetts.* Hanover, N.H.: University Press of New England, 1981.

Kagle, Steven E. *Late Nineteenth-Century American Diary Literature.* Boston: Twayne, 1988.

Katz, Michael B. *The People of Hamilton, Canada West: Family and Class in a Mid-Nineteenth-Century City.* Cambridge, Mass.: Harvard University Press, 1975.

Kelsey, Darwin P., ed. *American Agriculture, 1790–1840: A Symposium Edited by Darwin P. Kelsey.* Berkeley, Calif.: Agricultural History Society, 1972.

Kennedy, Charles J. "Commuter Services in the Boston Area, 1835–1860." *Business History Review* 36 (Summer 1962): 153–70.

Kenzer, Robert C. *Kinship and Community in a Southern Community: Orange County, North Carolina, 1849–1881.* Knoxville: University of Tennessee Press, 1987.

Kett, Joseph F. *Rites of Passage: Adolescence in America, 1790 to the Present.* New York: Basic Books, 1977.

Keyssar, Alexander. *Out of Work: The First Century of Unemployment in Massachusetts.* New York: Cambridge University Press, 1986.

Kirk, Gordon W., Jr. *The Promise of American Life: Social Mobility in a Nineteenth-Century Immigrant Community, Holland, Michigan, 1847–1894.* Philadelphia: American Philosophical Society, 1978.

Kirkland, Edward C. *Men, Cities and Transportation.* 2 vols. Cambridge, Mass.: Harvard University Press, 1948.

Knights, Peter R. "Ethnic Massachusetts." In *The Commemorative Guide to the Massachusetts Bicentennial.* Boston: Yankee Press, 1974, pp. 74–77.

———. *The Plain People of Boston, 1830–1860: A Study in City Growth.* New York: Oxford University Press, 1971.

Knobel, Dale T. *Paddy and the Republic: Ethnicity and Nationality in Antebellum America*. Middletown, Conn.: Wesleyan University Press, 1986.

Kuznets, Simon S., Dorothy S. Thomas, et al. *Population Redistribution and Economic Growth: United States, 1870–1950*. 3 vols. Philadelphia: American Philosophical Society, 1957, 1960, 1964.

Lane, Roger. *Policing the City: Boston, 1822–1885*. Cambridge, Mass.: Harvard University Press, 1967.

———. *Violent Death in the City: Suicide, Accident, and Murder in Nineteenth-Century Philadelphia*. Cambridge, Mass.: Harvard University Press, 1979.

Laslett, Peter, with the assistance of Richard Wall, eds. *Household and Family in Past Time: Comparative Studies in the Size and Structure of the Domestic Group over the Last Three Centuries in England, France, Serbia, Japan and Colonial North America, with Further Materials from Western Europe*. Cambridge, Eng.: Cambridge University Press, 1974.

Leavitt, Judith W. *Brought to Bed: Childbearing in America, 1750 to 1950*. New York: Oxford University Press, 1986.

Lebergott, Stanley. *Manpower in Economic Growth: The American Record since 1800*. New York: McGraw-Hill, 1964.

LeBlanc, Robert G. *Location of Manufacturing in New England in the 19th Century*. Hanover, N.H.: Dartmouth College Geography Department, 1969.

Lerner, Monroe, and Odin W. Anderson. *Health Progress in the United States, 1900–1960: A Report of Health Information Foundation*. Chicago: University of Chicago Press, 1963.

Lowe, Richard G., and Randolph B. Campbell. *Planters and Plain Folk: Agriculture in Antebellum Texas*. Dallas: Southern Methodist University Press, 1987.

McMurry, Sally Ann. *Families and Farmhouses in Nineteenth-Century America: Vernacular Design and Social Change*. New York: Oxford University Press, 1988.

Mahon, Richard Michael. "Class and Context in Nineteenth-Century Urban Out-Migration: Madison, Wisconsin, 1860–1870." M.S. thesis, University of Wisconsin–Madison, 1985.

The Maine Atlas and Gazetteer. Yarmouth, Me.: De Lorme Publishing Co., 1982.

Martinius, Sture. *Peasant Destinies: The History of 552 Swedes Born 1810–12*. Stockholm: Almqvist & Wiksell International, 1977.

Mayer, Martin P. *Making News*. Garden City, N.Y.: Doubleday, 1987.

Modell, John, Frank F. Furstenberg, Jr., and Douglas Strong. "The Timing of Marriage in the Transition to Adulthood: Continuity and Change, 1860–1975." *American Journal of Sociology* 84 Supplement (1978): S120–S150. This supplement appeared separately as *Turning Points: Historical and Sociological Essays on the Family*, edited by John Demos and Sarane Spence Boocock. Chicago: University of Chicago Press, 1978.

Modell, John, and Tamara K. Hareven, "Urbanization and the Malleable Household: An Examination of Boarding and Lodging in American Families." In *Family and Kin in Urban Communities, 1700–1930,* edited by Tamara K. Hareven, pp. 164–88. New York: New Viewpoints, 1977.

Nesson, Fern L. *Great Waters: A History of Boston's Water Supply.* Hanover, N.H.: University Press of New England for Brandeis University, 1983.

The New Hampshire Atlas and Gazetteer. Yarmouth, Me.: De Lorme Publishing Co., 1981.

Norris, James D. *R. G. Dun & Co., 1841–1900: The Development of Credit-Reporting in the Nineteenth Century.* Westport, Conn.: Greenwood Press, 1978.

Paludan, Phillip Shaw. *"A People's Contest": The Union and Civil War, 1861–1865.* New York: Harper & Row, 1988.

Parkerson, Donald H., and Jo Ann Parkerson, "'Fewer Children of Greater Spiritual Quality': Religion and the Decline of Fertility in Nineteenth-Century America." *Social Science History* 12 (Spring 1988): 49–70.

Rorabaugh, William J. *The Craft Apprentice from Franklin to the Machine Age in America.* New York: Oxford University Press, 1986.

Rosen, Christine M. *The Limits of Power: Great Fires and the Process of City Growth in America.* New York: Cambridge University Press, 1986.

Rosenberg, Charles E. *The Care of Strangers: The Rise of America's Hospital System.* New York: Basic Books, 1987.

——. *The Cholera Years: The United States in 1832, 1849, and 1866.* Chicago: University of Chicago Press, 1962.

Rosenkrantz, Barbara Gutmann. *Public Health and the State: Changing Views in Massachusetts, 1842–1936.* Cambridge, Mass.: Harvard University Press, 1972.

Ross, Steven J. *Workers on the Edge: Work, Leisure, and Politics in Industrializing Cincinnati, 1788–1890.* New York: Columbia University Press, 1985.

Rothenberg, Winifred J. "The Emergence of a Capital Market in Rural Massachusetts, 1730–1838." *Journal of Economic History* 45 (December 1985): 781–808.

——. "The Market and Massachusetts Farmers, 1750–1855." *Journal of Economic History* 41 (June 1981), 283–314.

Rothman, Ellen K. *Hands and Hearts: A History of Courtship in America.* 1984. Reprint. Cambridge, Mass.: Harvard University Press, 1987.

Russell, Howard S. *A Long, Deep Furrow: Three Centuries of Farming in New England.* Hanover, N.H.: University Press of New England, 1976.

Sablonsky, Irving, ed. *What They Heard: Music in America, 1852–1881, from the Pages of *Dwight's Journal of Music.* Baton Rouge: Louisiana State University Press, 1986.

Salmon, Marylynn. *Women and the Law of Property in Early America.* Chapel Hill: University of North Carolina Press, 1986.

Salsbury, Stephen. *The State, the Investor, and the Railroad: The Boston & Albany, 1825–1867*. Cambridge, Mass.: Harvard University Press, 1967.

Sanborn, Melinde Lutz. "The 1860 Census for Ward One, Boston, Massachusetts: Some Special Features and Flaws." *New England Historical and Genealogical Register* 142 (January 1988): 25–28.

Saum, Lewis O. *The Popular Mood of Pre–Civil War America*. Westport, Conn.: Greenwood Press, 1980.

Schapiro, Morton O. *Filling Up America: An Economic-Demographic Model of Population Growth and Distribution in the Nineteenth-Century United States.* Greenwich, Conn.: JAI Press, 1986.

Schivelbusch, Wolfgang. *The Railway Journey: Trains and Travel in the 19th Century.* 1979. Reprint. Berkeley: University of California Press, 1986.

Schlebecker, John T. *Whereby We Thrive: A History of American Farming, 1607–1972.* Ames: Iowa State University Press, 1975.

Schwarzlose, Richard A. *The Nation's Newsbrokers.* 2 vols. Evanston, Ill.: Northwestern University Press, 1989–90.

———. *Newspapers: A Reference Guide.* Westport, Conn.: Greenwood Press, 1987.

Shammas, Carole, Marylynn Salmon, and Michael Dahlin. *Inheritance in America from Colonial Times to the Present.* New Brunswick, N.J.: Rutgers University Press, 1987.

Shannon, Fred A. *The Farmer's Last Frontier: Agriculture, 1860–1897.* Economic History of the United States, 5. New York: Rinehart, 1945.

Shaw, Robert B. *A History of Railroad Accidents, Safety Precautions and Operating Practices.* 1st ed. 1961; 2d ed. 1978. Potsdam, N.Y.: The author, 1978.

Siracusa, Carl. *A Mechanical People: Perceptions of the Industrial Order in Massachusetts, 1815–1880.* Middletown, Conn.: Wesleyan University Press, 1979.

Slater, Peter Gregg. *Children in the New England Mind in Death and Life.* Hamden, Conn.: Archon Books, 1977.

Solomon, Barbara Miller. *Ancestors and Immigrants: A Changing New England Tradition.* 1956. Reprint. Boston: Northeastern University Press, 1989.

Soltow, Lee. *Men and Wealth in the United States, 1850–1870.* New Haven: Yale University Press, 1975.

Spear, Dorothea N., comp. *Bibliography of American Directories through 1860.* Worcester, Mass.: American Antiquarian Society, 1961.

Stannard, David E., ed. *Death in America.* Philadelphia: University of Pennsylvania Press, 1975.

Steckel, Richard H. "Census Matching and Migration: A Research Strategy." *Historical Methods* 21 (Spring 1988): 52–60.

Stephenson, Charles, Richard J. Jensen, and Janice Reiff Webster. "Social Predictors of American Mobility: A Census Capture-Recapture Study of New York and Wisconsin, 1875–1905." 2 vols. Chicago: Family and Community History Center of the Newberry Library, May 1978. Mimeographed.

Stilwell, Lewis D. *Migration from Vermont*. 1937. Reprint. Montpelier: Vermont Historical Society, 1948.

Story, Ronald D. *Harvard and the Boston Upper Class: The Forging of an Aristocracy, 1800–1870*. Middletown, Conn.: Wesleyan University Press, 1980.

Taylor, George Rogers. *The Transportation Revolution, 1815–1860*. Economic History of the United States, 4. New York: Rinehart, 1951.

Thernstrom, Stephan A. *The Other Bostonians: Poverty and Progress in the American Metropolis, 1880–1970*. Cambridge, Mass.: Harvard University Press, 1973.

Thernstrom, Stephan A., and Peter R. Knights. "Men in Motion: Some Data and Speculations about Urban Population Mobility in Nineteenth-Century America." *Journal of Interdisciplinary History* 1 (Autumn 1970): 7–35.

Thornton, Tamara P. *Cultivating Gentlemen: The Meaning of Country Life among the Boston Elite, 1785–1860*. New Haven: Yale University Press, 1989.

U.S. Bureau of Economic Analysis. *Long Term Economic Growth, 1860–1970*. Washington, D.C.: U.S. Government Printing Office, 1973.

U.S. Bureau of the Census. *Historical Statistics of the United States, Colonial Times to 1970*. Washington, D.C.: U.S. Government Printing Office, 1976.

———. *Twenty Censuses: Population and Housing Questions, 1790–1980*. Washington, D.C.: U.S. Government Printing Office, 1979.

U.S. Library of Congress Catalogue Division, comp. *American and English Genealogies in the Library of Congress: Preliminary Catalogue*. Washington, D.C.: U.S. Government Printing Office, 1910.

Verbrugge, Martha H. *Able-Bodied Womanhood: Personal Health and Social Change in Nineteenth-Century Boston*. New York: Oxford University Press, 1988.

The Vermont Atlas and Gazetteer. Yarmouth, Me.: De Lorme Publishing Co., 1981.

Vinovskis, Maris A. *Fertility in Massachusetts from the Revolution to the Civil War*. New York: Academic Press, 1981.

———. "Have Social Historians Lost the Civil War? Some Preliminary Demographic Speculations." *Journal of American History* 76 (June 1989): 34–58.

———, ed. *Studies in American Historical Demography*. New York: Academic Press, 1979.

Vogel, Morris J. *The Invention of the Modern Hospital: Boston, 1870–1930*. Chicago: University of Chicago Press, 1980.

Warner, Sam Bass, Jr. *Streetcar Suburbs: The Process of Growth in Boston, 1870–1900*. Cambridge, Mass.: Harvard University Press and MIT Press, 1962.

Whitehill, Walter Muir. *Boston: A Topographical History*. 1st ed. 1959; 2d ed.

1968; 2d ed., enlarged, 1975. Cambridge, Mass.: Harvard University Press, 1975.

Wilkinson, Warren. *Mother, May You Never See the Sights I Have Seen: The Fifty-seventh Massachusetts Veteran Volunteers in the Army of the Potomac, 1864–1865*. New York: Harper & Row, 1990.

Williamson, Harold F., and Arnold R. Daum. *The American Petroleum Industry: The Age of Illumination, 1859–1899*. Evanston, Ill.: Northwestern University Press, 1959.

Wilson, Harold F. *The Hill Country of Northern New England: Its Social and Economic History, 1790–1930*. 1936. Reprint. New York: AMS Press, 1967.

Winkle, Kenneth J. *The Politics of Community: Migration and Politics in Antebellum Ohio*. New York: Cambridge University Press, 1988.

Yasuba, Yasukichi. *Birth Rates of the White Population in the United States, 1800–1860: An Economic Study*. Johns Hopkins University Studies in Historical and Political Science 79/2 (1961). Baltimore: Johns Hopkins Press, 1962.

Index